Twitter Marketing

by Brett Petersel and Esther Schindler

A member of Penguin Group (USA) Inc.

ALPHA BOOKS

Published by the Penguin Group

Penguin Group (USA) Inc., 375 Hudson Street, New York, New York 10014, USA • Penguin Group (Canada), 90 Eglinton Avenue East, Suite 700, Toronto, Ontario M4P 2Y3, Canada (a division of Pearson Penguin Canada Inc.) • Penguin Books Ltd., 80 Strand, London WC2R 0RL, England • Penguin Ireland, 25 St. Stephen's Green, Dublin 2, Ireland (a division of Penguin Books Ltd.) • Penguin Group (Australia), 250 Camberwell Road, Camberwell, Victoria 3124, Australia (a division of Pearson Australia Group Pty. Ltd.) • Penguin Books India Pvt. Ltd., 11 Community Centre, Panchsheel Park, New Delhi—110 017, India • Penguin Group (NZ), 67 Apollo Drive, Rosedale, North Shore, Auckland 1311, New Zealand (a division of Pearson New Zealand Ltd.) • Penguin Books (South Africa) (Pty.) Ltd., 24 Sturdee Avenue, Rosebank, Johannesburg 2196, South Africa • Penguin Books Ltd., Registered Offices: 80 Strand, London WC2R 0RL, England

International Standard Book Number: 978-1-61564-157-4
Library of Congress Catalog Card Number: 2011938632

14 13 12 8 7 6 5 4 3 2 1

Interpretation of the printing code: The rightmost number of the first series of numbers is the year of the book's printing; the rightmost number of the second series of numbers is the number of the book's printing. For example, a printing code of 12-1 shows that the first printing occurred in 2012.

Printed in the United States of America

Publisher: *Marie Butler-Knight*
Associate Publisher: *Mike Sanders*
Executive Managing Editor: *Billy Fields*
Executive Acquisitions Editor: *Lori Cates Hand*
Development Editor: *Mark Reddin*
Senior Production Editor: *Kayla Dugger*
Copy Editor: *Jan Zoya*
Cover Designer: *William Thomas*
Book Designers: *William Thomas, Rebecca Batchelor*
Indexer: *Johnna VanHoose Dinse*
Layout: *Brian Massey*
Proofreader: *John Etchison*

Contents

Introduction

Hi, Esther here. I recently told the desk clerk at the Sedona resort that this trip was a retreat to crank out a few book chapters. “What’s the book about?” the woman asked politely, as she marked down *one more order of chocolate brownies* in the accounting ledger.

It took remarkable self-restraint to avoid answering, “About 300 pages.”

“It’s about Twitter marketing,” I finally said.

“Oh! I *need* to read that!” replied the absolute stranger, with surprising intensity and urgency.

Over the months that Brett and I worked on this book, the hotel clerk’s response was one that we heard repeatedly. And no wonder: Twitter mystifies many people, especially those who hope to use it to attract new business, build connections with customers, and get real-world feedback.

But they have no idea how to get over the fumble-fingered, awkward moment of “What the heck do I say?” It’s as bad as the first day of high school. Only without acne.

Twitter’s mantra is simple: 140 characters. You can type anything. And people do post anything and everything. News events. What they had for lunch (chicken tikka masala, thanks for asking). Conversations about business techniques and tools. Requests for help. The all-important kitty videos.

Savvy business marketers know that they need to be part of the conversation. With Twitter, marketers have a unique opportunity to establish real, meaningful relationships with employees, partners, and customers. Through ongoing engagement, knowledge-sharing, and constructive dialogue, Twitter has transformed some of the best businesses of our time.

But creating those conversations and getting that marketing traction? That’s another story. We are here to help.

Twitter at its core is a dinner party where everyone is invited. You might feel socially awkward, as if you don’t know how to meet anyone or what to say. In this book, we introduce you to the coolest people at the party, and teach you how to become the center of attention. Occasionally, you may even giggle.

What You'll Find in This Book

Part 1, The Big Picture of Twitter Marketing, explains why Twitter matters to any business marketer. You'll see what it can do for you, whether your business operates out of a home office or is a multinational corporation. And you'll learn the most common ways that social media marketing fails.

Part 2, Getting Started, teaches you about participating on Twitter. We help you establish a Twitter identity, with a focus on learning how the community works and the "netiquette" for a responsible (business) citizen. We also give you lessons in using hashtags, teach you how to mine your own business knowledge to tweet information that people *want* to share, and explain the steps in building a Twitter following.

Part 3, Twitter Marketing Campaigns, connects your marketing know-how to your newfound Twitter expertise. You learn the steps in a successful campaign, design a social media workflow, create social media policies that work for your organization, and solve the complexities of managing multiple Twitter accounts with a distributed team. We also help you understand which metrics assist in measuring progress toward your marketing goals, and which ones get in the way.

Part 4, Tailoring Twitter to Your Business Needs, drills into the unique needs of marketers based on company size, employee role, or the goal of your marketing campaign. We show you the freedom and limitations facing small businesses; what public relations professionals need to know about convincing the CEO that Twitter is the right plan; highlight opportunities for retail business owners, such as location-based marketing; and share the marketing advantage of a customer-service based Twitter campaign.

Part 5, Integrating Twitter into Your Marketing Mix, addresses the world outside Twitter. Learn how to integrate Twitter into your company website, to find employees with Twitter's help, and to make Twitter part of your essential offline persona.

How to Get the Most Out of This Book

We use several formatting conventions throughout this book to make it easier to understand. For example, actual Twitter accounts (such as **@estherschindler** or **@Brett**) appear in bold.

Throughout the book, we show sample Tweets, many of them drawn from real life. You'll also find a number of sidebars with extra content that read as such:

TWITTER TIP

Years of experience have taught us what works to get attention on Twitter. When there's something that is especially helpful, we draw your attention to it.

FAIL WHALE

These sidebars caution you about common mistakes and tell you how to avoid them.

DEFINITION

Twitter has its own terminology to describe its features. The community has come up with the rest. When we introduce you to a new term, we call out its definition.

MARKETING WIN

Many of our examples show a company's success, or identify useful ways to market a business using Twitter. In these sidebars, we highlight the lesson to take away.

Acknowledgments

From Brett Petersel:

I thank the following people for their inspiration, continued support, and sense of humor:

My parents, Sheldon and Gail Petersel, who are not on Twitter, my sister Danielle Petersel (**@dlpnyc**), and our dog Slim (**@slimthedog**). Also Ziggy, the amazing and talented Alexa Scordato (**@alexa**), Drew Olanoff (**@thatdrew**), Damien Basile (**@db**), Adam Ostrow (**@adamostrow**), Jennifer Schenberg (**@penvine**), Rachel Sokol (**@raymala**), Owen Stone (**@ohdoctah**), Khayyam Wakil (**@iamkhayyam**), Aaron Strout (**@aaronstrout**), Jason Keath (**@jasonkeath**), Howard Greenstein (**@howardgr**), Jennifer Wojcik (**@thejenatx**), Brian Simpson (**@bsimi**), Sarah Prevette (**@sarahprevette**), Oz Sultan (**@ozsultan**), Joseph Jaffe (**@jaffejuice**), David Armano (**@armano**), Erica O'Grady (**@ericaogrady**), David Spinks (**@davidspinks**), Francisco Dao (**@theman**), Jenn Pedde (**@jpedde**), David Weiner (**@davidweiner**), Ken Yeung (**@thekenyeung**), David Berkowitz (**@dberkowitz**), Ben Parr (**@benparr**), Steph Agresta (**@stephagresta**), Bill Sobel (**@bsobel226**), Joe Chernov (**@jchernov**), Liz Pullen (**@nwjerseyliz**), Mike Lazerow (**@lazerow**), Kyle Lacy (**@kyleplacy**),

Brian Solis (**@briansolis**), Mike Schneider (**@schneidermike**), Saul Colt (**@saulcolt**), Stu Tracte (**@stwo**), Josh Pelz (**@jmpelz**), and Sean Percival (**@percival**).

Thanks to the following artists for providing the best soundtrack in the world to accommodate the writing process:

Eric Powell (**@16volt**) of 16volt, Wade Alin (**@wadealin**) of The Atomica Project and Christ Analogue, Alec Empire (**@alec_empire**) and Nic Endo (**@nic_endo**) of Atari Teenage Riot (**@atr_official**), Chris Randall (**@chris_randall**) from Micronaut and Sister Machine Gun, Third Eye Blind (**@3eb**), Eve6 (**@eve6**), KMFDM (**@kmfdmofficial**), and Richard Patrick (**@richardpatrick**) from Filter (**@officialfilter**). #bestsoundtrackever

From Esther Schindler:

I give special thanks for the good stuff to Cindy Kim (**@cindykimPR**), John Prewitt, Karina Bohn, and Nancy Hubbell. Any errors, of course, are my own damned fault.

I also appreciate the ever-patient Land DuPont, Neil Chase, and Alex Forbes, all of whom resisted the urge to joggle my elbow while I was ignoring their projects at the expense of the book. And I cherish every single member of the Internet Press Guild (**@estherschindler/internet-press-guild**), most of whom plied me with chocolate, at least virtually.

I would never have finished this project without the loving assistance of my feline overlords, Meriwether and Shaka; a winning season by the Arizona Diamondbacks; and—especially—my beloved husband Bill Schindler, who made dinner appear at critical times, as if by magic.

Special Thanks to the Technical Reviewer

The Complete Idiot's Guide to Twitter Marketing was reviewed by an expert who double-checked the accuracy of what you'll learn here, to help us ensure that this book gives you everything you need to know about using Twitter in your marketing efforts. Special thanks are extended to Lorraine Ball (**@lorraineball**) of Roundpeg (**@roundpeg**).

Trademarks

The Big Picture of Twitter Marketing

Part 1

Online conversations are happening all over Twitter, reaching hundreds of millions of consumers and providing new opportunities for you to connect to customers. Many companies—both "household word" brands and the tiniest of startups—have used Twitter to attract attention, drive sales, and vastly improve their customer engagement.

Before you implement your own plan for world domination—or a more modest goal, such as building a passionate community of new customers—find out what you can achieve with Twitter marketing … and what can happen if you stumble.

Twitter Marketing Basics

Chapter 1

In This Chapter

- Learning how Twitter has disrupted "business as usual"
- Identifying Twitter's business value
- Inspiring examples of familiar businesses using Twitter

Once Twitter was considered a fad, another "shiny new object" for marketers and early adopters to flock to. It seemed silly: How could anyone say anything meaningful in only 140 characters? Why would anybody care about trivial status updates?

However, Twitter has maintained its prominence in both pop culture and the business world, holding its own against other social networks, such as Facebook, Google+, and Foursquare. In addition to individuals following each other for entertainment and conversation, Twitter has become an effective and affordable way for any business to attract new customers and to encourage existing ones to tell people how great you are. If you are willing to see past the initial superficial status updates, you'll find that Twitter is a valuable business tool. Each 140-character Tweet represents a firehose of business intelligence that every marketer can tap into.

Whether it's sourcing new customers or receiving feedback from existing ones, Twitter helps brand marketers engage in a one-to-one dialogue at an unprecedented rate and scale. It's deceptively easy to get started, but just as easy to stumble. The learning curve to using Twitter for marketing may be steep, but with the right set of guidelines and plenty of examples showing best practices (and fumbles, too), even the most novice user can master Twitter. We're here to help you do just that.

A Brief History of Twitter

Twitter is relatively young, which makes its significance even more remarkable. In 2006, Twitter was nothing more than a simple SMS service—what you think of as "texting" on your smartphone—meant to help individuals communicate in a small group. It asked users to answer the question "What are you doing?" in 140 characters or less and to text their updates to 40404.

At the time, Twitter was a side project; it wasn't even the founders' main gig. Co-founders Jack Dorsey, Evan Williams, and Biz Stone launched Twitter while working at podcasting company Odeo. At the time, the site was called Twttr. On March 21, 2006, Dorsey published the first Twitter message, "just setting up my twttr," and the rest is history.

Twitter Catches Fire

Initially, Twitter was just a curiosity. But it burst into the consciousness of the tech elite when, in March 2007, Twitter made its debut at SXSW interactive in Austin, Texas. Members of the digerati immediately took a liking to the service; the number of Tweets increased from 20,000 to 60,000 in two short days.

By 2010, Twitter's growth exceeded more than 100 million users and 50 million daily Tweets. Its high-profile users include the likes of Oprah (**@Oprah**) and Ashton Kutcher (**@aplusk**)—the first person to ever reach 1 million followers—as well as politicians (**@BarackObama**), journalists (**@Pogue**), and major Fortune 500 brands (**@Ford**).

Today, Twitter boasts more than 200 million active users with more than 450,000 accounts created every day. It's a ubiquitous channel of communication that extends far beyond the web professionals, science-fiction authors, jazz musicians, and early adopters who attended that long-ago SXSW conference. Over the past five years, Twitter has become a part of pop culture, influencing the way people share ideas, learn, and connect.

Twitter has become a news platform, delivering insights into global trends, conversation topics, and events happening in real time. In July 2009, TechCrunch reported an internal document from Twitter in which co-founder **@Biz** referred to Twitter as "the pulse of the planet." Even if Biz Stone didn't write that phrase, it's an accurate assessment. Twitter functions like a news network, often breaking stories several minutes faster than traditional media. Brian Solis, a new media strategist, calls Twitter "TNN"—The Twitter News Network. Twitter, he says, has "set a foundation for which news media can more effectively track, check, and report on breaking stories as they unfold."

On a frigid January day in 2009, Janis Krums snapped a picture of U.S. Airways Flight 1549 sitting in the Hudson River. Other people were taking pictures on their cell phone; that wasn't new. It wasn't Krums' picture that changed the perception and use of social media and citizen journalism; it's the fact that he Tweeted it. It was amazing to see how quickly Twitter was used to share information before traditional news networks could gear up to cover it. People shared images and on-the-spot observations and let the world know what was happening. This was just one example of showing how our tools to communicate are changing.

Twitter as a Business Tool

Beyond celebrity hype and citizen journalism, Twitter has had a huge effect on the business world. With so many people participating together in shared dialogue, businesses didn't want to be left out of the conversation. Nobody wants to know that others are talking about them behind their backs, after all! The service gives businesses like yours the ability to connect and engage with audiences at an unprecedented rate and scale.

Twitter is more than a way to "get the word out" about your products and services. For marketers in particular, Twitter gives brands new opportunities to interact with current and prospective customers, to find out about consumer trends and insight in meaningful and measurable ways, and to give the business a recognizable voice.

How Businesses Use Twitter

Twitter can help any business. It doesn't matter whether you have a small business that's just getting started, whether you work for a "household name" big business, or whether you help other businesses with public relations or sales and marketing.

That shouldn't really be a surprise, because Twitter is just another communications medium. You need to learn about its unique characteristics—and you will—but, overall, this is akin to the shift from magazines to radio, and from radio to TV. You can use these media in new ways, and everything you already know about marketing in those media applies here, too.

Like other channels of communication, Twitter lets your business establish its brand and promote products and services. However, what sets Twitter apart is conversation. Not only do businesses share their messages with their target audience, but customers and prospective customers respond and react in return.

What Twitter Can Mean for Small Businesses

Small businesses always have a hard time getting noticed. They have little money to spare for marketing, and often the business owners (if indeed there is more than one person) are more expert at their services (such as designing a great product logo or cooking a great steak) than at marketing the business. Twitter has been a godsend. Because it's so personal, it lives on word-of-mouth (just like small businesses), and, oh yeah—it's free!

Twitter success is as close as your neighborhood food truck. Take **@kogibbq** in Los Angeles, which discovered how Twitter could be a great driver of loyal fans and followers. The Kogi BBQ truck, which fuses Korean and Mexican cuisine, became famous for its use of Twitter to share its whereabouts with local patrons. By updating the truck's location, co-founders Caroline and Mike Miguera attracted devoted fans who would flock to the truck and bring friends with them.

> **@kogibbq** LUNCH RUUUN! 1130AM-230PM: *Roja@Mattel, City of Industry (15930 E Valley Blvd 91744); *VERDE@Downtown LA (9th and Hope St 90015)
>
> **@kogibbq** Rowland Heights! Verde is running 30 min behind. ETA 11
>
> **@kogibbq** CHEGO BURGER FOOD TRAILER: bit.ly/qTtd3q <— pLus dino gas, beat-up toiLet seats and surfing in vegas.

While amassing more than 90,000 followers might seem like an intangible feat to most small businesses, **@kogibbq** achieved it by doing the following:

- They had a quality product to begin with. (You can't create demand for something that isn't good.)
- They depended upon fans to drive the word of mouth.
- They established a personal voice. Although most of their Tweets are informational (essentially "Here's where the truck is!"), they also share their own experiences.

Twitter for Big Businesses

Twitter can work for anyone and any business. Why? Because it enables people to connect with companies, and companies can connect with their consumers. This is more than advertising or other broadcast media where the company shares what it wants customers to know; it's truly a conversation. The ability to connect in real time and receive a quick response to a question has made Twitter the online destination for immediate service.

As widespread as Twitter is, it isn't always easy to get senior leadership to buy in. Shifting traditional marketing dollars into social media, specifically Twitter, might raise an executive eyebrow or two.

The challenge isn't just the 140-character limitation or the lack of flashy media. Unlike traditional marketing, it's much more difficult (some might say impossible) to control the message on Twitter. In today's world, everyone has an opinion and a platform on which to publish it. Many large businesses (and some smaller ones) are wary of proposing a new Twitter initiative because the leadership team is not ready to accept that Twitter is a dialogue. That's a cultural change that the business may struggle with.

Yet Twitter has become a boon to many established brands because it has enabled them to create customer relationships that were impossible through any other means.

MARKETING WIN

JetBlue is a large company that was smart enough to recognize that the conversation of Twitter was more of an opportunity than a potential public relations (PR) nightmare. With the right strategy, executive buy-in, and purchase incentive, they created one of the first enterprise Twitter success stories.

Twitter for Marketing and Sales Professionals

If you're passionate about your business, some part of Twitter marketing may come easily to you. You know the product line intimately, you lie awake at night trying to think of new ways to create happy customers, and you are always thinking of new ways to engage with your customers. But frankly, you might use Twitter even if you are just a PR or marketing wage slave who wants to earn a big promotion.

And it makes good sense to do so, as Twitter offers so many opportunities to build a brand.

For sales and marketing professionals, Twitter is a bonanza of new ways to raise awareness, leads, and customers. Professionals at PR agencies are using Twitter to connect with journalists and to monitor news feeds for Mentions of their clients. Sales teams use Twitter to follow up with prospects as an alternate to email and phone calls. Advertising-centric marketers run promotional discounts and advertisements on the service.

The payoff is huge. Using Twitter for PR and marketing efforts can earn the business-referral traffic, brand awareness, consumer insight from real-time feedback, qualified leads with a greater conversion rate, and improved customer satisfaction, leading to better retention, job recruiting, and … well, you are limited only by your imagination.

Making a Mental Shift

The opportunities for marketers on Twitter are endless, but where does one begin? Let's start with this: approach Twitter with an open mind. Too often, new users get dismayed by the learning curve and give up. Or they insist on applying traditional marketing principles to the service. While a majority of marketing basics hold true, in many ways Twitter is a social experience unlike any other. Be prepared to engage with strangers and to expect the unexpected. Be open to serendipity and to reacting and responding in real time.

No matter what size of business you serve, don't expect Twitter to do everything for you. While it is a tremendous marketing vehicle for your business, Twitter alone will neither make nor break it. The onus is on you to deliver a product, service, and story that's worth sharing. Had KogiBBQ tried to sell food that was neither appetizing nor interesting, none of their efforts on Twitter would have succeeded.

Businesses are powered by people. Twitter isn't a robot that can automate itself. It's up to you, whether you're the marketing specialist or business owner, to communicate authentically. Twitter users respond better to your brand when the content is written in a personal tone versus just pure marketing speak.

Remember, your fans come first. Pay attention to customers who are advocates. They're the ones who tell their friends about your business, whether it's via text message, telephone, or Twitter. There's a big difference between the following two Tweets:

> I need to order more green beans for my coffee roaster
>
> I need more green beans for my coffee roaster. Fire up the **@sweetmarias** order form!

Identify your advocates and connect with them on a personal level. Twitter can give your loyal customers a call to action, which helps spread your story and amplify your marketing efforts.

We go into more detail about each of these points, and many more, in the chapters ahead.

How JetBlue Became a Leader in Twitter Marketing

Airline giant JetBlue turned to Twitter as one way to monitor its brand. Thousands of travelers were Tweeting about their in-flight experiences, whether on JetBlue or other airlines.

MARKETING WIN

"Made it to my gate at SFO, only to learn that my flight was canceled" is an example of a boring Tweet for most people. It's one step above the "I ate a sandwich" Tweet that those who disdain Twitter make fun of. But for those in the travel industry, "my flight was canceled" is an opportunity for public relations and customer service. It made sense for JetBlue to pay attention, and they were smart enough to do so.

The airline's social media team began by responding to customers one by one, startling the otherwise-disgruntled traveler in the nicest possible way. The outreach customer service established **@jetblue** as one of the first large companies to truly have a voice on the social web.

> **@jetblue @travismurdock** Thanks for the shout-out. We'll make sure Mario and his supervisor are aware of your appreciation.
>
> **@jetblue @djbarrett** We're sorry our service did not meet your expectations. We'll be sure to pass along your concerns to our Airport Leadership.

Moving from Customer Support to Marketing

JetBlue's leaders didn't stop there. They also realized that Twitter could be more than just a customer support channel. They were smart enough to see Twitter as an effective way of driving sales and revenue. In July 2009, JetBlue launched **@JetBlueCheeps**, an account dedicated to promoting real-time deals.

> **@JetBlueCheeps** $109 AUS to JFK next Sat. JFK to AUS next Mon. or Tues. 25 seats avail or til 6 pm EDT. http://bit.ly/JBCheeps Taxes, Fees, Rest. Apply

By giving Twitter users a clear incentive to follow the account, JetBlue grew its follower base quickly. Today, JetBlue has the largest Twitter audience of any airline, with more than 1,600,000 followers, even though they are a much smaller business than competitors Delta and United. JetBlue is proof that big brands can drive business results, 140 characters at a time.

Secrets to JetBlue's Success

What factors have led to their success? Here are just a few:

- JetBlue's corporate culture embraces feedback. They sincerely want to know about customer experiences, and the personnel genuinely want to help them resolve problems. Furthermore, they use customer data to fix internal workflow issues that can improve the customer experience.
- Leadership took a risk and thought about long-term results. The social media effort could never have succeeded without corporate executives' encouragement.
- They emphasize value for the customer. Although JetBlue clearly has the aim of getting people to buy plane tickets on its airline, nothing in their Twitter feed sounds that way. Everything is presented as a service they are doing to make their customers comfortable, happy, and get the most for their dollar.

How Ben & Jerry's Used Twitter to Promote Its Ideals

Twitter can help an established brand underscore the ideals it believes in (and uses to its marketing advantage). Ice cream manufacturer Ben & Jerry's noticed that millions of Tweets contained unused character space, so they created a campaign that promoted fair trade (using the hashtag #FairTweets). They easily could have stopped there and used #FairTweets to encourage a grass-roots movement toward Fair Trade (the organized social movement and market-based approach that works to improve life for producers in developing countries). That might have been enough.

However, Ben & Jerry's took their effort a step further, beyond Twitter. The company created a micro-site (at http://fairtweets.com).

Ben & Jerry's integrated its Twitter campaign with one of its charitable projects.

It encourages Twitter people to Tweet as they normally would; the website fills in any unused character space with an explanation that the individual is using unused characters to promote fair trade, along with a customized URL linking to the Fair Trade Resource Network. This appeals to socially responsible users (at least in their own mind) by letting them contribute something to a good cause, even if it's only a few spare characters.

By mid-2011, the *micro-site* had generated over 500,000 Tweets.

DEFINITION

A **micro-site** is a "site within a website," which usually has a specific purpose. For instance, a company blog is a micro-site, as is a page dedicated to one particular marketing campaign.

Ben & Jerry's Multifaceted Twitter Presence

The fair trade Tweets aren't the company's only presence on Twitter, of course. Ben & Jerry's has several Twitter accounts, including a corporate account (**@cherrygarcia**), a rolling free ice cream truck (**@BenJerrysTruck** and **@BenJerrysWest**), and regional offices (such as **@BenAndJerryOz**). Each of these is well thought out for attracting people to the company's ice cream, and they also acknowledge the contributions from retailers.

> **@BenAndJerryOz @coontastic** Don't forget to ring your local store to check if the new flavours have arrived!

What Ben & Jerry's Does Right

Ben & Jerry's efforts demonstrate several things that a company can do right in a PR campaign, whether it's for a specific event or for ongoing branding:

- Ben & Jerry's highlights a product "feature" that had very little attention, and used it to promote a cause to which the company is committed.
- The Twitter campaign extended past the micro-blogging site itself. By drawing visitors to the FairTweets page, would-be customers can look at other things the company has to offer, whether in social media (such as a Facebook Like), fair-trade activism, or the company's home page. That's far more than they could accomplish with any stream of 140-character messages.
- The business doesn't try to make every marketing campaign fit under a single corporate umbrella. Different "departments" have their own Twitter IDs, letting each of those identities engage with its own target market in the appropriate manner.

The Least You Need to Know

- Twitter can help your business reach new audiences no matter what size your company is.
- It's important to give your account an authentic voice and understand the people you're communicating with.
- Twitter works best when the company genuinely wants to connect with customers—not lecture at them.

The Rewards of Twitter Done Right

Chapter **2**

In This Chapter

- Learning how a small business earned more local clients
- Discovering how a sports team found new ways to engage with fans
- Turning a news feed into a community service

Before you start drinking the social media Kool-Aid, let's consider the many ways your business might use Twitter.

In this chapter, we use case studies to demonstrate how Twitter can produce business results—no matter what size your company is, or what type of business you're in.

A Bevy of Business Benefits

Imagine how businesses reacted when the telephone first became available in the late nineteenth century. The speed of communication must have been astonishing, because issues could be resolved so fast. Suddenly it was possible to maintain relationships—not just telegraph messages, our precursor to texting—over long distances. A business owner could contact a customer or supplier immediately ("Where are the buggy whips you promised us by this morning?"), instead of relying on the post office or in-person meetings.

The telephone was not immediately embraced, however. Only a subset of people and businesses could afford them (in 1900 there were about 600,000 phones in Bell's telephone system; that number shot up to 5.8 million by 1910). And it played havoc with the rules of business etiquette, which had already suffered major disruption by the industrial revolution. Previously, "everyone knew" the rules for presenting a calling card, but new telephone users had no idea even what to say when they picked up the receiver (the word "Hello" was invented precisely for use with the phone). And just think about the first telephone cold sales call.

Nowadays, we could not imagine running a business without a phone. Its business advantages are taken for granted.

Twitter hasn't reached that point, yet. As with our grandparents and great-grandparents who tried to wrap their heads around this new tool, we're all just making up the rules as we go along—and exploring what can be achieved with this new way to communicate.

Let's look at a few ways businesses are using Twitter to help their organizations succeed.

Twitter for Information Dissemination

For some organizations, it's important to spread and collect data. One example beyond news organizations is the Toronto police (**@torontopolice**), which is using Twitter to catch criminals.

Constable Scott Mills told *The Toronto Sun* that social media is a powerful tool for cops, particularly for getting tips about crimes. Sgt. Tim Burrows, who's working on developing policy for police use of social media, described Twitter as "a resource we can use to help augment our abilities to spread messages, to educate, to help raise awareness."

In addition to general cautions ("Think safety-first in choosing a Halloween costume!") and news items (arrests made), the police invite people to share information, and they link to documents that might help solve local problems. Social media enables residents to send anonymous tips, too. "Anything video-related, I put on YouTube, and then link into Facebook and … Twitter," Mills told the *Sun*.

> **@TorontoPolice** 0929 13:49 Missing Woman, Maureen Beck, 73 is.gd/auK4OL
>
> **@TorontoPolice** Confirmation #MissingTSEAR has been LOCATED. Thanks to EVERYONE who shared the information and helped in the search. ^tb

MARKETING WIN

Don't think of Twitter as an RSS feed of press releases. Encourage your followers to use the information you share.

"Your follower base just keeps getting bigger and bigger, so the power of one becomes greater," the Toronto police told the newspaper.

Leverage Word of Mouth

Grasshopper (**@grasshopper**) is a small company, with just 45 employees. They sell a virtual phone system that, they promise, helps entrepreneurs sound more professional and stay connected from anywhere.

It would have been easy for Grasshopper to exert all its energy telling followers how wonderful their service is. Certainly that's the route that many businesses follow—with little payback.

Instead, says Stephanie Bullis, "the ambassador of buzz" at Grasshopper, they're using Twitter to connect potential customers with dedicated users.

"By going above and beyond for our customers—providing exceptional service, hosting events, and doing anything we can to make our customers happy—we've been fortunate enough to create an army of brand loyalists," says Bullis. "On any given day, we see a handful of Tweets asking for recommendations about our service, or a service similar to ours. Rather than responding directly to these questions—and offering self-serving, biased reviews and recommendations—we connect these potential customers with our happy passionate brand loyalists." The happy customers boast about their experience with Grasshopper's service and ultimately turn prospective customers into actual customers.

TWITTER TIP

Testimonials work online just as they do in any other marketing venue. Your happy customers' advice to choose your product has more credibility than you do, simply because the customers don't have a sales agenda.

Zappos Finds a Perfect Fit for Shoe Sales

Zappos (**@zappos**), an e-commerce store that began by selling shoes, was one of the first brands to master the art of relationship-building. In March 2008, CEO Tony Hseih Tweeted this:

> **@zappos** Hello zappos people at SXSW. Please twitter "follow zappos" to follow me.-Tony

As an attendee at the influential South by Southwest conference, Hseih engaged with others both offline and online. A big proponent of establishing a healthy company culture, Hseih saw Twitter's potential to help Zappos employees and customers connect in a new format. Shortly afterward, twitter.zappos.com was launched, transparently sharing a directory of all employee Twitter accounts, brand Mentions, and employee Tweets. Hseih encouraged employees to talk to one another and to be responsive to customers' needs online.

Twitter wasn't meant to be a silo for the company that focused only on customer support. Rather, Twitter became a marketing vehicle for Zappos as a whole, positioning the company as more than a shoe retailer. In an 2008 interview, Hsieh said, "We're not really looking at Twitter as a way of driving additional traffic—it's really just a great way for employees and customers to see that we are real people, and it makes the relationship a lot more personal, which is what we ultimately want people to feel about the Zappos brand."

Hsieh's comment perfectly captures the opportunity big brands have on Twitter. They can change brand perception, empower employees, and drive customer loyalty.

So can you.

Cleaning Up by Finding Local Customers

You don't need to be a high-tech company to use Twitter to attract new business. It's hard to think of a topic that's less sexy than laundry—and yet one high-end dry cleaner in New York City has used Twitter to grow its business.

"We use social media to introduce potential clients to our personality, raise our brand profile, and offer social proof of our services," says James White, Meurice Garment Care's (**@ClothesDr**) director of marketing.

Meurice Garment Care specializes in couture and custom cleaning. It has about 50 employees in four locations around the metropolitan area.

In the two years since the company began marketing on Twitter, it's garnered 2,300 followers. "We've reached a ton of people that we never would have heard from without Twitter," says White, "And it comes in handy for reaching journalists and influential people in our industry."

Twitter wasn't a hard sell to management, because the company owner already understood the value of community. Meurice's owner, Wayne Edelman, has always had an interest in sharing his knowledge both online and off, says White. "We realized that this was a big opportunity for us to build the Meurice brand as an expert in clothing care, and to be part of the conversation when our highly Internet-savvy customers had a need."

Most of the company's Tweets share their knowledge of fabric and its care; they also tap into customers' interest in fashion.

> **@ClothesDr** Be careful w nametags at conferences ... don't put them on materials like leather or silk that the adhesive can damage—#MM #garmentcare

> **@ClothesDr** Tweed three-piece racing suit: I love this! http://ow.ly/6FqB4 And if they need anyone to clean off the grease ...

And they quietly underscore the company's commitment to service.

> **@ClothesDr** You'd never believe what people leave in their pockets ... here's a hint! ow.ly/i/iiPz

MARKETING WIN

Don't beat your drum too loudly. Says White, "We didn't want to go for a hard sell, and create a super-self-promotional presence, but rather add something of value to Twitter and rely on other users to spread the word."

Twitter is about communication and branding more than exhortations to buy now. Many of its business benefits are in people watching how you present yourself and interact. "Not every favorable Twitter outcome involves adding a follower," White says. "Many customers and partners just skim the account to get a sense of our personality and popularity before doing business with us. I'd estimate that for every participant on Twitter, there are 10 users sitting on the sidelines and observing—and that's fine for us!

Even a small business needs to track its results, and the dry-cleaning company staff are self-professed metrics junkies.

Initially, they focused on a big follower count and driving traffic to the website. "But over the years we've realized Twitter is really a marketing channel separate from the website," says White. "It's better to continue a customer interaction where it started."

Now **@ClothesDr** is more concerned with statistics that measure engagement. They track Retweets (currently they average about 10 weekly, most often their garment care tips and blog posts), @Mentions (20 to 25 per week), and customers in the store who mention Twitter. "This happens (mentioning Twitter) at least every week, which leads me to believe there are many Twitter lurkers who keep their social media presence to themselves," says White. "We can also see some Twitter users who check in through FourSquare."

Even a small business needs to establish a workable workflow. White's biggest challenge used to be team communication. "When Twitter users interact with **@ClothesDr**, they assume he (we!) knows about everything that's going on at Meurice; in reality, we hear only a bit of what goes on in our three stores." It was possible to announce a coupon or contest through the Twitter account without the store representatives being aware of the promotion.

To combat the issue, they've learned to send an email message to the entire company before they post anything "worth Tweeting about." They follow up with phone calls to make sure everyone has the message.

Meurice is also training the staff about social media. "Most folks we hire are fluent in Facebook, but less so in Twitter," he says. "We have meetings to show our reps the ropes of social media, and encourage everyone to play around with their own personal accounts. This way, they learn by doing (and can follow our Meurice accounts, too!). It's a great way to keep our team engaged and on the same page as our customers."

Explains White: "I love getting instant feedback from our customers, and being able to solve problems on the spot. The immediate-gratification aspect of Twitter is definitely addictive!"

Engaging the Community with the Arizona Diamondbacks

Large organizations sometimes are nonplussed by the tenets of social media. Public relations teams aren't used to sharing what goes on behind the scenes (it's too much "inside baseball," they're sure), or transparency, or letting their subject matter experts and company executives speak for themselves. Even when the corporate culture is relatively open, the logistics of orchestrating contributions from several departments can be somewhat overwhelming.

The organizations that "get" social media thus are worth looking at in some detail. Let's take a closer look at how one organization is succeeding.

The Arizona Diamondbacks (**@dbacks**) have done a lot of things right with their Twitter campaign. It's been a huge success in regard to engaging the team's baseball fans—and putting more butts into seats at Chase Field. They make clever use of hashtags, and encourage staff to Tweet (from baseball players like Justin Upton [**@realjustinupton**] to the TV announcers [**@dbacksbooth**] to management [**@DHallDbacks**]). And they back it all up by featuring all sorts of "follow us" messages in visible places offline, so fans know how to connect with the team.

A Social Media Home Run

They've done it in a relatively short amount of time, too. Initially, the **@dbacks** Twitter account was managed by the communication department, and, like a lot of large companies, it was full of a lot of factual information, such as press releases. Useful? Absolutely. Thousands of people followed the team. But it wasn't yet ideal.

In the 2010/2011 off-season, the social media responsibility moved to the marketing department, which set new goals for followers, Retweets, and other metrics (set as a percentage increase rather than a hard-and-fast number). They encouraged enthusiastic staff to contribute; one of the social media team members officially works in an unrelated department—"social media" doesn't appear in his job title.

During the 2011 season, the number of followers more than tripled.

That success surely was influenced by the baseball team's own playing season, which went from last place in its division in 2010 to the 2011 National League West championship. "There's no question that team play enters into it," says Karina Bohn, the Arizona Diamondbacks' senior director of marketing.

People like to talk about good things. "We can see a direct correlation between a winning game and the number of Tweets and followers," says Bohn.

Apply this to your own business: share your company's wins, even if it's a single and not a grand slam. People *want* to believe in you. Your company's allies will cheer for you, or at least be reassured that they're dealing with a thriving operation. Prospective customers will be motivated to contact you, because they want to work with winners.

The **@dbacks** own Twitter stream focuses on news, data (such as the game lineup), comments, and feedback to fans, as well as Retweets of fan responses, player commentary, and the occasional link to a news story, photo, or video. Plus, of course, a bit of rah-rah cheerleading:

> **@dbacks** RT **@JarrodBParker** Good day for baseball especially with **@DHuddy41** on the mound! #BeatMil lets go **@dbacks** #whynotus
>
> **@dbacks** For those that have been asking, the start time for Tuesday's #NLDS Game 3 has not been released yet. We'll keep you posted. #WhyNotUs
>
> **@dbacks** #dbacks vs. #Brewers: Bloomquist SS, Hill 2B, Upton RF, Montero C, Goldschmidt 1B, Young CF, Roberts 3B, Parra LF, Hudson RHP

Importantly, the **@dbacks** account works as a communication hub for the organization, and usually responds to fan questions, such as this one:

> **@funbrooksie @dbacks** Any game 2 viewing parties going on?!
>
> **@dbacks @funbrooksie** Nothing official going on, but we wouldn't be opposed if you started one … #GoDbacks #WhyNotUs

There's not a smidgen of doubt in followers' minds that the Twitter account is run by responsive people who care about the team—and the fans.

Let's Go #Hashtags!

Among the most brilliant things about the Arizona Diamondbacks' Twitter campaign—and what first attracted us to use them as an example—is its laudable use of Twitter hashtags. (You'll learn more about using hashtags in Chapter 9.)

The obvious hashtag is, of course, #dbacks. Anyone on Twitter can click on #dbacks in his timeline and find others Tweeting about the team. The Arizona Diamondbacks marketing organization didn't need to get that started.

But they could, and do, orchestrate and spread hashtags to connect the community, especially in and around baseball games. If the **@dbacks** account Tweets #GoDbacks, so do followers who respond. They mix it up, too: #BeatLA when the team plays the Dodgers, or, as you saw previously, #WhyNotUs during the National League playoffs.

"The specific hashtags have been our own idea," says Bohn. The marketing team creates some. But some have been organic. When shortstop Steven Drew was injured, a fan Tweeted a "go team!" message including #DoItForDrew; the **@dbacks** Retweeted the hashtag, and others picked it up. "We try to pick up on what they Tweet," Bohn adds. "Fans know what resonates with them."

On the Big Screen

The hashtags are used in the Twitter stream by the team and its players and contributors, of course. Even without that, it isn't difficult for existing Twitter users to find the **@dbacks** account; anyone in the Phoenix area is apt to see a Mention by baseball fans.

The organization does its best to let people who are not yet well connected or social media savvy to discover the team's activities, though. The Arizona Diamondbacks' "connections" web page helps fans find the Twitter accounts of their favorite players, and organizes the team's social media activities in a single site.

The Arizona Diamondbacks' social media webpage.

Also, the Twitter IDs are shown prominently during media broadcasts, and the announcers sometimes ask people to share opinions via the **@dbacksbooth** Twitter account.

Perhaps the biggest thing they do, however—at least in physical size—is display Tweets on the big screen before games, based on fans using the current game's hashtag.

Before the game, fan Tweets are displayed on the scoreboard, and the Twitter identity is highlighted.

Motivating Fans to Contribute by Sharing

Not everything is "Yeah team!" The Arizona Diamondbacks' marketing team has also used Twitter for ticket sales promotions.

On a few occasions (they're still experimenting), through social media (Facebook as well as Twitter), the team offered a promo code for 25 percent off the usual seat price for certain sections on certain dates. If the fan used the promo code, she was told that by sharing it, she'd get a *new* promo code that doubled her savings. Perhaps it's too much to say they created viral marketing in this manner; maybe it was a modest cough of a virus rather than full-blown influenza.

The same sort of offer was made through email marketing previously—just as you may do currently for your own business—and continues to be used. However, the social media promotion was marvelously effective, and "far outperformed" traditional email marketing, says John Prewitt, the Arizona Diamondbacks' Sales & Marketing Analyst.

A Team Effort

The Arizona Diamondbacks are not the only baseball team to use social media. Every team is using Twitter, under the oversight of Major League Baseball (**@mlb**), which itself is involved.

For example, Major League Baseball's first-ever "Social Media Derby" integrated social media into the State Farm Home Run Derby (**@StateFarm** #HRDerby), reported MLB.com. It resulted in a significant volume of online activity, considerable increases in Twitter followings for the participating MLB All-Stars, and (was this cause or effect?) increased television ratings and viewership.

Players on the field interacted with fans via social media during the home run derby competition, including video and pictures taken by players during the event. Twenty-three All-Stars actively Tweeted, gaining a combined 121,428 new followers over an 18-hour period, an average increase of 17 percent. The 23 All-Stars sent a combined 223 Tweets, which generated more than 18,000 @Mentions back to their accounts.

Keeping Contributors Independent—and Responsible

Perhaps your industry lacks an All-Star game (oh, so *that's* the problem!). But cross-team integration and business policies are relevant to any company that's large enough to have multiple product lines, vaguely interrelated business divisions, and subject-matter experts who are better at their technical area (whether it's chemistry, hardware design, or hitting a baseball) than public communication skills.

Some of the social media policies, and a few of the tools the team uses, are set by Major League Baseball (MLB) and an affiliated company, Major League Baseball Advanced Media (MLBAM). That creates consistency across the baseball industry, the same way each team's website operates under the MLBAM umbrella.

The marketing team sometimes has to tread a fine line. They don't want to quash the players' personalities and fan following; some of the players are wonderfully engaged with the community. Yet, as public relations representatives, the players (and sometimes management) can be … really great at baseball.

For instance, reported fan reporter Jim McLennan (**@AZSnakePit**) from the Arizona Diamondbacks' sponsored "Tweet-Up" gathering, pitcher Brad Ziegler described how he actually first heard about his trade to Arizona on Twitter, before Billy Beane called him into his office to tell him officially.

Nor is the not-always-comfortable oversight role particular to players. Arizona Diamondbacks president and CEO Derrick Hall told his own cautionary tale of the media, which resulted from a Tweet after star Justin Upton was ejected during a game with the Giants. Hall Tweeted, "Umpires need to realize they are NOT the center of attention. Tossing a MVP candidate in a pennant race for a call YOU blew is bush!" Reported McLennan, "That resulted in a phone-call from Commissioner Bud Selig the next day to discuss the matter."

MARKETING WIN

Get the boss involved! The baseball team has benefited from Hall's enthusiastic participation in its social media strategies. Hall has always been ahead of the curve in terms of responsiveness to fans, says Bohn, in that he answers every fan phone call, letter, and email, but Twitter has opened up a new world of possibilities for him to enhance that one-to-one relationship. Plus, Hall's example encourages other staff members to participate.

This is a rare relationship that not many CEOs have with their customers. If your executive staff groks Twitter, appreciate and encourage it!

All this creates tension for the organization's Twitter team. "Your employees are your best advocates for the brand," points out Bohn. "But Twitter blurs the line between 'work hours' and 'off hours.' You can't be speaking for the team and then flip a switch, and have people assume you're not speaking for the team."

"The general consensus of the [Tweet-Up] panel was that Twitter has changed the whole landscape, especially around the trade deadline, and that it's probably inevitable, at some point, that MLB comes in and imposes tighter restrictions in this area," wrote McLennan. "Though how they will enforce those on journalists might be interesting."

Yours may not be as visible an organization as the Arizona Diamondbacks, with a built-in fan base and on a topic that people love to talk about (sports). But the baseball team's success with Twitter contains lessons for businesses of any size. Throughout the rest of this book, we show you how to emulate the many things they've done right.

The Least You Need to Know

- Use an authentic voice that represents the value of your brand.
- You don't have to "sell" anyone on Twitter. Share your knowledge, and the community will respond.
- Twitter is just as much about listening as it is engaging. Monitor your brand closely and be prepared to respond to feedback when appropriate.

Chapter 3

The Pitfalls of Twitter Marketing

In This Chapter

- Misguided business Tweets that lack expertise, compassion, and value
- Avoiding the silently sinking business failure
- How not to respond to PR flaps
- Learning how *not* to leverage the news

As with every communication medium that can be used for marketing purposes—from the telephone to a static website to door-to-door salesmen—Twitter is as useful, as smarmy, as obnoxious, and as fun as you make it. It's all in your hands.

It's just a tool. You can use Twitter for good, and you can use it for evil. The rest of the book explains how to use Twitter for the mutual benefit of your customers, business partners, and your bottom line. But here, we challenge you to consider what happens when Twitter goes wrong. Oh so very wrong.

We don't want to scare you off. We believe that Twitter is a wonderful way to share, connect, and learn. But before you learned to drive a car, you were told about the consequences of driving drunk, and your first lesson in rock climbing taught you how to fall correctly. In this chapter, we warn you about the things that can make you fail at Twitter marketing.

Public Relations Explosions

It's titillating to look at the many ways that a company can mess up in public. None of us can keep ourselves from rubbernecking at another company's fender-bender on the information superhighway.

But let's temper our blatant digital Schadenfreude with instructive "Today I Learned" moments. When you step back from these faux pas, the lessons are blindingly simple: Act ethically. Be careful what you say. Listen to your customers and respond quickly to complaints. Manage crises carefully, as if your life or business survival depends on it. Because they do.

Making a Hash of Hashtags

Twitter users commonly employ *hashtags*—quite literally, putting a hash mark (#) in front of a word or phrase—to label and identify the "topic sentence" of their posts. So one person might include #quote at the end of a favored "quote of the day," sports fans might include a team hashtag ("How did I miss the news of Charlie Weiss joining the #Gators coaching staff?"), and entire "conversations" are held using a hashtag as an identifier. (You'll learn more about how to use them in Chapter 9.)

DEFINITION

Using a word that starts with the # symbol, called a **hashtag,** marks keywords or topics in a Tweet.

Hashtags are simple. It's just a word with a hash symbol (#) in front, such as #Java, #EgyptUprising, or #IHateMonday. It's how hashtags are used that makes them innovative and exciting, because Twitter uses them to make it easy to search for information.

In particular, hashtags are commonly used to identify news events, such as #RoyalWedding or #earthquake. There are tasteful ways for a company to contribute to the conversation about a new event, but way too many ways to do it wrong.

For example, in 2009, UK furnishings retailer Habitat Tweeted promoting its brand using then-current hashtags. Habitat later apologized and blamed an "overenthusiastic intern" for inserting "#mousavi" (a 2009 Iranian presidential candidate) and "#iphone" into their promos.

And in 2011, the Twitterverse buzzed with anger in response to a Tweet on fashion designer Kenneth Cole's account that many felt treated the protests in Egypt as unimportant. The initial Tweet read:

> **@KennethCole** Millions are in uproar in #Cairo. Rumor is they heard our new spring collection is now available online at http://bit.ly/KCairo -KC

The Tweet was later removed, and the company apologized:

> **@KennethCole** Re Egypt Tweet: we weren't intending to make light of a serious situation. We understand the sensitivity of this historic moment -KC

This type of Tweet can draw attention to your company—though probably not the sort you want. When the much-publicized Casey Anthony trial finished with a "not guilty" decision, Twitter exploded with commentary on both sides of the issue under a #notguilty hashtag. Social media agency Likeable Media issued a single Tweet on behalf of its client Entenmann's that made a tongue-in-cheek joke:

> **@Entenmanns** Who's #notguilty about eating all the tasty treats they want?!

After offended Twitter users objected, the Tweet was taken down, and an apology issued. (Do you see a theme here?)

Despite that half-baked stumble, we must point out the Entenmann's Twitter account got a 35 percent spike in new users. They were probably from hungry people who were more interested in donuts than they were irritated by a news-related Tweet. The explosions were probably felt inside the company and with its relationship with Likeable Media, however, because the account went dark—no new posts—two weeks after the event.

These failures are not ephemeral; the effect on your business's reputation lasts far longer than the news story. Long after the Tweets were removed, the articles with the screen grabs of the original updates remain.

All people remember is that you screwed up. For instance, the Kenneth Cole story generated a lot more than Tweets; professional and influential bloggers wrote about the incident. Even now, a search for Kenneth Cole or Entenmann's displays blog posts criticizing the companies' insensitivity, with multiple comments and no counter post from the company.

MARKETING WIN

It's entirely possible to leverage current events to share your unique knowledge, when you can echo the value of your brand. But they should not be perceivable as insensitive and self-aggrandizing.

Oops, I Shouldn't Have Said That

Companies, or the people who Tweet on their behalf, sometimes forget that they are broadcasting to a worldwide audience. While most of us have learned (the hard way) to refrain from immediately clicking on **Send** after writing an angry email message, this lesson has not reached everyone who Tweets on business accounts. It's amazing how quickly you can anger your entire customer base in 140 characters or less.

For example, Emma's Pizza, a pizza place in Massachusetts, Tweeted:

> **@emmaspizza** where in 'substitutions are welcome' does it read it's free? Adding meatballs to a Pressed Veggie Sdwch is nasty and will cost u, dumbass.

One of the eatery's Twitter followers suggested they shouldn't call a customer a dumbass. But Emma's didn't know when to quit, with several more responses, such as these:

> **@emmaspizza** She made a scene in my store when she was told how much something that is not on the menu cost. Called like seen + MYOB.
>
> **@emmaspizza** I never mentioned names which hardly makes it a public berating. I'm wondering who asked you how to run my biz anyway? #MYOB

It only took one Tweet to draw the ire of the Internet masses. But it required five Tweets for the store's owner to craft an apology.

Everything you say on Twitter represents your company. If you are hostile, rude, threatening, or condescending, that's the branding your prospective customers will take away.

Public Shaming

In 2009, an apartment resident with only about 20 Twitter followers Tweeted (under the now-expired Twitter account name **@abonnen**) that her apartment had mold. The Chicago real estate company that owned her building, Horizon Realty Group, filed a lawsuit against its tenant to "protect their reputation" and sued her for $50,000 for slander.

By the next day, the story of Horizon's lawsuit hit trending topics on Twitter. A peevish remark made to 20 people found its way to hundreds of thousands. Almost instantly, Horizon made a worldwide name for itself by connecting its brand with callous disregard for its tenants.

FAIL WHALE

The rules have changed. Your company's public actions—both kindness and obnoxiousness—reflect upon you with a very wide audience. As blogger Sonia Simone wrote, "You don't get the old privilege of anonymity. You don't get to bury your story on page 47. There is no more page 47. Every story is somebody's page 1."

It used to be that a company could dispassionately distance itself from any minor fracas. No more. You cannot hide behind the public persona of your Twitter stream, because—whether you participate in it or not—your customers will comment. Loudly. Even if you think an incident is just a flash in the pan, remember that Tweets are searchable on both Twitter and Google.

After Hurricane Irene, the Long Island Power Authority struggled with rampant power outages. It struggled just as much with public opinion, because its Twitter feed (**@LIPANews**) failed to acknowledge customer concerns or respond (on Twitter or, apparently, in any other way). Residents Tweeted the following:

> **@JPZAMBETTI @LIPAnews** One of your reps just told me that the online outage map is wrong. East Hampton has a sub station problem, and there are far more
>
> **@Evanswweather** LIPA is not helpful with info.
>
> **@EastMeadowMom** Amazed that **@LIPAnews** used a 30 year old disaster recovery plan. Simply. Unacceptable. #irene

Instead of using its customers as a source of information who could help the power company map and publish problems and enable customers to assist one another, the Twitter feed proclaims, "This is LIPA's news and info feed. It is NOT monitored 24/7 for replies."

MARKETING WIN

Smart companies have alerts set up to search for their names because they know that every customer counts, even the smallest single resident. If customers are unhappy—or just mildly irritated—step in early to offer assistance. They will talk about your organization's behavior under stress whether you respond to the emergency well or poorly; you might as well contribute to the conversation with hard data and compassion.

Poor Branding

Think of everything you ever hated about Marketing Gone Wrong. The slimeballs. The come-ons. The obnoxious salesperson who wouldn't take "No" for an answer. The marketing campaigns that battered you with information that didn't help you make a decision, and instead substituted lofty claims ("We're the best!") for technical specifications, business hours, or other information that might help you, y'know, spend your money.

You can do all of those things on Twitter, too, of course. But Twitter offers unique new ways to screw up.

Sell, Sell, Sell

Perhaps the most common misuse of Twitter is when businesses, who so desperately want it to generate revenue, act like snake-oil salesmen.

Yes, you can find people on Twitter who are interested in your type of product. But every individual "cold call" Tweet should be considered carefully.

Savvy marketers look for people who talk about topics with which their business can serve them. Esther once Tweeted about the problems she had with a swimming pool pump; a pool supply company followed her and offered advice. (It wasn't very helpful advice, but the intention was fine.) The emphasis should be on "How can I help?" rather than "What can I get?"

Just because someone mentions that he went to a dude ranch doesn't mean that your dude ranch is of immediate and fervent interest. One Twitter user (see the following figure) was annoyed enough to receive an unsolicited commercial message that he Tweeted about his annoyance to his followers. (The other person who received the Tweet said he "kind of liked it." Go figure. The problem is you never know which response you'll get.)

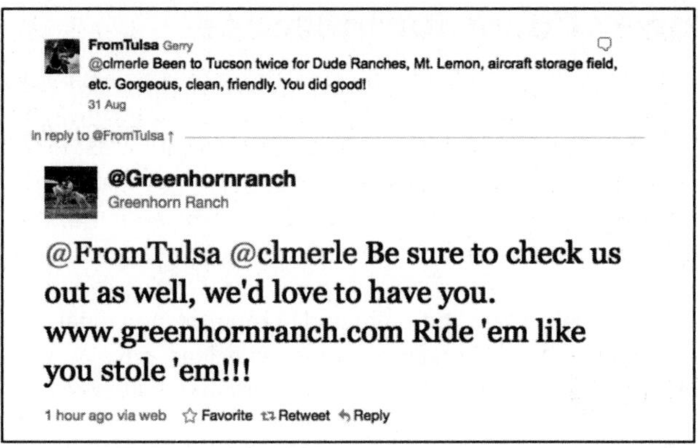

The Greenhorn Ranch sends a purely sales message—it falls flat.

Faking Sincerity

We all hate getting form letters and canned email responses, especially when we took the time to create a carefully thought-out personal message that asked for human input. And we resent the insensitivity even more when the message pretends to be personal: "Gosh, thanks for writing to us! You can find the answer to every question about our product on our FAQ. But don't respond to this message because nobody actually reads the email."

Why would you expect people would react differently to the same poor communication practices on Twitter? And yet, some people do.

Some individuals and businesses imagine that it's important to acknowledge a new follower, and—either manually or with some sort of automated system—send a private message to every new follower, like "Thanks for following us, @YOURNAME! Check out our great deals at www.notsuchagreatdeal.com!"

Such auto-Tweets are irritating because it's obvious there's no human soul behind the effort. It feels as though someone pressed her business card into your hand three minutes after a party introduction. Many people hate canned responses so much that they immediately unfollow any source of one.

Mistaking Follower Count for Influence

A more egregious misstep is to try to appear more influential than you are in order to establish *social media reach.* More followers mean more bragging rights and at least the appearance of more credibility.

DEFINITION

Social media reach means the estimated number of individuals (or target readers, businesses, etc.) that are contacted or touched at least once during a specific period of time, or in social media terms, the sphere of influence.

Attracting not-quite-active followers isn't always a nefarious activity—unless you're already under public scrutiny and bragging about how connected you are.

For instance, opponents claimed that most of the followers of former U.S. Speaker of the House Newt Gingrich (**@NewtGingrich**) were "fake" (or, it turns out, inactive). Gawker's John Cook quoted an anonymous former campaign staffer who claimed Gingrich paid "follow agencies" to create 80 percent of his followers. The allegations were made a few weeks after Politico published a glowing story about "Gingrich being miles ahead in the Twitter primary," with "an impressive 1.3 million followers."

Astroturfing—fake "grass roots" activities—long predates Twitter or the Internet. Twitter gives the "planted review" a new twist, though, because proving someone's online identity is such a challenge. That was demonstrated when the office of a former Nebraska senator working for the American Petroleum Institute appeared to set up two dozen fake Twitter accounts to promote the KeystoneXL tar sands pipeline.

This isn't about your or our political views. In neither case was anything "proven" except the power of the rumor mill, and the effect it has on the individual's or organization's reputation.

MARKETING WIN

Any company or individual in the public eye must stay aware of its brand identity on Twitter. If you're tempted to build a Twitter following using anything other than charm and passion and good works, think again. If you are in the public eye—and any business is—build your online reputation with the same attention and openness that you apply to your "real world" dealings.

Nothing Happens

Most Twitter failures don't get tagged as #PRFail, and few are listed in a Google search for "Twitter debacle." Instead, they are failures because nothing happens. Nobody says anything. It's as sad as a 5-year-old's birthday party in which none of the invited guests arrive—and it's almost always avoidable.

The Abandoned Twitter Page

We could show a screen shot of a real company's Twitter account demonstrating just how empty it can be, with infrequent posts, buy-my-stuff entreaties, and a desperate air. That's too depressing, and it's unfair to the business. (We like to think they will have seen the error of their ways.)

So let's consider a real account in which, apparently, the business forgot to show up. We won't name the business specifically, but it is a recognizable brand within its niche. It's a company that manufactures semi-custom items for woodworkers.

In three months, the company posted only five (count 'em, five) Tweets:

- An announcement about its new updated website (a month ago)
- A link to a (relatively cool) video they recorded at a trade show (a month ago)
- Thanks to everyone who visited them at the trade show (a month ago)
- An announcement of their intention to attend the trade show: "Come by booth 1439, say 'Tweet shirt' to get your T-shirt!" with a link to a show flyer (six weeks ago)
- A "thanks for the follow" to a famous name in woodworking (three months ago), including "Be sure to check out everything new we are doing at [their website] !!!"

What do they imagine they are accomplishing? Who do they think is listening, after all this time? You don't have a conversation that happens one statement per week. Not a good one. The first element in communicating on Twitter is to add new content regularly.

That's it. What personality do they portray? What information do they provide? Who matters to them? We'll let you draw your own conclusions.

None of these are terrible Tweets. They aren't awesome or especially effective, but there would be nothing wrong with them—as long as they had been posted within, say, a single week.

MARKETING WIN

A business getting started on Twitter should post at least twice a day. Ten posts is common. Some incredibly popular Twitter users post four times per hour.

It's especially frustrating to see such poor performance when this business operates in such a creative industry. The manufacturer could, instead, consider who they're selling to: woodworking enthusiasts, largely hobbyists. The business could share its own enthusiasm for woodworking, with photos of what customers built using their equipment. They could post staff video demonstrations on how to use their tools, and point to blog posts with how-to instructions (on nearly anything related to woodcraft). They could Retweet interesting facts from relevant but noncompeting businesses, such as from exotic wood suppliers. They could respond to people who use the #woodworking hashtag, either to offer help or just to say, "Wow, what a great-looking project!" Instead, there was nothing.

We are certain you have seen plenty of examples on your own. You glance at their Twitter stream and think, "Who cares? Why ever would I follow these people?" Don't be these people.

Don't abandon a Twitter account. While it is easy to create an account, it can be very difficult to maintain an active profile. Before jumping in, be prepared to spend the time to maintain your account for the long haul.

Lacking Engagement

Twitter is a fantastic way to get the word out about your work. But just as you don't subscribe to a magazine that is full of advertisements, people don't follow you just to hear that you have something to sell. It's an uncreative mind that uses Twitter just to say "Here's my stuff—take a look at it."

It isn't a mortal sin to treat Twitter as a billboard, and to fail to connect with anyone else. But you can do so much more when you engage with the community.

For example, Franklin Art Glass (**@FranklinArtGlas**) almost gets Twitter right. The company has a beautiful background, a truly descriptive description ("Manufacturer of fine stained glass and distributor of wholesale and retail supplies for the stained glass industry for over 85 years"), and plenty of information about the business in its Twitter stream (including a photo of the shop cat, which is always a nice touch). The interest of any stained glass enthusiast is sure to be piqued.

Franklin Art Glass's Twitter identity is great. But its Twitter stream doesn't recognize anyone besides themselves.

That is, until you read their Twitter stream, which can be summarized as, "It's all about us."

The company does a good job at keeping you informed about what it's doing: holiday hours, new products in stock, a short-term sale. But it barely acknowledges anybody else. The business currently follows 660 other Twitter accounts, including glass artists, museums, other local-to-them Ohio businesses, and their own glass-oriented suppliers. Surely they have something to remark to one of them?

It's obvious from the company's website that Franklin Art Glass knows its stuff and is passionate about glass. But you would never know that from its Twitter stream, and few people will click through to discover more.

If this business showed more of its own personality, replied to people who might care about glass as much as they do, or tipped its hat to partners and allies occasionally, it might get a lot more business from Twitter than it does today.

In Chapter 6, we go into a lot more detail about what you can and should Tweet about. With everything you learn in that chapter, you won't have an opportunity to be boring.

The Least You Need to Know

- Twitter gives you a very big megaphone. Consider carefully what you are broadcasting to the world.
- An empty, rarely updated Twitter feed makes your business seem uninterested … or out of business.
- Your goal for Twitter might be to increase sales. But displaying a sell-sell-sell attitude chases people away rather than drawing them in.

Part 2

Getting Started

It takes five minutes to create a Twitter ID. However, creating a business identity that resonates with your target customers takes a little more thought and preparation.

You can zoom out of the gate, of course, and plenty of businesses have successfully bonded with their communities that way. But it's far smarter to learn Twitter "manners" before you act like a social media boor, to consider how to present your company to the world, and, of course, to understand the myriad ways to Tweet things that make people want to follow you. Learn the virtues of brevity, whom to follow, and how Retweeting can attract people to your Twitter presence … and your front door.

Chapter 4

Building Blocks of Using Twitter

In This Chapter

- Setting up a Twitter account for your business from start to finish
- Understanding basic Twitter terms
- Considering the best persona for your Twitter account

By now it's obvious why your business should be on Twitter. You're ready to make it happen.

In this chapter, we help you set up a new Twitter account—with the business in mind—and introduce you to Twitter's basic functions. Don't worry, this is the easy stuff.

Basic Setup

Setting up a regular Twitter account only takes a few minutes. It's meant to be straightforward enough for the most technology-averse newbie to achieve with confidence. You simply go to the home page of Twitter.com, fill out your name, email ID, password, and hit **Submit**. Optionally, you can customize your account with a photo, biography, and other information—all to an individual's whim.

But you aren't just an individual; you represent a business with a marketing presence. And you need to present the business accordingly.

FAIL WHALE

Each Twitter account must be associated with an email address. If the person creating your account already has a personal Twitter handle, you need another email alias to associate with the account—and someone to be responsible for its upkeep. After all, if you assign this to an employee, what happens when he leaves the company?

One solution, appropriate especially for small companies: when you set up the business Twitter account, assign it to an email ID used only for this purpose, to which multiple people have the password.

Creating the actual account is easy and straightforward. When it comes to setting up a business Twitter handle or ID, there's a lot more to think through. By the way, a Twitter name, handle, and ID are all synonymous terms.

Choosing a Business Twitter Handle

In some cases, choosing a business Twitter handle is dead simple. If you have a well-known company name that is also descriptive and rarely confused with anyone else, this becomes a "duh" step. For easily recognizable brands like Starbucks or McDonalds, it makes sense for the Twitter handle to take on the company name. However, in some instances, the choice of a Twitter name is more complicated.

What happens when your company name is generic or easily confused with another brand? Do Twitter users expect **@delta** to belong to Delta Airlines or Delta Faucets? (It's the former.)

TWITTER TIP

Name squatting or trademark infringement is unfortunately not an uncommon occurrence. If your business name has been claimed by a fake or inactive account, fill out a support request at https://support.twitter.com/forms/trademark.

One example is Columbia, a sportswear company headquartered in Portland, Oregon. If they were to create a consumer-facing Twitter account (right now they have only **@columbiapr** for interaction with the media), they would find the handle **@columbia** is already used by Columbia University. As a result, the business would have to put on their creative hats and think through the following:

- Can other words or descriptors be added? Columbia could create **@columbiasports** or **@columbiagear**. (They seem to have camped on **@ExploreColumbia** but have not yet begun using it.)
- Should divisions of the company be promoted and used to differentiate the business by region or other criteria? For example, there's **@virgin** and then **@virginamerica**.
- Can you own a category name, where prospective customers might go without awareness of the brand behind it? For example, Burger's Smokehouse Tweets as **@smokehousemeats** rather than trying to use a variation of the company name.
- Does your account have a specific purpose that should be reflected in the handle? The customer-support-focused **@comcastcares** is a great example of a business handle where the purpose is clear in the name.
- Choose a username that's memorable. There's no point in being unique if no one can remember who you are.
- Shorter names are better, both for type-ability and because it's easier to Retweet your messages.

Another complication you might encounter is if your business is commonly misspelled. To avoid confusion, sign up with Twitter IDs for every variation of your company's name. Then post a single Tweet on each of the "wrong" ones that points the visitor to the correct account.

The name should also reflect your long-term plans. It's common for the owner to Tweet, in very small businesses; but as the business grows, others need to be represented as well. As the company becomes more than "just the owner," the owner needs her own Twitter identity.

MARKETING WIN

If these issues give you a sense of déjà vu, we aren't surprised. They are precisely the same questions you had to answer 15 years ago when the company chose a domain name for its first website. These concerns apply to your brand across all digital identities, not just Twitter.

Among them are several matters of intellectual property such as name squatters. It could keep the lawyers occupied for months. So if your "obvious" name is taken, get the lawyers on the case early.

Creating Your Twitter Home Page

Twitter is just one way for your brand to present itself online. In the same way we consider the impact of the clothes we wear, brands on Twitter should think about how they "dress" their account. On Twitter, that's composed of three things: a photo, a bio paragraph, and a background for the Twitter page.

Create an avatar. An avatar is any image meant to represent you. For an individual, it's usually a personal photo. For a business, the avatar is generally the company logo.

Most people only ever see a tiny square that represents your business on Twitter. Use this space wisely. If you have a large logo, consider creating an image that is a clean and simple version. Most companies use a staid corporate logo, but nothing says you have to do so. The Chilean Avocado board puts a little zest in its avatar.

The Chilean Avocado board's avatar.

Write your Twitter bio. This is the first thing users read when visiting your page. Make it clear what your business is, why you're on Twitter, and why someone should follow you. Are you there to share news? Are you there to share deals? Don't leave users guessing about your purpose or identity.

If your brand is generally well known, be sure to disclose that yours is an official account. There are lots of Twitter imposters!

Create a branded background. The default choices for Twitter backgrounds are fairly dull, and they do nothing to identify your company. Work with a design team to create an image that displays behind your Timeline.

MARKETING WIN

For authenticity, the best step is to get Twitter to mark you as a "verified account," as they have done with celebrities such as Yoko Ono (**@yokoono**) or fiction author Neil Gaiman (**@neilhimself**). Unfortunately, Twitter's process for doing so keeps shifting, so it's difficult to give you the How-To steps.

At a minimum, linking to your Twitter profile from your official website is the easiest way to confirm your identity to your followers. Somewhere on the company website you should list the employees who Tweet and their roles, linking to the Twitter account—a practice that has plenty of other benefits, too.

The background gives you additional real estate to relay information to Twitter followers and page visitors. Here's a few ways to use the background to enhance your business presence:

- Describe your business in greater detail.

Twitter's bio paragraph has a fixed number of characters. Consider using the background to offer more information.

- Use it as a portfolio or billboardlike advertisement. This is primarily suitable for businesses that are inherently visual, such as a photography studio or web design business.
- Visual branding—the background can reflect or emphasize the company's existing color and design themes.

The New York Times *has dozens of Twitter accounts, held together by a consistent professional background based on the company logo.*

- Point visitors in the direction of other properties, such as your Facebook page.

MARKETING WIN

Do not underestimate the importance of getting your ID, bio, and photo right. When you follow someone, most people get an email notice letting them know about their new follower. (It's a system preference, but most people do leave that turned on.) The email message they receive says that @SoAndSo is following them. All they get is the Twitter ID, photo, and bio.

Think of it as if it were a direct-mail piece. If you don't capture their interest with that information, the person you follow will not click through to see who you are, what you offer, or the chuckle-worthy Tweets you wrote. This is the front door to your business for most people, so don't blow it!

Using Twitter Elements Properly

A number of elements on Twitter might not seem very intuitive to a newbie. Twitter has a whole language of its own, consisting of things such as "@ replies" and hashtags. We get into more detail about how to use these to benefit your business in later chapters; right now it's only important to identify them.

A Look Around

When you log in to your account, you see at the top of the screen the prompt, "What's happening?" with a field below it. Here's where you write and post your Tweets.

Immediately below that text box is your main Timeline: a stream of Tweets posted by the individuals you follow. If you don't see anything here when you set up your account, it's only because you haven't started following anyone yet!

TWITTER TIP

You can use the Twitter.com website to access Twitter, and many people are happy with it. However, an entire ecosystem of specialized applications give Twitter a different user interface and extend its functionality. These Twitter clients run on mobile devices and computer desktops; we discuss them later. In general, we show you how to do things with the default Twitter website because it's accessible to everyone.

The tabs pertaining to the Timeline include Home, Connect, and Discover. Let's go through these one by one.

The Home tab returns you to the main Timeline, which shows the Tweets from the accounts that you follow.

The Connect tab has two options: Interactions and @Mentions. Interactions shows who followed you, mentioned your Twitter handle, Retweeted a Tweet of yours, or added you to a Twitter List. @Mentions highlights messages to a specific Twitter ID. Simply put an @ in front of the account name, such as @brett. Twitter highlights @Mentions in that user's Twitter stream.

The Discover tab displays the latest stories that people on Twitter are Tweeting about, and includes a link (outside of Twitter) so that people can read about the topic(s) being discussed.

If you are mentioned in someone's Tweet, the Tweet appears in your Twitter stream under the @Mentions tab. When you click on the @Mentions tab, you see all of the Tweets where you're mentioned. For instance, if Esther wrote the following Tweet, Brett would see it in his @Mentions tab.

> **@estherschindler** I sure wish **@brett** would bring me chocolate.

And obviously, Brett would immediately fetch her the very best dark chocolate, because he is a loyal friend who knows what's good for him.

Ordinarily, you don't get an email or text message or other offline notification about @Mentions. You can change it in your settings, but it's turned off by default. You can choose whether you want to receive notifications when you're mentioned in someone's Tweet and when your Tweets are Retweeted. Most people leave it turned off.

To directly acknowledge or address someone else, Tweet with an @ in front of her username. ("That's a really good idea, **@estherschindler**!") Otherwise, she is unlikely to find out you were talking about her.

TWITTER TIP

A variation on the @Mention is a direct message, or DM. A DM is a private message sent only to the individual account. Twitter sends an email to the recipient letting him know you wrote to him.

To send a DM, type D, space, the person's account name (**D Brett**). (Not **DM Brett**, which is a frequent mistake by new users; they shortly discover their "private" message was posted to the world.)

The catch is you can only send a DM to someone who is following you. If Brett is not following you, Twitter gives you an error message.

Retweets (RT). When you look at the Tweets in your Timeline, you see a Retweet button. Clicking on it enables you to repost that Tweet. Think of Retweets as a way to share worthy news, ideas, or links while attributing them to the original source.

Searches. With so many millions of Tweets posted every day, you naturally want to discover the topics, people, and conversations that are of interest to you.

Type your keywords or names, or what have you, into the Search bar located at the top of the page, such as "Complete Idiot's Guides." Twitter shows you both "people" matches (such as **@IdiotsGuides**) and text matches (such as the Tweet of anyone mentioning the phrase "complete idiot's guides," surely in the most glowing of terms).

From a marketing point of view, searches are useful to monitor Mentions of your brand, product category, or other keywords that matter to your business. It's also a good way to find people you care about.

You can save the search by clicking the "Save this search" button at the top right.

Lists. You can create lists of people you follow based on interest or context. For example, you can group together co-workers, journalists, news feeds, suppliers, etc. Lists make it easy for you to spend quality time catching up with a single set of people.

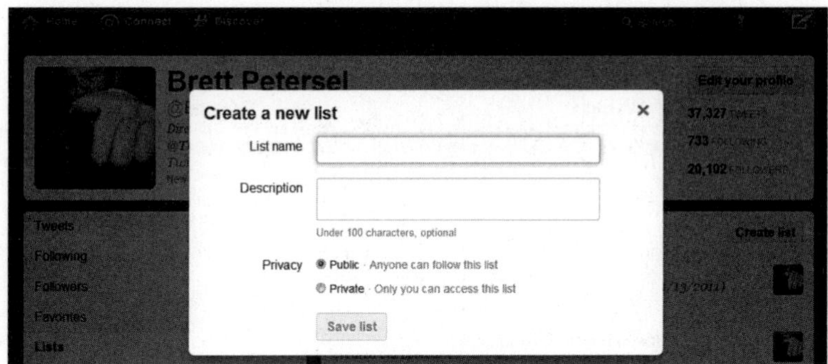

You create or add to a list from the user's profile.

To add a user to a list, go to his profile, and click the button that looks like a person's silhouette beneath his bio. A drop-down menu appears with the option to "Add to list." You can create a list from scratch or add the user to an already existing one.

Lists can be public ("computer-tech journalists") or private ("My clients"). You can follow other people's public lists, which is a shortcut way to use someone else's collation wisdom.

TWITTER TIP

Don't worry about posting a lot of @replies on Twitter. Unless a Twitter user is following the person you @reply, she won't see the message come up in her Timeline. For brands and individuals who engage frequently on Twitter, this eliminates any worry or concern that their general updates or announcements are drowned out or that they'll alienate followers with too many Tweets.

Understanding Hashtags

Hashtags are deceptively simple. It's nothing more than adding a # to mark keywords or topics in a Tweet.

Hashtags let the Twitter community categorize information, especially to show information more easily in a Twitter Search.

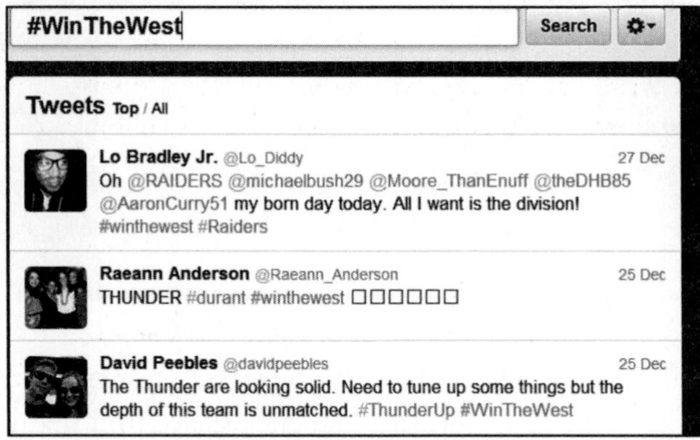

Searching on a hashtag brings up all Mentions of that tag.

Clicking on a hashtagged word in any message shows you all other Tweets in that category. By including hashtags in your own Tweets, you can attract interest from people who might not discover your existence otherwise.

Defining Your Twitter Persona

Professional authors often speak of having a "voice," a way of presenting themselves through their words. One person writes in a matter-of-fact manner; someone else imparts useful information interspersed with jokes to liven things up. Even if you don't envision yourself as a writer, you are using Twitter to communicate to the world about your business, so it's important to consider your demeanor.

In other words: How do you want to present your business to the world?

Most business Twitter accounts are set up as a marketing function: to drive awareness, new business, and customer loyalty. Your Twitter account is an extension of your brand and a tool to deliver key messages to a relevant audience. The tone of your

Tweets sets expectations. Become cognizant of how your account is perceived and how it might impact your overall goals.

Tweeting with Purpose

You should know exactly why you're Tweeting, who you're trying to reach, and the message you'd like to get across. These form a premise that underlies your business strategy and your campaign's goals. If the goal of your activity on Twitter is to increase sales, then your account should help support this objective. If your business is trying to build brand advocates, then your Twitter account should support this as well—sometimes to the exclusion of other good ideas that are off-purpose.

The content and tone of your Tweets make all the difference when it comes to setting audience expectations. Here are a few examples of how a business's Tweets create a brand's persona.

@LuxorLV, the official account of the Luxor Hotel & Casino in Las Vegas, puts its emphasis on helping guests make the most of their stay. They offer personal greetings and customer recommendations. On a rainy day, they might Tweet an indoor exhibit or special spa discount. They acknowledge guests when they Tweet a positive experience at the hotel. The account is focused on the needs of existing customers, rather than an outreach in which the hotel staff aims to convince people to visit Las Vegas. It's friendly and personal, and modeled on a virtual concierge service.

> **@LuxorLV** Glad you are enjoying your stay. What have you done/seen so far? RT **@GLopezSantana** Staying **@LuxorLV** **#**WONDERFUL!

In contrast, the **@chicagobulls** Twitter account focuses on fans and real-time experiences such as game time. The Chicago Bulls' Tweets offer fans news and insight into the basketball team that they might not otherwise get. They share links to news and sometimes post exclusive photos of players at events. Their Tweets still have a "business personal" tone to them, but their engagement is less frequent than **@LuxorLV**.

The Chicago Bulls' Twitter account informs its fans about schedule updates and posts information about special pricing for official merchandise.

> **@chicagobulls** Bulls announce 2011–12 preseason schedule http://bit.ly/nwwlbR

At news sources like the Wall Street Journal (**@WSJ**), **@CNN**, and **@huffingtonpost**, the content is almost exclusively headlines: informational versus conversational.

> **@CNN** Secret life of D.B. Cooper hijacking witness includes disappearing to a nunnery: on.cnn.com/p4NF0A

There's nothing wrong with putting less emphasis on one-to-one dialogue—if that is what your audience expects. For some companies, this makes complete sense. Consider what your targeted Twitter followers need from you, and what you need and want from them.

Again, it all goes back to why you use Twitter. If it's to push news and information, then this approach is appropriate. (Information-sharing is also the easiest way to get started, at least in organizations that are not yet comfortable with the idea of user interaction.)

Keep in mind, though, that the true benefits accrue in using Twitter for conversational marketing.

@HRBlock both shares information and engages with followers. On any given day, **@HRBlock** shares relevant tips about financial fluency. It also serves as a resource for taxpayers by encouraging followers to ask tax-related questions.

> **@HRBlock** Did you know the IRS requires you to keep your tax records for a minimum of three years? Multiyear transactions records must be kept longer.

Often, a company's senior leader, perhaps the CEO or its most public expert, uses Twitter to carve out thought leadership in the industry or to get a better pulse on employee and customer sentiment. This type of account, although business-related, usually has a much different style—often a much more personal one.

Your Personal Brand

Twitter is a community. It is a community of real people who have things to say, things to learn, and interests that just so happen to encompass products and services you might be able to supply to them.

Many companies go into Twitter treating it as just another form of advertising. They have a "message" they want to get across, and they imagine that if they browbeat people with their self-absorbed needs, the world will beat a path to their doors.

It doesn't work that way. Twitter is attractive to millions of users because it helps them learn and it entertains them. It's not an ad campaign. It's a conversation between real people who have personalities, and they expect to see your personality, too.

TWITTER TIP

Ambrose Bierce defined an egotist as "a person more interested in himself than in me." Write to your followers' interests, not your own. A rule of thumb: no more than one in four Tweets should be about you.

No matter what your company size, let yourself show. Include your personality in your Tweets.

Sure, get the business message across. Help people discover what your company can do for them. But don't be afraid to recognize the world outside your office. The world knows vast details about Esther's cats (who are, we should mention, the most adorable cats anywhere), and interspersed with "work" messages she includes links to those all-important silly videos on Friday afternoon.

FAIL WHALE

"Let yourself show" does not mean "Get drunk in public." Separate your personal and business personae. Have a personal ID if you must talk politics or you want to share reviews of wine bars. (Just tell us where the good wine bars are.)

The Least You Need to Know

- When setting up a Twitter account for your business, ensure that you have added all of the appropriate information about yourself and the service you offer.
- Define how you want to use your company's Twitter account. Make it come alive by communicating with your followers and providing proper information.
- Twitter is a community. It's up to you to embrace it—humanize your company, and the rest will fall into place.

Understanding the Twitter Community

Chapter 5

In This Chapter

- Getting up to speed on Twitter etiquette
- Using direct messaging rather than Tweeting publicly
- Greeting new followers without a breach of manners

Most traditional marketing methods are essentially a broadcast medium. You send a press release, you schedule a TV commercial, you place an ad in the local PennySaver. You communicate what you want heard—and then, for the most part, it's out of your hands. All you can do is wait for a response from your target market.

Twitter is different. Despite our frequent analogies to radio, Twitter is not solely a do-it-yourself radio station. Twitter is an ongoing, worldwide conversation in which you are welcome to participate.

Like all communities, Twitter has its own etiquette and tacitly accepted behavior. When you're new in any community, it's easy to fumble in public. In this chapter, we prevent you from making the most common mistakes.

Twitter Manners

If you have been in business for any length of time, you already know how important it is to get along with people. In person, you have learned to dress like your peers (and when not to), to perfect your handshake, to make idle chit-chat before a conference call starts.

Twitter society has similar conventions for what is "done" and "not done." Here are some of the unspoken rules, especially as they apply to businesses.

Using Direct Messaging for One-on-One Conversations

Most messages you post on Twitter are public, viewable by anyone in the world. With direct messages (DM) you can send a private message that is readable only by the recipient.

It's simple enough to do: type d, space, and the recipient's name, such as d estherschindler. If she is following you, the message appears in Esther's Direct Messages tab, and (assuming her Twitter preferences have the default settings) she receives an email message with the contents of the DM.

When to use direct messages, however, is a little less cut-and-dried. You need to be cognizant of two things:

- Your Twitter followers' perception of the public conversation
- Your relationship with the person you're DMing

TWITTER TIP

In general, use direct messages for one-on-one conversations when there's no value to Twitter at large to hear the conversation.

DMs are ideal for conversing about semi-private information. A customer support representative might request (publicly) of an unhappy user: "Please DM me your account number so I can find out what happened." One reason is for the security concerns regarding publicly posting private information such as account numbers. Also, seeing the account data on a public Timeline doesn't help anybody.

The same reasoning applies to two-way conversations that span several public messages. It's fine for you to have a back-and-forth conversation with a follower, but unless you are both scintillating or insightful, take it one on one in a DM. Asking a colleague, "What time do you expect to arrive at the conference hotel?" doesn't need to appear in other followers' Timelines. They don't care.

The usefulness of DM conversations shows up even more when you find yourself disagreeing with someone. Unless your discussion enables you to illuminate a product advantage ("Ah yes, unenlightened one, but you didn't know about this nifty feature in our ProductGizmo 3.0!") your followers see only that you squabbled with a customer. Even if the customer deserved it (our technical term for these people is bozo), it rarely enhances your reputation.

TWITTER TIP

If you're unsure whether it's time to take a conversation private, apply this rule: if you were a panelist at an industry conference, answering questions from the audience, at what point would you tell the questioner, "Let's take this offline"?

Don't Auto-DM New Followers

In early Twitter days, individuals and businesses sometimes sent a DM to new followers, usually with a marketing message attached.

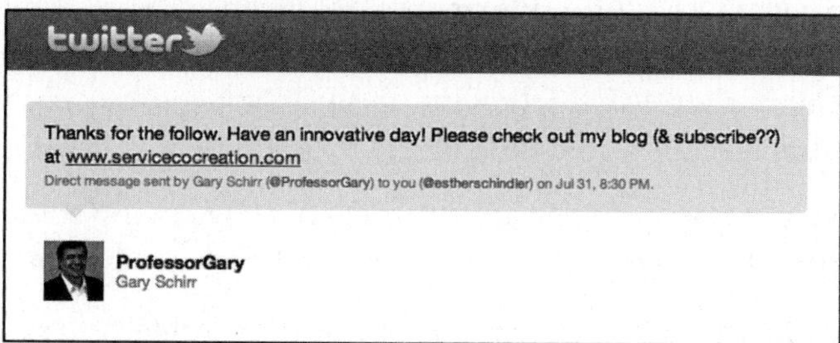

A private "Thanks for the follow."

The practice has, thankfully, become uncommon. It's considered pushy marketing, at best. Many followers who receive an automated or "sales" DM immediately unfollow you. They may block you entirely. Some people make a point of complaining about spam DMs. It's a lose-lose situation. Save DMs for personalized messages.

Right, you're thinking. Maybe that's true for other people. But if I set up an auto-DM for new followers, saying, "Welcome aboard! You might like to read our B2B Marketing Manifesto [link]" (or "our white paper on healthy teeth" or "Five ways to improve your golf score"), I'm sure to get a marvelous response. After all, chances are that the new follower is a B2B marketer (because that's what we do, as reflected in our Tweets) so he really would like the B2B Manifesto. Why not let him know it exists?

However, even if Auto DMs seem to convert better than other marketing messages, you will alienate 40 people for every successful click. Really, you will.

If you're truly interested in cultivating new business contacts, then send a truly personal message. Tell me why I will be interested. Cite something in my Twitter stream or other public contact information to demonstrate your certainty. Otherwise, you are sending unsolicited commercial messages—which rightly would be banned as spam if they arrived by email.

Don't Thank Followers for Following You

It used to be somewhat common for businesses (particularly small businesses, and especially marketing-centric businesses) to greet new followers publicly. We used to see Tweets like this:

> Thanks for the follow, @oneperson @secondperson @thirdperson @enoughalready!

Initially, it seems like good manners to welcome people who took the trouble to follow you.

But it isn't. This gives no useful information to anyone reading your Twitter stream—especially if you gain more than a trivial number of followers. Have you ever seen someone with more than 1,000 followers do this? No, you haven't. Can you imagine what their Twitter stream would look like if they did?

From the recipient's point of view, it's overkill. It's like having someone with a megaphone announce, "Julie just walked into our store! Everybody look at Julie!"

There are a few exceptions. One is when you want to publicly greet someone you know personally and professionally, who might be of interest to your followers.

For instance, French Wine Tours welcomed a new follower, a nearby Chateau, when the winery joined Twitter. We assume the tour company often brings its guests to this winery:

> **@frenchwinetours** Thanks for the follow **@Chateaudebreze** we send someone your way nearly every day! Welcome to Twitter!

Another irresistible "Thanks for the follow" message is when you are followed by someone famous in your industry. You can tell yourself that being followed by that person gives your company more credibility, especially if yours is a small business for which celebrity attention means a lot—and that's probably true.

But really, this feels good; we might indulge, too.

Even so, try to make the "Thanks" useful to your other followers, as the French Wine Tours did. A follower interested in wine tours would be happy to know about the Chateau as both a destination and a useful Twitter feed. Plus, their Tweet demonstrates that the wine tour company is well connected.

Or say something with substance that helps or supports the new follower. In this case, the second Tweet has a lot more substance:

> Thanks for the follow, **@kirstiealley**!
>
> Thanks for the follow, **@kirstiealley**! We think your weight-loss program is outstanding! You dance better than anyone!

Besides, if you sincerely praise the influential new follower, she is more likely to Retweet your message—to the very people you hope she influences.

Don't Thank People for Retweeting You ... Often

Some social niceties are clear-cut rules, like "Don't spit in public" (or the high-falutin' version, "Don't expectorate in front of the ladies if you expect to rate with the ladies"). Others are general guidelines, in which you should use your own judgment. This one is in the latter category.

In general, don't thank people for Retweeting you. If you are particularly grateful, and you think it will make the recipient feel all warm and fuzzy to get a private note of appreciation, send the person a simple DM ("Thanks for RTing my link to the article about birds in Belize!").

Some people do send these thank-yous publicly; however, they usually do it in a single Tweet thanking several people at once:

> Thanks for the RT of my birds in Belize blog post, **@brett @estherschindler @SlimTheDog**!

When it's an infrequent practice, a public thank-you has some benefits:

- It introduces people to one another who have at least one thing in common: interest in the item they all Retweeted.
- It's another opportunity to reference the item you wanted to get noticed. Someone who missed the item earlier in your Twitter stream ("Oooh! Pretty bird pictures! Must see!") might be inspired to go back and look for it. (But don't hold your breath.)
- It demonstrates that someone thought it was interesting enough to share.

Overall, however, Retweeting is now part of the conversation, and it rarely needs to be called out. For most of your followers, seeing a "Thanks for the RT!" in your Timeline is just noise. Resist the urge unless you are sure it makes a difference in your brand's perception.

Rather than a public thank-you, express your gratitude to someone who Retweeted you by looking at their Timeline for a shareable Tweet. Retweeting something they said gives them value and introduces them to a new audience.

The Dubious Merits of Follow Friday

Another debatable practice is "Follow Friday." In early Twitter history—say, 2008—when the only people on Twitter were the digital intelligentsia (that is, we cool people), it wasn't easy to find people who shared your interests or were in your extended social circle. That was long before Twitter lists were rolled out, blog posts commonly had links to "follow me," or articles such as "25 Software Testers to Follow on Twitter" were common.

The Twitter community evolved a nicety called #FollowFriday, almost immediately abbreviated as #FF. Every Friday people would Tweet a short list of people they believed others should follow, ideally with a clue as to why. So Esther might Tweet the following:

> For good insights on beer-brewing and consumption: **@FlagstaffBeer @OdellBrewing @FullSailBrewing @RealBeer** #FF

It was—and for many people still is—a shortcut way to recommend subject-matter experts, and to show the recipients that their Tweets are appreciated. We've both found interesting people to follow that way, though more often in the past than in the last year or two.

#FollowFriday has fallen out of favor, for a few reasons:

- It was overdone. Some people would Tweet five or six times with #FF recommendations in a row. They listed, apparently, everyone they knew, with no context for why anyone should follow those people.
- Some people used #FollowFriday to imply influence they didn't have. For example, a tawdry business owner might mention other accounts just to be noticed, because perception matters. The assumption went: "If I post a Tweet and include a Twitter celebrity's name, people will think I know them and then I'll be a celebrity, too!" Wrong! There is nothing special about including someone's name in a Tweet unless he or she reciprocates.

- Other Twitter functions such as Twitter lists largely made #FollowFriday superfluous.

TWITTER TIP

If you have sets of people who are top influencers on a particular topic, create a public Twitter list to which you direct your followers occasionally.

Still, there's nothing wrong with #FollowFriday. You won't upset anyone if you participate. It's just that there are far more effective ways these days to tip your hat to those whose information you rely upon.

Engage with the Community

The Twitter community is very much like a cocktail party. If you're new in town, it's important to meet people and to make a good impression. The same social rules apply:

- If you only talk about yourself, people at the party become annoyed or disinterested.
- If you only repeat what other people say (Retweeting), you'll be viewed as dull and avoidable.
- Rude behavior, offensive language, and off-color jokes are frowned upon. And when you're new, you can't be sure where the societal lines are drawn.
- No one wants to meet an insurance salesman at a party, so keep the selling to a minimum.
- Sitting by yourself in the corner and watching is creepy. So talk!

Want to be the life of the party and make new friends? Be the person who listens, communicates, and discusses topics of choice by the group, not just you.

Avoiding Heavy-Handed Selling

People don't want marketing materials shoved at them. If every Tweet is about how awesome your company is, people lose interest fairly quickly—as in, immediately.

"Twitter is an invaluable resource when you have something important, direct, or personal to get out there," American Apparel's Ryan Holiday told Business Insider. "It's important that you don't blow that opportunity with trivial updates or greedy thinking."

You have a lot more to share with your followers than "Buy my product." Show them why they should do business with you, rather than telling them to.

Don't Repeat the Same Things Over and Over

Some businesses mistake Twitter for a worldwide billboard, and repost the same messages. By now, you have probably figured out that this doesn't work, but plenty of other people haven't gotten that message.

For example, a company that sells point-of-sale software for bookstores Tweeted variations on the same all-sales-all-the-time text—three times in the same hour—with absolutely no other content:

> **@Bookseller_POS** Bookseller-touch POS Software; naturally Leading tiny.ly/YG5k (1 minute ago)
>
> **@Bookseller_POS** Bookseller-bank POS Software; easily A-1 tiny.ly/YG5k (13 minutes ago)
>
> **@Bookseller_POS** Bookseller-genius POS Software; ordinarily Matchless tiny.ly/YG5k (25 minutes ago)

What makes them think this will attract followers—or customers? It's a turn-off at a cocktail party, and it's a turn-off online, too.

A variation on this is the "personal" Tweet to advertise services—except it's [your name goes here] personal.

If this @Mention arrives unsolicited from a stranger—and it nearly always does—it's no more welcome than the junk mail in your post office box. And it gets even less respect.

Don't Tweet to everyone "individually."

Tweets Should Be Readable and Interesting

It ought to be obvious that nobody follows you unless you give them a motivation to do so. The best way to do that is to be interesting.

If you're unsure of what to Tweet, don't worry; we spend the entirety of Chapter 6 helping you discover how much you have to say. If your muse is still silent, however, you can be interesting simply by acting as a curator of good content. If you know people who do know fascinating things, and you share them with your followers, you'll soon be considered a subject-matter expert in your field.

Editing Tweets to Make Them Interesting

"Share interesting stuff" doesn't mean you can attract people by Tweeting never-ending streams of "Check out this cool link!"

If you are Tweeting something that is already published, such as a page on your website or a review of your product, don't automatically assume that the existing headline or article title is appropriate as a Tweet.

For example, we saw someone Tweet "iPhone iOS 4 Security" and a link. We thought, "Yeah? What about it?" and we had not the slightest urge to click.

In particular, don't confuse headlines that appeal to Google with headlines that appeal to social media audiences. Twitter is not about *search engine optimization*.

DEFINITION

A whole area of website promotion is called **search engine optimization** (SEO); that aspect has little relevance here, but you should know what SEO is so you can contrast it with Twitter marketing.

SEO aims to attract people who are looking for information to land on your website. The idea is to match the phrase (or keywords) that an individual types into a Google search field, and end up with your site on the first page. End result: articles stressing descriptive words, often ahead of cleverness.

Social media participants, including Twitter users, are not Google. They are individuals who need to be cajoled, entertained, surprised, and so on. For social media promotion in particular, go for the emotional component in your Tweets. That doesn't mean fear, uncertainty, and doubt (though those obviously work) but also humor, mystery, and just-plain-odd.

For outstanding and usually funny before-and-after headlines, visit fark.com and look at the headline on the (usually seriously reported) story to which fark points. Often the fark headline is too long for Twitter, but the site indirectly shows you how to write for the people whose attention you want to attract. (It's also a good way to lose an hour of productivity by giggling. Don't say we didn't warn you.)

For example, here's the headline of the actual news story from the *New York Daily News:*

> Bling and a miss: Yank ring stolen

That is pretty terrible in regard to SEO, even if it's a decent summary. But that title is nowhere near as compelling as the fark headline:

> Lesson #1: Don't leave your $10K Yankees World Series ring in a desk drawer in your office. Lesson #2: Don't leave your $10K Yankees World Series ring alone with two hookers you just met.

Which one of those headlines would you have clicked on?

Letting Your Personality Show

Your company might sell a service that's perceived as a commodity. There are a finite number of ways that you can make a hair salon stand out from the crowd, or to distinguish your chiropractic business from competitors.

But one thing is a unique differentiator for your brand, impossible for others to take away or duplicate: you. Or, for a larger business: you and your employees.

That's why we keep beating this drum: the best way to make your company stand out on Twitter is to communicate your own passions and enthusiasms. Most of that passion, presumably, is about your products and services (we do assume you think they are great), but it also extends to the technology or techniques that drive your industry (fashion and hair trends, for the salon, or natural health, for the chiropractor). And sometimes it's about the people who sell and provide these services—who have other activities and interests.

In short, you want to be likeable. Not just because you are charming (at least we assume you are), but because most of us choose businesses based on people reasons. People want to work with and give their business to trustworthy, likeable people.

MARKETING WIN

What you share should perform at least one of these functions: inform, entertain, support others, add value. Whenever possible, each should be imbued with your personality.

Saying Something Original

It isn't hard to find business accounts in which every Tweet starts with "RT." Yes, Twitter is about sharing. However, if you only repeat what others say—especially if it's from only one or two sources—you give no one a reason to listen to you.

A Retweet only shows what others have created. Add your own thoughts, include your response to the item, and give it context for your business.

For example, if a friend Tweets something that'd be useful and interesting to your own followers, you might be tempted just to Retweet it:

> RT **@MitchWagner** A bunch of very useful Instapaper tips http://t.co/W3MB6uM

There's nothing wrong with that, but you can make it better.

Instead, add something that turns this into a conversation. Disagree. Express an opinion. Respond, don't just repeat.

> You turned me on to **@instapaper**. This makes it even better. RT **@MitchWagner** A bunch of very useful Instapaper tips http://t.co/W3MB6uM

> *snort* RT **@julielerman** "I skipped the first 400 pages of your book and the stuff I'm reading doesn't make sense" #facepalm ;)

> **@Beaker** RT **@bryanrbeal** Deutsche Telekom Wants 'German Cloud' to Shield Data From US tpt.to/ahKFP4 < erecting walls to contain clouds

Interact with those who respond to you or interest you. Comment. Share what you feel and observe.

Tip your hat whenever possible: bring others into the conversation.

> WebSite Story (video) bit.ly/naoQq3! This is LOL funny. I hope the folks at **@eharmony @evite @pandora_radio** notice it.

This isn't just good business practice; it's also what the Twitter community expects and what makes Twitter so special.

Write as if your audience doesn't already love you and could unfollow you at any moment.

Don't Make Your Twitter Account Only About Personality

While we are all for communicating that your business is staffed by real people with real lives, don't take it to extremes.

A business Twitter account needs to keep its focus. If a social media influence report shows that your topics of influence are model-railroad-related and your company has nothing to do with trains or hobby sales, then you're off the rails.

While you shouldn't talk solely about your company, stay on related topics and industries; that builds you an audience who actually cares about your product. At least let the diversions be infrequent.

If you are a small business or a solo shop, you can get away with more personal information in your Twitter persona. If you stick to a few unlikely-to-offend topics, they can be a bit like a company mascot or a sign of the company's values. These snippets of your life give Twitter followers the sense they know you.

Still, limit yourself so that these are diversions rather than the core of your Twitter stream. Utter strangers have commented on Esther's cat updates. But she mentions them once every few days, not every few hours, even though the cats are adorable 24×7.

For example, we found a patent lawyer whose Twitter page indicates interest in legal matters. Except he posted for a solid week about what his favorite sports team was doing—and about nothing else. It's fine to show your enthusiasms, but if you're selling law expertise, it's rude to not talk about law most of the time.

TWITTER TIP

Many people, even in small businesses, maintain more than one Twitter account: one for business, and another for friends and family. There, you can rant about politics, express your spiritual preferences, and talk about other controversial subjects.

Being Trustworthy

If you are a business on Twitter, people understand that you are interested in selling your products and services. They hope you want to do more than that—to connect with people, to help, to learn—but most people understand that making money is the business's primary agenda. They're okay with it.

What they aren't okay with is when a business (or simply another person) appears to hide things.

For example, be sure to disclose conflicts of interest. Make sure that it's easy for a casual follower to be aware of the relationship, when, say, you Tweet on behalf of a client, you are a company employee Tweeting under the organization's authority, or you praise the achievement of a business that happens to be your customer. Sometimes this disclosure needs to be in the body of a Tweet ("Note: @ABC is a client"); other times it may be included in your Twitter bio ("An ABC employee; my words are my own").

Openness also matters in smaller ways. For instance, don't shorten your web address on your bio page with bit.ly or another URL shortener. Your (would-be) followers want to know where they are going, so include the complete address.

Don't Blur Twitter with Other Social Networks

Social media descended on businesses all at once, with companies suddenly waking up and realizing, "Oh no! We're missing the boat!" As a result, they began marketing on several online services at the same time and in the same way.

But Twitter is not exactly like Facebook, and it's not like a lot of other social networks. Don't make the mistake of treating them as if they are identical.

On Twitter, you share ideas largely with strangers who don't care as much about you as they do about what you say. Facebook status updates are shared with friends (or at least people with whom you have some sort of relationship), and Facebook business accounts aim to encourage communities of like interests. With Twitter, your ideas must sparkle to catch people's interests; with Facebook, most connections are already interested in you.

Twitter users don't mind that you also market your wares on another service. But they don't want to be treated as secondary citizens. We've seen companies post Tweets that link back to Facebook. We've seen company bios that link to a Facebook page. Don't do this; it only advertises that your attention is on another site rather than Twitter.

The same applies to respecting people on other services. Don't push content from one to the other. The strings of @Mentions, #hashtags, and Retweets will make no sense to your Facebook friends.

TWITTER TIP

You might feel that you're doing all the right things, but how can you know? One Twitter tool—which exists primarily to help you clean up follower lists—has a free service that lets you know if you break the rules of Twitter etiquette, tells you exactly how you're doing, and gives you tips on how to improve. Log into The Twit Cleaner (http://thetwitcleaner.com/howami); on its home page is the link, How Do I Look To Twit Cleaner.

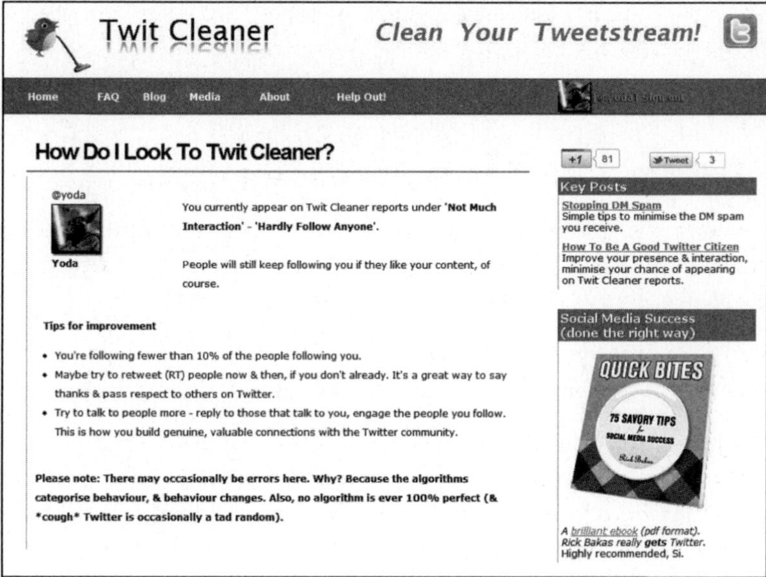

Strong the Force is with Yoda. The Twitter manners, not so much.

The Least You Need to Know

- Be a friend rather than a salesman.
- Add to the discussion rather than repeating what others say.
- Behave as you would at a social business gathering, by showing interest in other people more than talking about yourself.

Chapter 6

What to Tweet

In This Chapter

- Getting into the whole brevity thing
- Effectively including links that users want to click on
- Including photos and other media in your Twitter stream
- What do you mean, you don't know what to say?!

It's entirely possible that this was the first chapter you turned to.

When we mention using Twitter a lot, people tell us, "I tried Twitter, but gave up. I just didn't know what to say." And a moment later, they add, "And how can you say anything meaningful in 140 characters?"

Yet millions of people are saying plenty, every day, and they're getting new business from it, too. In this chapter, we help you understand what to actually Tweet, without being trivial or boring, and with proven methods that generate happy customers.

Learning to Be Concise

It seems like such an arbitrary limitation: all you can write is 140 characters! But that's actually a sentence or two, and you already say useful things that would consist of 140 characters all the time. Really, you do.

What Twitter does is teach you brevity, and to get to the point. We don't promise that this skill comes easily (and note that this advice is offered by two people who were willing to write 100,000 words), but it does come with practice.

Focus first on what you want to communicate to your followers, a topic we get to in the next chapter. It's more important to say something interesting and useful, initially, than to worry about how to say it with elegance, wit, and verve. Not to mention to fit it in a little tiny box.

When you start out, expect to write out a Tweet and then edit it to make it fit. When you are new to Twitter, this takes time. Even today we struggle to fit 10 pounds of message in a 5-pound bag. You will find yourself spending several minutes trying to shorten a Tweet to fit. That's truly okay. Take the time.

FAIL WHALE

Sometimes you will be tempted to give up on making the text fit. You will be tempted to split your text across two or three separate Tweets. Don't do it!

Or at least, don't do it more than, say, once a month. It's poor form. It makes it impossible for someone to Retweet what you said. And we bet you a bar of the very best dark chocolate that you can make your message fit.

For example, recently Esther wanted to Retweet a relevant newsworthy item written by a friend:

> #FEMA urges use of #Twitter, #Facebook bit.ly/piejHI Social media more reliable than cellphone in emergencies like #Hurricane Irene

That fit in her friend's Twitter stream, barely. But Retweeting it with her friend's ID exceeded the character limit, and she felt it was important to give him credit for the link.

She spent five solid minutes on editing (why, yes, she does need a life, thanks for asking) and managed to get all the important bits in, including the hat-tip to Alfred.

> #FEMA urges Twitter, Facebook use bit.ly/piejHI Social media more reliable than phone in emergencies like #Hurricane via **@AlfredPoor**

Our point is this: not everything fits in 140 characters the first time, but that doesn't mean you can't make it fit.

Finding the Magic Number

You hope for your Tweets to go viral, for people to Retweet your posts. But they can't do that if you used up all 140 characters—or at least not without effort, which lowers the chance they'll bother.

This is one reason it's better to choose a short Twitter name. Adding "RT @ABC" to the front of a post causes less stress than "RT @ABCDEFGHIJKLM."

Some experts advise you to take the time to figure out your "magic Retweet number," the total number of characters you need to leave blank at the end of every Tweet to ensure maximum Retweetability. To give yourself the best possible chance of a Retweet, make sure that you leave this many characters free at the end of each and every Tweet. The formula is this:

Your Number = Length of Username + Five Characters

So in Esther's case (**@estherschindler**), the magic Retweet number is 20; Brett's (**@brett**) is 10. If she passionately wants to make something Retweetable, Esther has to keep her posts under 120 characters.

It's okay to break this rule. Don't agonize over it. Don't sacrifice a really quality piece of copy to squeeze your Tweet under that ceiling. Just keep it in mind for the important Tweets. That is, if you're merely entertaining your followers with a link to a fun article on the **@PhoenixZoo**'s new acquisition of a male African lion and an Andean bear, write as long a Tweet as you want. If it's a coupon to your business's Spring sale or the teaser for your online contest, make sure that it's as easy as possible for a follower to Retweet.

Maintaining Good Grammar

In an effort to be concise, inevitably you will be tempted to use Twitter as if you were texting on your smartphone. Don't do it!

Avoid text-speak at all costs. Take an extra minute to elegantly craft your message and to squash it into the desired 140 characters. Otherwise your business persona sounds like someone who dropped out of high school (and then banged his head).

Oh, sure, Twitter has plenty of acronyms and abbreviations, not the least of which is RT for Retweet and #FF for Follow Friday. But just as in any other business interaction, people judge you (and your company) on how well you write.

Spell correctly. Use good grammar. Include proper punctuation. This is still business communication, after all.

TWITTER TIP

Writing well on Twitter is more than "making a good first impression." It has a direct impact on whether your links are clicked and your updates Retweeted.

Retweets contain more punctuation than normal Tweets. In one 2009 study, social media scientist Dan Zarrella compared a random sample of over a million "normal" Tweets to a sample of over 10 million Retweets. He found that while 86 percent of Tweets contain some form of punctuation, an overwhelming 98 percent of Retweets do as well.

Linking to Deeper Content

Try as you might, you can't always fit everything you need to say in 140 characters. The base Twitter limitation works fine for uttering a sentence or two, or for a conversation with other individuals. But it is a very, very tiny podium.

In 2010, Twitter's Evan Williams said that 25 percent of Tweets included a link. By now, that percentage may be higher. Certainly it is for both of us.

And it's no wonder that links are popular:

- A link lets you direct people to longer-form media, such as a blog post, website, or video.
- When someone clicks on your link, you can track the clickthrough to learn who's responding to your message.
- They make the Tweet more readable. URLs can be messy, especially if the URL is mostly numbers. A short URL lets the reader focus on what you say rather than the formatting of the link.

Every Link Needs a Teaser

It's tempting to include a link in every Tweet, and in some circumstances it's appropriate to do so.

Remember, though, that while you know how valuable the information is, your Twitter followers do not. You are asking them to click on something to start up a new window in their web browsers, which takes longer than glancing at a 140-character Tweet.

The Tweet has to have value and interest in addition to the link. Ask a question, add a comment, and then explain what's coming next.

For instance, don't Tweet this:

> Check this out! bit.ly/l6ZldL

Why should anyone bother? Most people won't just choose not to click the link. They will unfollow you, assuming that the Tweet is spam.

Instead, make it interesting:

> Han Solo in Carbonite Ice Cube Tray bit.ly/l6ZldL I need this. NEED IT, you hear?
>
> 66% of HR pros cite legal risks as reason they don't use social media in final hiring decision. http://t.co/CZ2vMiO

A Tweet has to stand alone and inform or entertain even if the follower doesn't click. You want her to click, and it's your marketing goal to make her do so. But she will not click unless she knows where she's going and she knows what she will find there. Every link has to be descriptive. The link is the "to learn more ..." button; it's not the message itself.

Be informative, but include a mystery. Make the reader feel she has to click on the link to find out, that she will get some sort of reward for doing so.

This isn't easy. Crafting a good I-must-click-on-this-or-I-will-surely-die headline is why journalists earn the big bucks.

Using Link-Shortening to Track Twitter Referrals

Plopping a link into Twitter might not save you any characters, if the link is particularly long. Most Twitter clients include tools that automatically shorten the URLs, such as bit.ly or tinyurl. That gives you more characters to write your update, which is useful enough on its own. Consider the following Tweets.

How to Defend Against the Apache Killer http://h30565.www3.hp.com/t5/Security-the-red-haired-step/Defending-against-the-Apache-Killer/ba-p/357

How to Defend Against the Apache Killer http://bit.ly/onRXHU

The second Tweet not only fits within the character limit, it also offers ample space for more information if you need it. Keep in mind that if you post to Twitter from the web page, your URLs are automatically shortened. But not every Twitter client does so by default.

For marketing purposes, URL shorteners have additional value. Many let you view the number of clicks, so you can see how many people followed the link.

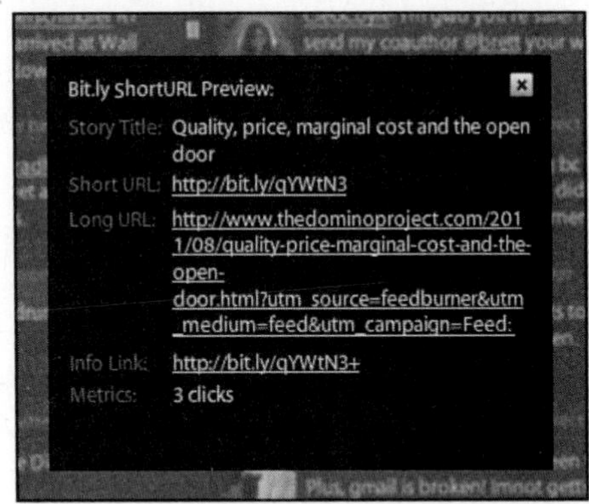

When bit.ly shortens a URL, it also provides information about how many people have clicked on the link.

It's likely that many of the links you post to Twitter are to information on your own website, such as blog posts. The analytics tool you use for site traffic (such as Google Analytics or Omniture) gives you *referrer* information, letting you know how many people came to this page from Twitter, but usually with very little granularity. That is, you might learn that Twitter sent people to the site, but not which Tweet did the job.

DEFINITION

A **referrer,** or referring site, is a source of traffic to your website. If a blogger mentions a specific page on your site ("Read a great blog post today about …"), that blog post becomes a referrer, and your website analytics will show how many people clicked on the blogger's link. Similarly, a link in a Tweet—whether your own or someone else's—is a referrer, though you may not always be able to tell who Tweeted the link.

Going Beyond Text

Another way to expand outside the stricture of the 140-character limitation is to link to multimedia and photos.

It's easy to get lost in the multimedia options, which are admittedly cool. However, photos and other nontext media are still content; if they don't serve the needs of the Twitter marketing campaign, we urge you to resist the temptation to post them.

Don't post a continual stream of product photos. That makes you look like a catalog. You can get away with product images occasionally—especially if they are photos taken by customers—but a nothing-but-pictures stream makes you a catalog, not a conversation. Need evidence? Popular e-commerce sites like **@1800flowers** and **@thinkgeek** rarely post product images.

Every photo should be posted for a reason. Is it a fun photo? (Nothin' wrong with that!) Will it entice your audience to buy your products? Do you expect the photo to engage them into further conversation, leading to conversion?

MARKETING WIN

The photo you share should be good, but it doesn't need to be professionally staged or high resolution. Most people won't see the detail in a photo with a billion megapixels. You're posting to Twitter, not to the front page of *The New York Times*. It's more important to crop it for visibility on a small screen.

The best photos on Twitter give people an insight into your business or your expertise, and thus promote the brand. Show some "backstage" scenes people normally wouldn't see at your conference. Post photos of the design team for your new product. Show the line around the block on its release date.

Posting Media

Video sharing is still largely a link, as Twitter doesn't host video files. However, tools like TweetDeck can play a YouTube video from within the client application, rather than sending your followers to another website.

The web client (Twitter.com) plays videos in the details pane when they are shared from YouTube, Vimeo, Ustream, Justin.tv, Twitlens, and Twitvid; your followers can see your video without leaving their Timeline. Most video tools can post a video directly to Twitter.

Photos are a little different.

You can, of course, link to a photo as if it were any other URL. Most Twitter clients can display the photo within the tool, so your followers don't have to fire up Flickr or go to your website or some other site.

Or you can upload a photo directly from the web Twitter client.

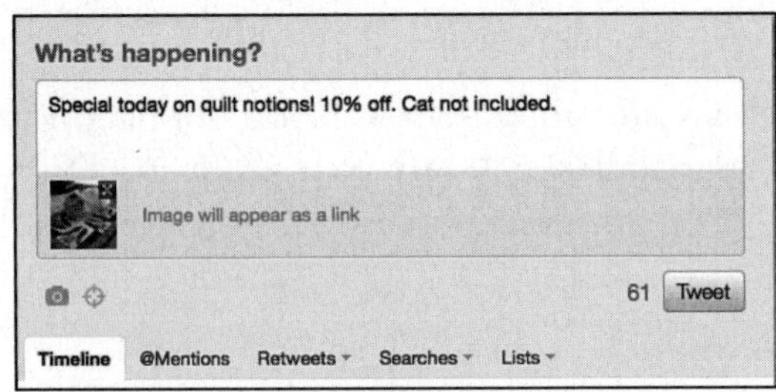

To upload an image, click on the small blue button underneath the "What's happening?" box.

Photo Grids: Your Company's Photo Album

Twitter's image galleries collect the 100 most recent images you uploaded into your Tweet stream. The images are organized on a single page, and displayed in chronological order. The user gallery includes images from Twitter, yFrog, TwitPic, Instagram, and other image-sharing services.

Your followers can get a visual impression of your company and its interests by looking at your photo grid. For example, the "recent photos" from the Te House Of Tea demonstrates how devoted to tea the small business is.

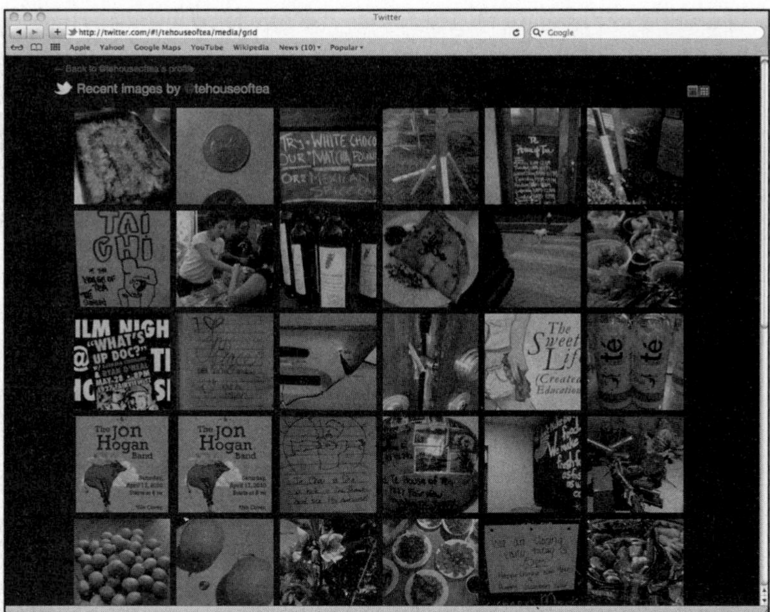

Te House of Tea's photo grid.

One useful tool for posting photos to Twitter is Twitpic. You can post photos or videos to TwitPic from your phone, from the site, or through email. All popular Twitter clients have built-in support for TwitPic, so it's easy to, say, snap a picture at the ballpark and email it to a special-for-you ID (e.g., yourcompanyname.1865@twitpic.com). The photo appears in your Twitter stream, along with any text you put in the subject line.

With all those options, it's hard to imagine that 140 characters is too narrow a pipeline to express your message.

Who Wants Ads?

Elsewhere, we describe Twitter as radio, with every one of us as an independent radio station. You can "tune in" to the stations that interest and inform you (such as the all-news station or the hippie folk music station). Your followers can "tune in" to your broadcast, too—assuming that you offer something worth listening to.

We use that analogy primarily to get across the issues in choosing who to follow and in attracting followers. But in this context we want to stress two important points:

- By participating in Twitter, you are a broadcaster.
- Nobody turns on the radio to hear the ads.

Before we advise you on the specifics of what to Tweet, we want to knock into your head that what you want—more business—is not necessarily the same goal as what your followers (and would-be followers) have in mind. You want to improve your brand perception and increase sales. They want entertainment and education. And a pony.

You can convince people of your unutterable goodness during the "ad breaks" in your Twitter stream. But they aren't going to follow you if you only Tweet about yourself. That is, don't be boring. We wish we had a nickel for every time we looked at a company's Twitter stream and thought, "Why would anyone care what they say?"

The potential traffic to your website or office door is huge, but promotion is an art form. Promote your brand too heavily and turn off followers; yet don't promote enough and receive little attention. The way you achieve this is balancing your Tweets about …

- What matters to you, such as selling your products and expertise.
- What matters to your target audience, such as actionable information or saving money.
- What matters to both of you, such as using your products wisely, business category trends, or things that tickle your mutual fancy.

TWITTER TIP

Instead of answering the question, "What are you doing?" answer, "What has your attention?"

It's All About You

People who are nervous about promoting their business—whether a solo shop or a PR person who's uncomfortable with this "conversation" business—tend to Tweet primarily about what they are selling. It's far more effective (and also easier) to Tweet about what the company is doing.

When you Tweet about your business, make it useful. Give advice. Show how you have solved problems for other people. Demonstrate that you are wonderful human beings who deserve their trust (or at least a smile). Give people a reason to like you and to be interested in what you say—which, every so often, includes "Look what we have to sell."

Bragging

One easy way to convince people of your expertise is to show off that other people think you are experts.

MARKETING WIN

Many solo practitioners (especially techies) are uncomfortable with active self-promotion. This is not immodesty; think of it as "sharing what you're proud of: Yay me!" Remember, people want to do business with successful people, especially—oddly enough—those who are too busy to take on more work.

Tell people about company accomplishments, especially when the Tweet includes some measure of personal pride.

> **@infinimedia** New blog post: Infinimedia CEO one of top 20 leaders under 40 http://bit.ly/bMGnpd

These Tweets don't have to be about an award. They can be anything you're proud of (and which, by the by, gives followers a warm and fuzzy feeling about the company).

> **@google** How our transportation programs help Googlers get to (& around) work while leaving their cars at home goo.gl/0bdVc

> **@The_Pig_Hotel** Our New Forest Truffle Risotto is proving to be a firm favourite with guests recently!

It's even better when you Retweet or respond to someone's praise of your ever-so-brilliant actions.

> **@dermalogica** We couldn't be more honored to be featured today on **@WellandGoodNYC**! Read about their experience here bit.ly/nwaK0W We're blushing :)

Tweeting Company Activities

Keep your followers up-to-date with the company's activities, whether it's business news, a conference in which you participate, or any "happening."

> **@ATT** Live @ #TPIAspen, ATT Labs president/CEO, Krish Prabhu, speaking on innovation at ATT & our vision for the #network of the future
>
> **@PHXPublicMarket** Join us for the Open Air Market tonight, 4-8 pm. If you haven't been before, we're on Central just south of Roosevelt in Downtown Phoenix!

Not all of your company activities fit in Twitter's 140 character window, of course. It's fine to link to the company newsletter or website articles for more depth.

> **@Mortons** Did you know? We feature #wine tips, pairings and recipes in our weekly #WineWednesday Blog. Check it out: http://ow.ly/6hM0m

Asking for Action

In marketing terms, you might call this "asking for the sale." Tell people what you want them to do, whether that's to nominate your exec to speak at a conference or to donate to your nonprofit.

> **@asmartbear** If you haven't yet, thanks in advance for upvoting (and commenting?) for my #sxsw talk on being honest in business: bit.ly/qpYHQu
>
> **@Heifer** Need an easy way to give? Text 'Give' to 41010 to donate $10 to Heifer to help give a family a future out of #hunger.

The key to asking for action is to do so with personality and transparency.

For example, **@DogsTrust** promotes rescue dogs, shares dog videos, and raises funds. The relatively small UK nonprofit has 28,000 followers, and is a poster child of using a personal touch while also communicating its message.

> **@dogstrust** Lots of little tweaks and updates to make to the main website. *headphones on, bingley bingley beep-y music activated*
>
> **@dogstrust** One more time, we'd love to ask you to watch and share our #JustTextGiving puppy-filled video. youtube.com/watch?v=X-999s … Still in 2nd place *ulp*

They are very clear about what they want you to do. They also make you feel as though the nonprofit has caring people behind it ... so you want to do it. (And besides: puppies!)

Announcing Sales

The most obvious Tweets are commerce related: telling followers how spending money at your business is the smartest decision they could make all day. Offering coupons and deals helps people discover your business and take direct action.

> **@fatquarterworld** Last Day of Simple Savings Event—20 Off—http://eepurl.com/m5R1

MARKETING WIN

Online discounts are popular and effective. But it's best to incorporate some way to track the source of the Twitter promotion. It might be a specially coded URL that your web analytics software can track, or sending Twitter followers to a unique Twitter Discount page. Or just incorporate it in the promotion, such as Tweeting, "Say 'Twitter Tuesday' and get a free appetizer."

Sharing Your Knowledge

All of the preceding suggestions are much like traditional PR and marketing: you tell people what you want them to know, and give them an incentive to take action. Here's where we veer away from the PR pro's comfort zone.

One of the best ways to attract Twitter followers is to give away information, especially information that only you can share.

This might mean updates on information that you are charged to gather. For instance, the Los Angeles Fire Department (**@LAFD**) Tweets alerts such as traffic collisions and lost hikers.

> **@LAFD** *Traffic Collision* SB 5 FY x 118 FY; MAP 502-D6; FS 98; Overturned dumptruck. Driver self-extr ... Read more at bit.ly/rdirD1

Demonstrate your expertise, publicly. Followers can tell that you know what you're talking about as long as you are talking about it.

Tweet how-to information that just so happens to show that you know what you're talking about. No matter what your industry, people appreciate short and sweet tips. Make it actionable and simple, and they'll thank you even more. They will also remember that your company was the one who knew how to make something happen.

> **@crwnptcabinetry** Watch Corey, one of our talented cabinetmakers, assemble glass doors! http://ow.ly/6hSw3

Some businesses worry that they are "giving away the store" when they share their knowledge. Quite to the contrary: it's how you establish yourself as a subject-matter expert. Both of us got consulting work because someone reading our Twitter stream decided we were the right people.

Sharing Company Information

Is your business hiring? Link to new job openings, using hashtags to attract people with the key skills you need or geographical location.

> **@IndySOW** We're hiring a Development & Grants Manager! http://ht.ly/6cB2A #indy #nonprofit #jobs #fundraising

Link to information on your website that is itself informative (not necessarily about marketing). Not everything you post has to be directly about your products or services. For example, the online real estate service Zillow regularly links to blog posts about disarmingly interesting topics. (Admit it: you want to look.)

> **@zillow @goldiehawn** and Kurt Russell List Exotic Malibu Retreat for $14,749,000 (PHOTOS) bit.ly/oBDyB0 #Zillow #realestate

MARKETING WIN

In general, every company blog post deserves to be Retweeted. But before you can link to interesting content, you have to have some. This may inspire an in-house editorial project to write blog posts, run a contest, or even create your own independent publication (as American Express did with **@openforum**).

Once you have a Twitter community established, consider asking your followers if they would care to craft a guest blog post or otherwise contribute content.

Remembering to Be Human

Tweets are not press releases. They don't need to be read and revised by three people before being sent out. In fact, most Tweets are spoiled if they are edited in such a way.

Twitter is about being authentic. It's conversations between real people. And in your case, your real people work for a company overflowing with folks who know their stuff and want to share it with customers.

For instance, the Pampers brand is a household word. You don't need an introduction to the diaper company, and if you need its products, then you probably don't need to be "sold" on it. So Pampers has made its Twitter stream a community service for parents, interacting with followers and letting its own staff act like, well, real people.

> **@Pampers** Jonas, 5 yr old, asked me this & I'm curious how others might answer. "Mommy, if you could do one "cool trick" what would you do?" ^Angie
>
> **@Pampers @Bubafettt** Look at him in that pic! Quite a comedian already! ^Angie

It doesn't have to be all business. This harkens back to our earlier advice about the brand's personality. Your corporate culture may not make it easy to let your hair down. Smaller businesses usually can do so with more freedom. For instance, the world knows about Esther's cats, her quilting, and her baseball preferences (Go DBacks!). Share what is happening in your lives.

> **@olivemagazine** Let the olive team summer lunch commence! yfrog.com/h0h68hwj

It's a particularly good opportunity for small personality-based businesses. Author Lynn Flewelling may Tweet primarily about her science fiction books, but she can draw her followers into her world with a quiet personal Tweet:

> **@LynnFlewelling** Up at 4 am to go to Santa Cruz for hiking and research. The world is dark and smells of sage and wet grass.

Your company is not "too big" to be personal. "[Zappos'] goal is to form personal connections with customers and employees, and Twitter is one tool we use to do that … [but our approach can be] summed up by 'Be real. Use your best judgment,'" Aaron Magness, Zappos' director of brand marketing said in 2010. "We want people to be able to get the sense of who we are by following our employees and seeing what our personality is like."

It's All About Them

Largely, your followers don't care about your company's agenda. They care about the things that matter to them, such as their problems, distractions, work, and family. Fortunately, your business can help them solve the problems and enjoy the happy times.

The best way to get attention—and followers—is to talk to people about their interests. It won't always sell more widgets in the short term, but it builds loyalty, lets people know you can help, and captures their attention.

Sharing Their Wins

Whether you actively solicit input from customers (as California Bamboo does with its Project of the Month) or you find success stories online, share customer experiences with your followers. It lets people know that others use your products, which doesn't hurt your marketing effort. Also, the happy customer is likely to be so glad of the praise that he will Retweet it to his followers—earning you even more attention.

> **@Cali_Bamboo** POTM Howard K (Arlington, TX) wanted a low-maintenance deck & he achieved that w/ Caramel BamDeck Composite decking bit.ly/fEXGWf

Don't limit these posts to customers. Share information about business partners and other allies, too.

> **@WholeFoodsPV** Our local vendor, Adventures in Roasting will be here to sample their amazing Iced Coffee from 11-3. http://fb.me/19xhlmUEy

Asking for Help

Don't be shy. Asking your followers a question is a great way to break the monotony of a Timeline full of links; it's also a good way to increase engagement. Most of us do want to help one another, especially when we can *crowdsource* wisdom.

DEFINITION

Crowdsourcing refers to the practice of making decisions or causing effects based on "the wisdom of crowds," which you may think of as "many hands make light work." The premise is that groups of people make better decisions and can accomplish more than small numbers of individuals. New cloud technologies and intertwined social networks have supercharged how people collaborate. For example, instead of sitting idly in a traffic jam, Waze enables users to report traffic problems to other app users; NotchUp helps companies recruit executives by crowdsourcing information from online networks; and Quora encourages people to ask and answer specific business questions.

@GetYourPHXCrew We had so many great suggestions of "hidden gems" in the #cenpho area! Are there any more out there that we are missing?

@ModelRRNews Friends: We had a modeler post to our wall asking for some help with installing fiber optic lighting. Any suggestions for him?

It's perfectly fine to ask for personal help, too. If your CEO is traveling in San Francisco, she can ask her followers for restaurant recommendations. (Just tell us about the good ones.)

Making Friends

Don't wait for others to talk to you. If you find someone interesting among the people you follow, @reply to her. Respond to people who interest you. Be the one to start a conversation.

It's likely that you'll do this in the process of searching for people conversing about your business, but don't feel constrained by "work." If someone asks for advice about the best restaurant in San Francisco and you have an opinion, go ahead and share it.

Answering People

This ought to go without saying, but you should respond to people who write to you. Answer people's questions. Be helpful. That earns you personal appreciation from the recipient and public admiration from those who can see that your company cares about quality.

Engage, connect, communicate! Cool, someone is listening!

If you have zillions of followers, you can't reply to every single comment, but at least make an effort. If you never talk to anyone, how are you any different from an RSS feed?

Responding to Relevant Tweets

As we have said repeatedly, pay attention to people who Tweet about your product or its category. You can do so just for market research reasons, but it's far more effective to find those people and respond to them—and, usually, offer help.

Using Twitter's search tools or other monitoring software, look for people having trouble with something in your knowledge domain ("I spilled coffee in my computer keyboard, what now?") and—as your first communication with them—give them advice ("Get the vacuum cleaner NOW!").

You'll need to determine what advice to offer, but don't underestimate the marketing value of doing this. A personal response from a brand is one of the best ways for a business to earn loyalty and trust.

The individual doesn't need to mention your brand to earn your attention. It's just as effective to respond to people who Tweet about your category. For example, the Behr Paint team found someone having trouble with a painting project and offered personal expertise in solving his problem.

> **@Jake_Bevan** ANYONE WANT TO GIVE ME SOME TIPS ON GETTING PAINT OFF!!! I CANT GET IT OUT OF MY HAIR AND IT HURTS!!!
>
> **@BehrPaint @Jake_Bevan** Water-based paint will soften up w/soap & water. Shampoo your hair, let it sit, then wash. Rinse & repeat if an oil-based paint.

Look for people who have trouble, publicly offer assistance, and, when necessary, privately work very hard to address the issue.

> **@BofA_Help @TarynTalbott** Please DM your name, zip, phone and we'll give you a call to see how we can help. No account numbers. ^lw
>
> **@Rubbermaid @marison459** Follow me and I will send you contact information for helping with the Reveal mop

We go into more detail about the marketing value of an outreach customer support program in another chapter.

It's All About Shared Interests

Whatever your business, you care deeply about the product category. Sure, you care most about your business doing well, but you also pay attention to anything that affects it. If you sell software consulting, you care about programming trends. If yours is a boutique hotel, you care about local community events. If you sell consumer goods to young parents, you get passionate about child care.

So does your target market.

Tweeting About What You Have in Common

There's just so much you can say about yourself. At least when you are drumming up the Twitter campaign, you have limitations about what you can say about or to your followers. But you can always write to the interests of the people you want to attract.

You know your market—and not just in terms of its buying habits. Software people have a tropism toward science fiction, so a custom consulting business could link to an update about the upcoming Hobbit movie.

For instance, among the appeal of the novels by fiction author Gail Carriger (**@gailcarriger**) is that they are set in Victorian London; her heroine (married to a werewolf) is very fashion-conscious. Gail's Twitter stream is full of the things that get her excited: a link to a YouTube video showing how to make a crocheted parasol, and a link to a photo exposition of Victorian fashion (to die for, really).

> **@gailcarriger** Rings made from vintage spoons! kingdomofstyle.typepad.co.uk/my_weblog/2011…

Oh yes, Carriger certainly lets you know about her book signings and the progress of the next book in the series, but in between, you cannot help but connect with her on the topics that make her books appealing (assuming you care about steampunk, Victorian fashion, and undead mysteries—and certainly you do!).

Talking About Trends

You undoubtedly care about trends in your industry; you have to pay attention to news relevant to your business category using RSS feeds or other media. Some of it will be interesting to your Twitter followers, too.

For instance, if you have a restaurant, your customers might not care about the uptick in your area dining. But a standalone factoid might be entertaining, such as "Americans eat twice as many eggs today as they did 20 years ago." That's a Tweet (assuming it's true; we just made it up).

MARKETING WIN

It's an even better Tweet if you attribute the source: "According to @MyIndustryNews, Americans eat twice as many eggs today as they did 20 years ago." It's always a good idea to tip your hat in appreciation—and @MyIndustryNews might begin following you.

People love a good statistic. If you have an interesting stat jangling around in your head, let it out on Twitter. Ninety-five percent of people polled say this is a good way to add variety to your Timeline.

> **@SDLAirFair** Did you know that aviation represents 10% of Arizona's total employment?
>
> **@Rubbermaid** Check out this Woman's Day article about morning routines—I am definitely a iSnooze. What type are you? http://rbbr.md/8e

TWITTER TIP

Anything that makes you say, "Hmmm!" or "How about that?!" is a likely candidate for a Tweet.

If you act as a curator of good content, you will soon be viewed as a subject-matter expert in your field. Expertise implies competence, and that leads to new business.

Sharing What You Learn

In the "It's All About You" section we encourage you to share your experiences. Don't limit that only to experiences where you are the Source of All Knowledge. Demonstrate your ability to learn, too, and share the learning process.

For example, when you attend a conference, "live Tweet" what the speakers discuss. It's become common for conferences to adopt a hashtag to enable attendees to find one another and to help people on Twitter follow the live conversation. Using Twitter at events helps people build an instant "backchannel."

Deb Bryant is board director at the nonprofit organization DemocracyLab.org, and part of her job is to promote open government. She wasn't speaking at the Government Open Source conference (#goscon), but that didn't keep her from sharing information that her followers care about:

> **@debbryant** Maughan: if we fund Research they need to build it to share and is useful to the public. #goscon
>
> **@debbryant** Matthew Burton "Code is not data." releasing code as open source is not a security or privacy issue. #OSS #gov20

If you were in Deb's target readership—anyone involved in open government—you would easily recognize her as an authority. Not because she always knows the answer, but because she has the access to find out.

Note that Deb Bryant used hashtags liberally in her Tweets. This let people who don't know her, but who were following anything related to the Government in Open Source conference (tagged #goscon), discover her and her Tweets.

Noticing the Real World

Don't be callous. The world is not always about the things that affect us personally, whether it's business issues or the frivolities that attract us. When a news event happens—and on Twitter, you'll be the first to know—respond. Tastefully.

Don't try to "take advantage" of the event for personal gain. (We could tell a few horror stories about that.) Your response can be as simple as, "We wish the best to everyone suffering from this awful weather!" If your organization can offer useful (or even entertaining) information, you look even cooler, as the Sierra Club did here.

> **@Sierra_Club** You all know it, but let's say it again—animals are awesome. "National Zoo Animals React to the Earthquake" http://ow.ly/6byii

Retweeting with Savoir Faire

You are not the source of all information. If you are listening to other people on Twitter, you will learn things, too. Some of them are pragmatic; some of them are funny. Share.

All it takes to Retweet is to type RT and then the account's name, followed by their original Tweet, such as this:

> RT **@estherschindler** I wish I had chocolate.

The Retweet shows up in your Timeline and appears as an @Mention in the Timeline of whomever you Retweeted.

Gosh, Thanks!

Retweet praise for your product, or most anything where a customer connected with you. That doesn't mean you should Retweet every Mention—how boring would that be?! But when the follower offers new information that might help someone else, it's definitely "RT-worthy."

> **@Rubbermaid** New use :) Thxs for sharing! RT **@andrea_w** Thank you **@rubbermaid** for making the perfect to-go Tums container! http://rbbr.md/89

> **@Cali_Bamboo** Project of the Month Contestant: Billy S (Sea Girt, NJ) built an island-style bar, watch the video at: bit.ly/oMsEAP

For most people new to Twitter marketing, Retweeting is almost too easy. That's because you almost certainly follow people who Tweet things of interest to your other followers. For instance, the aforementioned **@dogstrust** Retweeted this post:

> **@wearefordogs** Check out our blog post on how microchipping works and why it's important, (featuring **@dogstrust** and **@RSPCA_official**) bit.ly/na2J2m

If it makes you say, "Gosh, I wish I wrote that," then it probably is worth repeating. Yet, your Twitter Timelines should not be solely Retweets, or people will assume you have nothing original to contribute.

Adding Something of Your Own

It's fine to simply Retweet someone else's post when she said everything that needs to be said or, more likely, when she used up all 140 characters.

But it's far more effective for you to add your own voice to the conversation.

> **@Rubbermaid** Great tips for any project :) RT **@OrganizerSandy** Five Easy Steps To Organizing bit.ly/pZARH8 #organize
>
> **@craftbeer** Great animated gifs that tell a story. RT **@beerinator** Sam Calagione's arm NEVER gets tired! (via **@Zimmerino**) j.mp/n1yqgj"

Adding your own comment to the Retweet makes it easy for your followers to know your own opinion, answer a question, or otherwise insert your own personality.

Getting Your Name Out ... or In

One marketing benefit to Retweets is that it helps people find one another. If Esther Retweets Brett's Tweet, you see the **@brett** in her Timeline. If Brett wrote something clever (and he always does), you might say, "Hey, I don't know that Brett dude. Let me see what else he's said." You click on the **@brett**, look at his Twitter stream, and, likely, decide to click on **Follow**.

That's precisely what you want to make happen. If you say something Retweetable, people discover you, and you make new friends.

It's another reason to add a short comment when you Retweet. In addition to making it easier to follow the conversation, if someone Retweets your Tweet, your ID displays and other people find out about your existence.

FAIL WHALE

Twitter has made it possible to Retweet direct from the Twitter website. The Tweet shows up in your Twitter stream but with their avatar.

The advantage is, you don't have to worry about character count. The downside is, Retweeting this way doesn't including a "RT @MyAccount" at the front of the Tweet. If your followers Retweet the item, nobody knows it came from you. This isn't a problem for minor items (that is, you Retweeted something because it was funny), but other times you want to be included (such as in breaking news).

Always Giving Credit

Not everyone writes concisely enough to be easily Retweeted. But they often say useful things, as **@AlfredPoor** did in the example we used earlier in the chapter.

> #FEMA urges use of #Twitter, #Facebook bit.ly/piejHI Social media more reliable than cellphone in emergencies like #Hurricane Irene

Often it's possible to edit their Tweet (such as deleting hashtags) to make the Retweet fit. Sometimes—well, not so much.

It isn't necessary to Retweet someone verbatim. Don't be afraid to rewrite the other's "headlines." Just because someone else (who you trusted) wrote "This is funny [link]" doesn't mean you are obligated to repeat that text. If you can do it better, do it better. Nobody will object if you're sending them solid traffic.

But you must always acknowledge the source; it's good manners.

There's no one right way to "tip your hat;" several are acceptable, such as these:

- Computers to pinpoint wild weather forecasts reuters.com/article/2011/0… #hpc via **@rikkikite**
- Computers to pinpoint wild weather forecasts reuters.com/article/2011/0… #hpc (HT **@rikkikite**)
- Computers to pinpoint wild weather forecasts reuters.com/article/2011/0… #hpc /**@rikkikite**

Just be sure to thank the people who help you … always.

Asking for Retweets

If you know someone who can help you amplify your message, don't be shy. Ask. In most cases, it makes sense to ask a well-placed friend (who has far more followers than you do) to share an item of importance. For instance, if you're friends (ideally "in real life") with someone influential in your business, send a direct message or email asking, "Could you Retweet my message about web design?"

Some people take this to extremes. AZ Motor Trendz (**@azmotortrendz**) wanted to be noticed by everyone in the Phoenix area. So they asked baseball pitcher Jarrod Parker for a Retweet: "Can we get an RT for our Biz finally being on Twitter?" Parker only had a few thousand followers at that point, but it was better than AZ Motor Trendz's 3. (The auto customization company has plenty of things wrong with its Twitter feed, but chutzpah is not among them.)

Don't be shy about asking for Retweets, even from celebrities.

Just don't do it too often. Pioneer Power Tools asks everyone to Retweet everything they post without any particular reason why we should comply. They link to a product page; it isn't information, just sales blather.

> **@pioneerpowertlz** (RT This) Northern Industrial Bench- or Wall-Mount Saw Chain Sharpener bit.ly/odqrG8 #tools

Appealing to Self-Interest

Twitter is the ultimate "networking" opportunity. The entire point of its conversations (at least in a business context) is connecting with other people, with the idea that at least some of them can help you. And you help them in return.

So in the context of enlightened self-interest, if you Retweet people who don't follow you, they may very well begin to follow you. It's an indication of shared interest—hey, you cared about this, too!—and thus the person who finds your Retweet in his Mentions Twitter stream will at least check out your profile.

TWITTER TIP

An early Twitter community practice was to thank people for Retweeting something you posted, such as "Thanks for the RTs, **@brett @estherschindler**!" It's no longer expected, but no one will be offended if you do so. The main advantage is that it helps the people you mentioned discover one another (Oh, so who's this guy **@brett** who thought her Tweet was funny, too?); anything that helps like-minded people discover each other is good. On the down side, it can clutter up your Twitter stream, especially if you thank everyone in sight.

Do you still believe you have nothing to say? We doubt it.

If you engage, entertain, educate, and interact, you will build a community of people who will listen to you, trust you, and care about what you're doing.

The Least You Need to Know

- Write the Tweet that you wish would fit in 140 characters, then edit to make it fit.
- Every link needs a "headline" that informs followers what they're getting and cajoles them to click.
- Use photos and multimedia when they contribute to your marketing message, not as distractions.
- Your Tweets should have a balance between topics that are about your company, the things that matter to your target audience, and the subjects about which you both care.

Finding the Right People to Follow

Chapter **7**

In This Chapter

- Determining the Twitter accounts to follow
- Finding influential connections
- Keeping up with the flow of updates

If you're using Twitter to market your business, it's because you want to be noticed. You want to engage with the right influencers and build relationships that can maximize the impact on your products, brands, and business.

But before you can get others to notice and listen to you, you have to find them. You can't define or contribute to a community you don't belong to. You can't learn from those you listen to if you're not listening. And you can't get the word out that your business is on Twitter and ready to communicate if nobody knows you exist.

Following matters more than followers. If you follow the right people (which is what we show you how to do in this chapter) and you Tweet appropriate and interesting things (as discussed in the previous chapter), the "being followed" goal largely takes care of itself.

The Community You Listen To

Twitter is unlike most social media in that it doesn't require a two-way connection. On LinkedIn, for instance, if you accept a colleague's connection request, you both show up in one another's updates, others can see your connection, and so on. In contrast with Twitter, you can follow someone without him following you back. And you can be followed without paying the slightest attention to your follower.

Think of Twitter as a radio with an essentially infinite number of radio stations. You can tune in and listen to (follow) any radio station you like—any "station" you think is interesting or useful or important.

You're a radio station, too. Others can listen to you (that is, they can follow you) if they think you're interesting or useful or important.

Very often, these two sets intersect. That is, in an ideal world, the people you think are interesting (Tweeting about things that matter to you) also think you are interesting (because you care about the same things).

TWITTER TIP

Don't expect everyone you follow to be interested in following you back. It would be strange if they did. It's rare to have a one-to-one ratio of follower to follow-ee. That's because we don't have identical interests even when we're in the same business. You and a business contact may both be real estate lawyers, but you are interested in commercial properties while the lawyer you follow specializes in farmland. Not to mention that one of you has a model railroad hobby while the other is involved with live-action role-playing games, with both of you Tweeting about these topics occasionally.

When it comes to choosing followers, you can be somewhat selfish. This is your personal radio station, and you shouldn't have anyone on it you don't find useful, interesting, or entertaining. You are under no social or business obligation to listen to someone who doesn't say things you want to hear, or even to include him in your Twitter stream.

What to Look For in People to Follow

When you use Twitter for your personal gratification, you don't need to think about the criteria you use to choose followers. Whoever is interesting, or funny, or makes you say, "Oh, that's cool!" a lot—it's all fair game.

As a business, you need a more deliberate approach. It's much like the thought process you give to traveling cross-country for a business meeting. If you attend industry conferences, you contemplate which ones can yield the best contacts and enable you to learn the most from its speakers; you balance those benefits with the investment of travel and time.

With Twitter, the cost is zero, but your time is finite. While you can unfollow another account with a single click—with less effort than deprogramming a station on your car radio—you might as well do it right in the first place. When we talk to people who gave up on Twitter, it's often because they were following people they considered trivial. That's like throwing out a radio because the one station you tune into plays music you dislike.

In a moment we show you how to find the right people. But first, consider who those people or organizations should be. These include—with a lot of overlap—people and businesses in the following categories:

- People who help you get smarter, become more knowledgeable, or make you giggle
- People who share your interests, especially those you can help or inform
- People who can spread your message

Each of these encompasses several opportunities.

Oh No, Not Another Learning Experience!

Naturally, we begin by suggesting you follow those you can learn from. We've shared plenty of advice throughout this book about the need for a listening program, especially in the chapter about designing your Twitter marketing campaign. By now you know that one of your initial and ongoing marketing goals is to learn what customers are thinking, what they care about, and—with some good brain sweat on your part—how you might use that knowledge to better serve customers.

So yes, this means you should pay attention to the Twitter feeds of those who can give you a "meta-view" of your business ecosystem and the world at large. The second half of this chapter helps you identify and find these people for your particular industry.

But "learn" includes personal learning, not just organizational knowledge.

No matter how good you are at your profession—as a business owner, marketer, or technical practitioner—you don't know everything. Follow people (and brands and organizations) who encourage you to get better at your job, too.

MARKETING WIN

Not everyone you follow needs to be aligned with the business goal of building its marketing presence. It's also fine to use Twitter to improve your own competence.

Twitter can be an ongoing personal-training class that keeps you in sync with your industry and improves your skill set. This is one way in which it can be personally rewarding as well as an effective marketing tool.

If you are a computer consultant, it's a good idea to follow other programmers who share their technical expertise, news, and opinions. A documentary filmmaker usually is motivated to learn about new video cameras, without urging. If you're a public relations pro who represents a large business, you probably care about (and can learn from) PR bigwigs and social media experts—even if the business you work for is a manufacturing firm.

Even before you consider how to find industry experts whose Twitter Timelines can become a personal mentor, look to one obvious way to stay up to date: news feeds. No matter what business you're in, you probably care about current news items (such as you get from CNN's Breaking News, **@CNNBrk**) or your local news (perhaps the Arizona Republic's **@azcentral** or the Jefferson City newspaper **@NewsTribune**). You rarely will share the information you glean from these sources, unless a news item has an impact on your community, which usually means local customers and followers:

> Hey folks: **@azcentral** says another monsoon storm is headed our way. Drive safely on your way home!

Most industries have their own niche publications, and by now the majority also have a Twitter feed. It might be MediaBistro (**@mediabistro**) for writers and media mavens, Software Development Times (**@sdtimes**) for IT directors, or American Farriers (**@Hoofcare**) for the horse-minded. If you're in the music business, whether you run a used record store or promote a jazz band, it behooves you to follow Billboard (**@billboard**) for industry news. The websites and newsletters for these trade magazines usually direct you to their Twitter feeds.

MARKETING WIN

Trade journals and other research Twitter feeds can be a handy source of "what to Tweet." When something happens in your industry that's relevant to your customers, Retweet the news item, with a comment explaining why it matters.

A historical novelist who's on Twitter primarily to promote her newest title can use Twitter to learn more about her story's era, and share what she learns with her followers. She might follow the Musical Instrument Museum (**@MIMphx**) primarily for historical research; but if the book's characters go to Bali, her followers are sure to be charmed by a Retweet about the museum's Balinese Gamelan Workshop.

Do these appear in the list of Twitter accounts you follow? Sure. But that isn't a problem. Your followers may not care about those industry journals. But they do care that you stay up to date. It's evidence of your commitment to improving your own expertise, which can only be reflected in the quality of service you provide.

You'll also find plenty of Twitter-only feeds and blogs, such as Wine Lover's News (**@GetYourWineNews**) and Music Daily (**@iMusicDaily**). A simple Twitter search helps you find these quickly.

TWITTER TIP

Pay attention to those the niche media news feeds Retweet, who they follow, and who follows them. It's an easy way to find others who share your interest in these topics. They may be noncompeting businesses (such as a similar business to yours, in another region), suppliers, or even prospective customers.

What about following your personal interests? If yours is a smaller personality-driven business, such as most solo proprietorships, you can follow anyone who makes you say, "Oh, cool!" To a point.

If *you* are the brand, then anyone who interests you is part of who you are. You might be an authoritative architect—the expertise you sell—but you might also be a woodworker, horror film movie buff, and champion Scrabble player. No one is apt to think less of you for following Fine Woodworking Magazine (**@fwmagazine**) or Bloody Disgusting (**@BDisgusting**), much less local-to-you businesses (such as the pizza delivery joint with splendid specials for Twitter followers). For small businesses, the line between self-marketing and business marketing is fuzzy.

Larger businesses with more conservative outlooks or several people tracking the Twitter account may be more reluctant to follow "irrelevant" feeds. It's your call.

FAIL WHALE

There's no way to "invisibly" follow another account; it's public information. And people do look at who you follow.

That can have an impact on who you choose to follow as well. Just as you wouldn't Tweet about politics or religion on a business account, be cautious about following Twitter feeds on controversial topics, such as the political candidate you personally support. Do you want to lose a sale because a prospective customer votes the other way?

Use a personal account for these, unless you are ready for your affiliations to affect your business.

Enlightened Self-Interest

The lion's share of the people you follow should be the people you want to personally connect with. These include people who can help you, those you can help professionally, and your business allies.

Follow those who depend upon you and who you depend upon, such as your clients, business partners, and suppliers. The business reasons are largely obvious:

- You keep up with the changes in their world, especially those that affect you.
- They appreciate your loyalty and interest.
- Your followers see how well connected you are.

So if you own a restaurant, follow your produce supplier and the company that makes your ice cream. (You do want to know that the new crop of peaches is ready, right?) If yours is a professional services firm, follow your clients to discover what projects they're crowing about (some of which might just happen to include an opportunity for your business). An educational nonprofit organization can follow other nonprofits to learn what they do differently for fundraising.

Among your allies, hopefully, are the people who work at your company. Most people follow their work colleagues, in our experience. That's as much a matter of internal politics and company policy as it is business manners.

If your business encourages its experts to Tweet and participate, it's usually a good idea to motivate them to correspond online. And they usually want to, because conversations among company experts both amplify the business message and help each expert's Twitter followers learn about the breadth of the company's knowledge.

MARKETING WIN

There's more than a grain of "enlightened self-interest" in doing this. We like to think that your primary motivation in following people is the sincere desire to share your interests and to help others. Certainly that's true for us authors, because we are warm and wonderful individuals whose spiritual generosity is exceeded only by our good looks and our modesty.

But in following others and communicating with and to them, stay conscious that you are representing your business. This is old-style networking at its finest, in which "I can help you" implies, "And perhaps you can help me, sometime."

In your outreach to find people to follow, look for those you can help. That's a large part of what customer service Twitter marketing is: searching for people who are happy or unhappy with company or product, and either offering to help resolve the issue or sharing their public pleasure. Those are "who to follow" in a shorter time frame, however.

It's more important to be noticed by those who might need or want your professional services, though they may not know it yet. First, you can learn from their perspective (what pain are they complaining about?). You can be the first to communicate to them by, say, offering a technical tip based on your expertise. The intent is to create an ongoing dialogue, with—enlightened self-interest, again—someone who can spread your message, at least saying aloud, "Gosh, aren't they nice folks who know all about this topic!"

Tasteful Sucking Up

In deciding who to follow, don't forget the influencers in your industry and business domain.

Follow the people you hope will follow you, such as prospective customers, market analysts, and journalists. In a just world, these are the people who ought to understand that you are fascinating and irresistible.

You probably want to follow these influencers even without a marketing agenda. After all, if someone is any sort of industry or business pundit, her opinion is worth listening to (even if your private opinion is that she's a jerk).

From a selfish perspective, there are other people you want as followers because of their social media reach: she has a bigger Twitter follower list than you do, or he has connections to an audience you haven't reached. That's just as it is in the "real world," of course: make friends with those who can help you. Thus a high-end restaurant likely follows the city's tourism Twitter feed, a political lobbyist follows area politicians, and start-up firms follow venture capitalists.

You probably also want to follow the press and media that cover your industry—both the trade publications and the reporters who write about your type of business.

Journalists tire quickly of perky PR people calling them on the phone (The phone! Imagine! In this day and age!) to ask, "What are you working on?" If you follow a reporter whose attention you want to attract, you'll know what he's working on, what issues captured his attention recently, and whether he is as much of a wine expert as you. Every PR pro knows the importance of creating a relationship with the press. And here, it's easy to listen and respond to the media.

MARKETING WIN

Journalists are all over social media. According to one study reported by Poynter, a survey of 371 journalists working for newspapers, magazines, and websites found a large majority of reporters and editors now depend on social media sources for story research. Half the journalists use Twitter and other microblogging sites.

Don't try to pitch via Twitter, either publicly or by direct message. Most journalists are put off; email is still the best for that role. But you can engage with them as individuals, and gain your company some mindshare.

Finding People to Follow

You don't need to find everyone to follow all at once. For most of us, following is a quiet, ongoing activity. Start out with a few obvious candidates, and when they @Mention someone else, click on the ID to learn more about that individual. If they're interesting, follow; if they don't stay interesting, unfollow.

Twitter gets interesting once you follow about 100 people. By that point, your Timeline shows enough diversity that it is not dominated by one or two noisy people.

TWITTER TIP

Even if you want to, you can't follow everyone at once. When you're new on Twitter, you can only follow 2,000 Twitter IDs. After you pass that limit, Twitter looks at the number of those who follow you, and permits you to follow up to 10 percent of that number. That is, if 100 people follow you back, you can follow another 10 accounts.

Twitter's policies on these matters can be capricious, so the numbers might be different by the time you read this. The bottom line is, don't try to follow everyone in the world at once.

In fact, the entire philosophy of finding people to follow could be summarized this way:

- Follow top Twitter users and "thought leaders" in your field and related fields.
- Follow who they follow.

Given these guidelines, however, it helps to know how to locate the people you want to reach.

Using Twitter's Search Tools

Start with people who Tweet in your topic. Overall, Twitter's native search does a good job here. One drawback is that, because of the sheer volume of Tweets generated, Twitter only provides access to a few days' worth of archives.

Regardless, a basic search for keywords, names, industry terms, and hashtags will yield dozens of people who care about the same things you do.

If your topic area is exceedingly general, however, or your business is geography focused, you can dig deeper with Twitter's Advanced Search (http://twitter.com/#!/search-advanced).

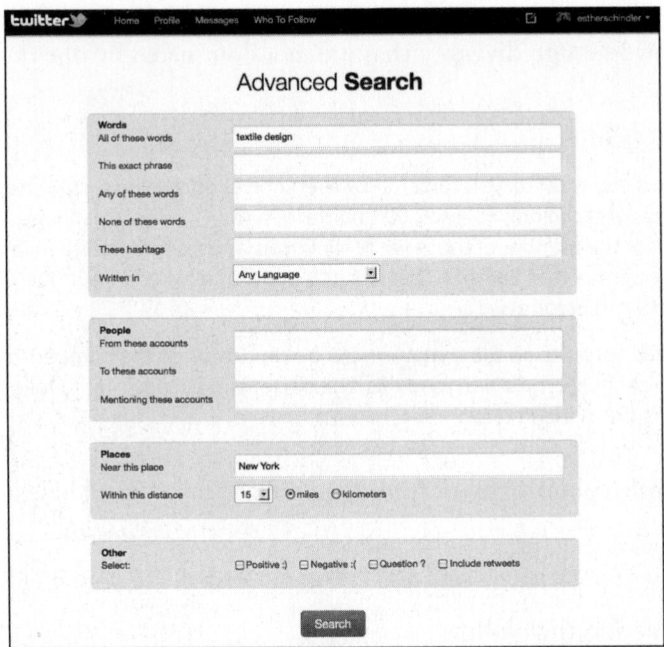

Twitter's Advanced Search lets you find people Tweeting about relevant topics limited by location, account name, language, and other criteria.

Bloggers and Other Influencers

Perhaps you aren't sure how to find the "influencers" in the first place—or at least you don't know how to find them on Twitter.

Start with offline means. A growing number of people include their company Twitter ID on their business cards (we do), as well as websites, brochures, and other offline media.

One helpful tool to find the online doyennes is The Archivist (http://archivist.visitmix.com/dfb76a35/1), a website with a visual interface that enables you to identify and click through to Twitter accounts of the top users organized by category. It identifies the top words in use, too, so you can see which accounts generate the most buzz.

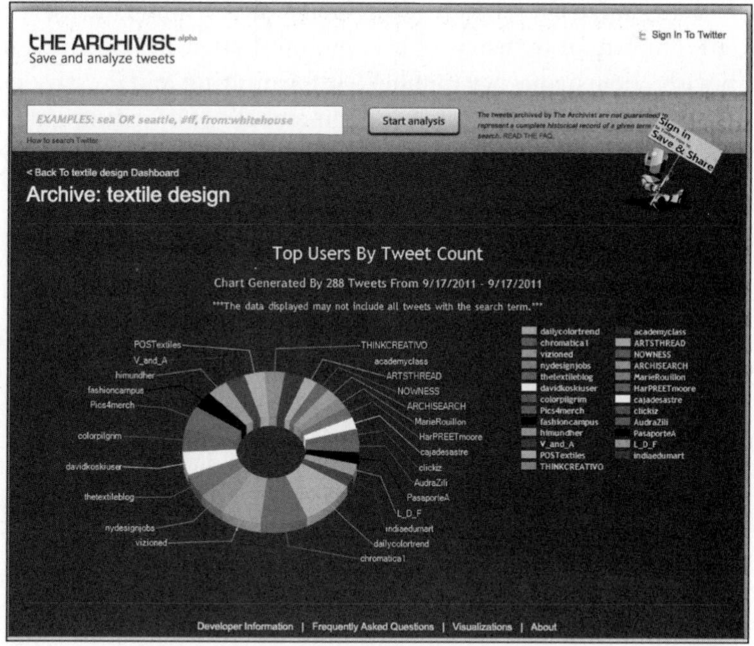

The Archivist shows who Tweets most often with a given phrase, so you can find the people who are most vocal, if not influential, about the subject.

Twitter Lists

One of Twitter's most useful enhancements has been the *Twitter list.* You're sure to find these helpful to organize information. In addition, they're an important discovery mechanism for great Tweets and accounts.

DEFINITION

A **Twitter list** helps you group together, follow, and find Twitter users. For example, you can create a list of the funniest Twitter accounts, local businesses, your clients, or any compilation that makes sense. Lists are public by default, but can be made private. The public lists you create are linked from your profile; other Twitter users can then subscribe to those lists.

We use lists to organize the various components of our interests. Lists are defined by a topic, an interest, an industry, or an opinion. Esther has one (private) list to help her keep up with clients, another (public) list for quilting and creative crafts, another for software developers, and yet another for members of a writing guild she belongs to. Brett keeps a "Daily News" list in which he collects the Twitter accounts he most cares about.

A Twitter list is a micro-Twitter, in that it displays all the updates from a subset of users.

Lists help you focus. When you want to catch up with your industry news, look at the Law News list you created. A few minutes with your Tech Update list can bring you up to date on the latest computing equipment. It's up to you to define a list and add the people who ought to be on it.

But you don't need to do all that work by yourself, because plenty of other people use lists to categorize Twitter streams, too. You can follow someone else's list, without bothering to follow those accounts individually. If the person who collates that list is more organized or in the know than you are, you can rely on her to keep it up to date.

To find relevant Twitter lists, start with someone you already follow. It helps if he is prominent in the field, as the number of lists on which a Twitter account is included is a mark of its reach and engagement.

Look on that expert's Twitter page: On the left side of their profile, you will see a Lists option. When selected, you will be able to view what lists that person is subscribed to as well as what lists they appear on.

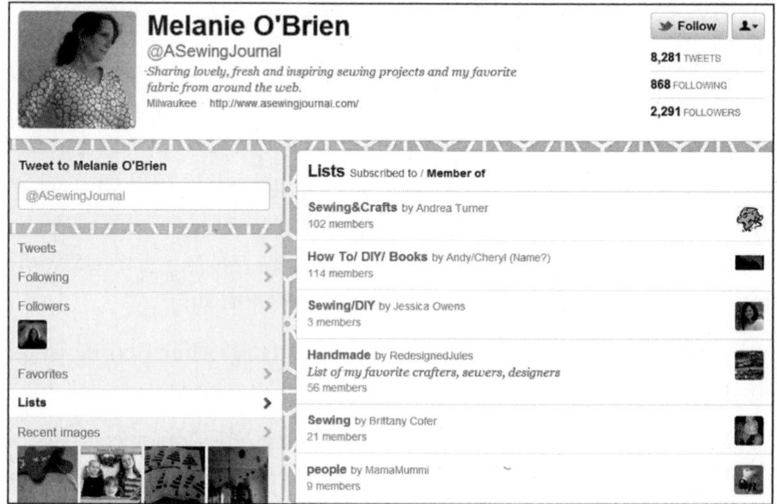

Twitter lists let you follow someone else's collection of experts.

Another way to find Twitter lists is to visit the account of someone you already trust, and click on her Lists tab to see which lists she created.

Finding a list that suits your own interests can take a bit of clicking and prodding, but it's less time-consuming than creating your own—especially when you're new to Twitter.

Note that you can add someone to a Twitter list without following him. So you can create a private "Our Competitors" list, and the competing business will never know. And because you aren't following every account on your lists (even the public ones), you can't be direct messaged by those accounts.

TWITTER TIP

Does that seem like too much work? Formulists.com builds Twitter lists according to a set of preset or user-defined variables. You can use it to create lists according to geography ("Scottsdale"), keywords in Twitter bios ("technology editor"), and other variables. Formulists keeps those lists up to date as you follow more people who meet your criteria; if you follow another person in Scottsdale, your Scottdale list magically grows. Handy.

Curated Lists

There are lots of places to find people worth following. In truth, your problem is going to be resisting the urge to follow everyone. Here are some additional resources.

Do a Google search for "People to follow in [your industry]" and variations on that phrase, such as "who to follow on Twitter for lawyers" or "… for software testers." Someone is sure to have written a blog post with suggestions and, usually, included an explanation of why these people are worth your attention.

Several websites help you categorize yourself and find other people by keywords. Among them are these:

- WeFollow.com is a popularity list, showing who has the most followers in a region or category. You can add yourself to WeFollow.com to ensure you're included on these lists.
- Twellow.com is more like the Yellow Pages of Twitter, emphasizing categories rather than tags or phrases.
- Listorius.com lets you search by topic, region, or profession, powered by data from tens of thousands of list curators. It also curates the most popular lists by category.

While you are searching these directories for people to follow, take a few minutes to ensure you are listed appropriately, too. Make it just as easy for others to find you!

Keeping Up with the Twitter Stream

If you adopt all of our advice in this chapter, you soon will be following a lot of people. It's likely that you're daunted less by Twitter's rule that you can follow 2,000 people than the idea of actually reading posts from that many people. After all, how many people can you reasonably keep up with?

There are two issues raised in this question, really: How many people do you want to care about? And how can you pay attention to those you follow and get anything else done?

How Many People to Follow

The matter of "how many to reasonably follow" is one area in which your faithful authors disagree with one another. Brett follows a few hundred people (though nearly 20,000 follow him). Esther follows a few thousand.

Brett follows fewer people because he insists on information density, business relevance, and their position in the industry. He likes to receive their news, and wants the opportunity to connect with them via direct messaging.

Obviously, Esther isn't so picky. But that doesn't mean she reads every Tweet that flashes by, or feels guilty about not reading them.

As with so many other things, it's your call. Whatever makes you comfortable and efficient. One exception might be customer service accounts. They tend to follow lots of people because a DM can only be sent to someone who is following them.

But before you decide to follow only a few dozen people, consider the ways you can prioritize the Tweets you see in your Twitter stream.

Managing Twitter Overload

It doesn't take too many follows to become overwhelmed with the deluge of content on Twitter. Following just 20 people can give you a lot of reading, especially if they are as loquacious as we are and they link to irresistible, cool stuff (Ooh, another kitty video! Business gossip! Breaking news!).

Fortunately, you can filter Tweets in several ways to identify the ones you care about most, and free yourself from being chained to a sometimes-irrelevant Timeline.

Just as in other areas of life, there are people who are of casual interest and there are true friends whose messages you don't want to miss. That's one reason to use a Twitter client (a topic we cover in Chapter 14) and Twitter lists. Whichever tool you choose, you can group people by topic or list or whatever makes sense to you.

For example, Esther has about 50 people in a Buddies column, and scrolls through that column several times a day to see what her clients, friends, and most-important-people are up to. Another column displays a Twitter list of hobbyist friends, which makes it easy to see the conversation in that community. Yet another tracks a client-related hashtag for which she captures social media metrics. Every so often (though not every day) she dives into a Twitter list to get educated in a topic area she needs to be briefed about.

Surefire ways to manage your Tweets, banish Twitter overload, and become a super-powered user in the process include the use of Twitter lists, following hashtags and keywords, and Twitter clients that filter and organize Tweets.

There are few situations in which you need to read every single Tweet. Some Tweets are more important than others. We urge you to experiment with tools and processes to help you percolate the vital ones to the top, leaving the less urgent Tweets to be of casual, "Hmm so what's happening?" priority.

The Least You Need to Know

- Choose people to follow who can make you smarter, who care about the same things you do, and who can connect you with more opportunities.
- Identify the people you most trust in your industry. Follow whoever they follow.
- Use Twitter lists to organize the Twitter stream by topic—and to rely on the expertise of others.

Building a Twitter Following

Chapter

8

In This Chapter

- Considering the importance of your follower count
- Motivating people to follow you
- Learning tasteful ways to engage with your target audience—and to attract their loyalty
- Balancing your follower-to-follow ratio

It's possible for you to Tweet fascinating, useful information that can make your target audience swoon and yet achieve none of your marketing goals. If nobody follows you, no one ever sees your Tweets, much less takes action on them. It's like singing your heart out on stage, with nobody in the audience.

In this chapter, we show you how to attract more people to what you're saying—which usually means being followed by as many people as possible—as long as most of those people are relevant to your business goals.

Quality Over Quantity

As a businessperson, you already know that having lots of customers is less important than having enough of the right customers. Few businesses are driven by counting the number of bodies that walk through the door; you care more about the size of the average sale, your repeat business, and other qualitative measurements.

Yet some people get into a quest to amass as many Twitter followers as possible. They mistake "follower count" for social influence or engagement or the business's true reach, and it just isn't so.

Twitter isn't about scalp collection; you are not judged by the number of trophies you have on your mantelpiece. What matters is how well you connect with your target audience, and how well you cajole them into doing business with your brand.

Your Follower Count Doesn't Matter

You might think it's odd, in a chapter that's about how to get more followers, to spend the first part of it explaining how unimportant this goal is. We don't mean to say that it doesn't matter if anyone pays attention to your Twitter feed. Rather, our message is: increasing your follower count should not be a primary goal.

So many businesses asking for help with social media marketing fret about their number of followers. Yet when we look at their Twitter feed, we think, "Dude, there's no reason for anyone to want to follow you. Who cares about what you're saying?" If, instead, those businesses lost sleep contemplating, "How can we better serve the people who do follow us?" they would have a lot more followers.

FAIL WHALE

If you judge your Twitter marketing campaign with "number of followers" as a primary metric, that measurement will sway you into making poor decisions. That's like marketing your business by papering the neighborhood with poorly designed sales flyers stuck into everyone's door jambs. Yes, that puts your message in front of a lot of eyeballs … for about a nanosecond. While the sales-flyer approach must be effective for some businesses, in 99 percent of cases it just becomes junk mail.

It's easy to get lost in "collecting followers" rather than helping the followers you have make decisions that help your business. Just as in offline business: serve your existing customers well, encourage them to communicate, and they'll share their joy with others.

Concern yourself with providing the best information possible and with the quality of the people who do follow you. It's better to be followed by 500 engaged, relevant members of your business community than by 5,000 people whose sole intent is to have a large number displayed next to their name.

Yes, that's easy for us to say; we both have an impressive number of followers. Perhaps you have only a few followers and nobody seems to read or respond to your Tweets, and surely the thing to do is to add more, lickity-split, before anything else?

Honestly, don't worry about the number of people who follow you. You certainly want a lot of followers, but if you apply the advice we share throughout the rest of the book, you will get a steady flow of new followers. The problem takes care of itself.

MARKETING WIN

Downgrade the importance of follower count as a success metric. While the number of followers is one meaningful statistic, others—especially those related to engagement—are far more important. Look to metrics that are aligned with user action (responses, Retweets, pageviews) because they show that you have an effect and not just a pigeonhole. Do pay attention to follower count; just don't make it the primary goal.

Monitoring Your Follower Count

Now that we've convinced you that the number of followers doesn't matter, we'll seemingly contradict ourselves by telling to you pay attention to it.

This isn't actually a contradiction. Gaining followers is, after all, a matter of getting attention on Twitter. The follower count is a measurement of your effectiveness in attracting that attention, as it's the first commitment that an interested person can make (that is, the commitment of "I will listen to these folks for a while and see if it's worth my time").

Don't worry about the number; pay attention to the trend. Don't concern yourself with daily up-and-down counts. As long as your follower numbers trend gradually upward, you are on the right track.

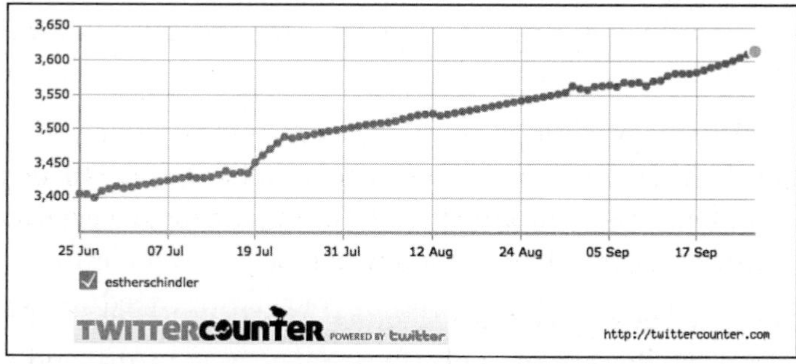

TwitterCounter shows a graph of your follower count over time.

As you implement your marketing plan, the follower count should increase. As you experiment with different techniques, it behooves you to measure the results. If one new action causes you to attract more followers, it's usually a good sign, particularly when accompanied by other measurements of engagement.

Many monitoring tools include features to report follower numbers over time. You can also find several standalone tools for this purpose, such as TwitterCounter.com.

FAIL WHALE

Never ask someone why he unfollowed you. That's like a teenage girl asking a boy why he didn't call back after a first date.

Even if the ex-follower has a conscious reason (besides "You just didn't interest me"), he won't likely tell you. And knowing the answer doesn't accomplish anything. As with teenage dating, you shouldn't expect everyone to care about you and what you say. Just move on to the next.

Getting Noticed

Getting followers isn't hard, as long as you are interesting, you offer something of value to your target readers, and you help those readers find out you exist. Concentrate on helping people learn that your company is online and Tweeting.

A few specific techniques can help people learn that your company is online and has something worthwhile to say.

Identify Target Followers

Who is your ideal follower? The more specific you are, the easier it is to attract people to your Twitter account. Tune your Tweets to the target followers just as you tune print advertising to a magazine's readership.

You'll pick up other followers on the way who aren't anywhere near the center of the bull's-eye—and that's fine. Unlike other marketing media, where it costs money to reach "wasted" eyeballs (such as a liquor store that discovers most of its ads are reaching teetotalers), anyone can pay attention to your Twitter feed without it costing you a cent.

Don't disdain followers who are "irrelevant" to your marketing plan. If you entertain people outside your target audience, that's great. It means you're entertaining and you're building a brand.

A follower may be a vegetarian who's unlikely to buy your company's delicious smoked hams, but she probably knows a meat-eater or two. If the vegetarian Retweets your oh-so-amusing and astonishingly useful tidbit, some of her followers will look at the source of the wonderfulness—you—and some subset of the tire (or ham) kickers will become your followers.

That's how Twitter works: it encourages serendipitous connections. And that's what makes it so cool.

Take the time to create a bulleted list of the people you want to attract. For instance, a commercial photographer might define his ideal followers thusly:

- Other professional photographers
- People who make photography gear or software
- People who purchase commercial photography services

Making this list helps you identify the needs of each audience (what do they care about?) and gets you to focus on responding to those needs.

It might be a long list; that's okay, as long as you have an overarching theme. One freelance journalist we know writes about science innovations, computing trends, and finance news. Her list of "people I want to follow me" stretches across several industries, but the theme is that they are all people who might hire her writing services or help her amplify her brand as a pen-for-hire.

It's also fine if the list is somewhat disjointed—to a point. If you're an accountant by day and an as-yet-unpublished novelist by night, your preferred followers list may be somewhat haphazard. For a solo shop, that might be fine; your writing-related Tweets show off your personality, which is a good thing. If one interest crowds out another, however, you may want to consider maintaining multiple Twitter accounts.

This is also true for larger brands. If the list of ideal followers for one product is very different from the ideal followers for another, it's time to create separate accounts for each product.

Focus on Relevancy

Tweet something of interest to each of your target audiences at least once a day. After all, if the photographer never Tweeted anything to pique the interest of prospective customers, none of those people would have a reason to follow him.

The target list tells you what topics are irrelevant or of lower priority. There's nothing wrong with a photographer who is looking for commercial projects to Tweet about wedding photography techniques or about baking cookies. That can show a breadth of interest, underscore that a real (cookie-baking) human is behind the business, and occasionally attract the "right" followers as the result of Retweets or @Mentions. But the target follower list should help you maximize the important Tweets and keep you from overloading your Twitter stream with off-message content.

Tweet as Though You've Succeeded

When you're on stage, it's easy to notice the empty seats instead of the ones that are occupied. "Hell is a half-filled auditorium," said poet Robert Frost.

If you have scarcely anyone following you, it's difficult to motivate yourself to Tweet. If *sniffle* no one is listening, why bother to say anything? Why not just wait until you do have followers before you "waste" a Tweet?

It's simple: tweet with the same dedication and the same Tweets whether you have 11 followers or 11,000. A professional singer with a small audience belts out his song with the same passion as he does to a packed house. Serve the followers you have and you will get more of them.

No matter how she learns about your Twitter ID, the first thing a prospective follower does is look at your timeline. If she sees several items that tickle her fancy, she is apt to follow you without regard to your follower count. (She cares whether your Tweets attract her, not what they mean to someone else.) If she sees a rarely updated page full of lonely all-about-me messages, she'll click off the page faster than a pilot ejecting from a burning plane.

Start the Conversation

If you want more followers, don't be shy. Find the people you want to talk with, and start talking with them.

Largely, that means following the people you want to follow you. Search for those who meet your criteria using Twitter search, hashtags, and other techniques (as described in Chapter 7) and follow them.

And then, for goodness sake, say something. Participate. Talk to them. Retweet them. Respond to the Tweets of the people you care about: answer their questions, praise their observations, politely disagree. Make the conversation about *them*, not you. If you sincerely care about the people with whom you want to connect, it won't be hard to find something to add genuinely to the conversation.

And there's always chocolate. Or coffee.

> **@aletheia_vox** Right there with ya. On my 2nd caffeine fix. RT **@estherschindler** I woke up tired. And it's gonna be a long day. Sigh.

When you respond to people you hope to gain as followers, you open the door for a conversation. The recipient might ignore your Tweet, in which case you haven't lost anything. In the worst case, your timeline showing the Tweet demonstrates to a would-be follower that you're interested in other people; that can only lead to good things.

Or the individual might answer.

She may answer you without following you. If she does, and she is influential on Twitter, some of her followers may click on the @Mention to see who you are. If your timeline demonstrates that you're follow-worthy, Ms. Influential's followers might click on that oh-so-important **Follow** button to add you to their own Twitter stream.

TWITTER TIP

It's tempting to attempt to engage with very famous people, which in this case usually means someone who has hundreds of thousands of followers. The motivation is obvious: if you succeed, and a well-known actor @Mentions you or Retweets you, it can generate a lot of attention.

But don't count on it. Most people with gobs of followers get so many @Mentions that they ignore most of them. They have to, or they would have no time to sing or act or do whatever it is that made them famous.

It's far more effective to respond to the famous people in your own market niche. They have more influence with your target followers, anyway.

One way to gain followers is to offer help based on your expertise. You can scan for frustrated customers or search for people for whom the appropriate response is, "How can we help?"

> **@VerizonWireless @MilfonDeck1** Unhappy with your network? Change is good. Switching to Verizon could get you a $100 gift card! Info: lo.cr/oT1kQS

> **@ClothesDr** We can clean/restore vintage! RT **@erincataldi** 'I would never recommend dry cleaning a civil war coat.'—wise words from antiques road show

Ask for Retweets

If you are new to Twitter, there isn't much you can accomplish by asking your non-existent followers to help you get noticed. But if your aim is to grow your follower base from modest to influential (or at least to "nothing to be ashamed of"), you can occasionally—and we do mean occasionally—encourage others to Tweet about you or to Retweet your post.

Pay attention to the way you ask for Retweets, as well as the items you ask others to share. Not all that long ago, "social media scientist" Dan Zarella broke down the most common words and phrases in 10,000 Retweeted posts. He discovered that the 10 most Retweeted words are: you, Twitter, please, Retweet, post, blog, social, free, media, and help.

"Retweets may seem like a small idea, and they are," he wrote. "But that small idea is the first real window into how ideas spread from person to person. We can study the linguistic traits, the topical characteristics, the epidemiological dynamics, and the social network interactions that take place when a person spreads a meme …. For the first time in human history, we can begin to gaze into the inner workings of the contagious idea."

In short, if you ask people to Retweet something that's important to you, often they actually do so. That puts your message in front of a new audience, and—assuming that your original Tweet is worth repeating—helps you find new followers.

It helps if you give your followers a reason to Retweet or share your content. For example, the Arizona Diamondbacks (**@dbacks**) had a sales promotion in which they offered followers a special price on baseball tickets. If the follower Retweeted the sales offer, the savings were doubled.

Advice throughout the book should inspire you to connect with Twitter users who can help you be discovered. Among these other techniques are these:

- Use hashtags in your Tweets. As we discuss in Chapter 9, including an appropriate hashtag helps people who care about a particular topic (#photography, #python, conference names) find others who share the same interest.
- Ask for an endorsement from an ally. If you have a relationship of trust with a business partner, customer, or supplier, ask the person to Tweet something about you with an @Mention. Testimonials matter online just as they do in "real life."
- Integrate "Tweet this" or other social media links on your website. You don't have to do all the work. Enable people who visit your website or other online properties to connect to you.

Following Back

We have written here about "whom to follow" and "getting followers" as if they are different things, and in most ways they are. Nothing requires you to pay attention to someone just because she pays attention to you—at least for yourself as an individual using Twitter.

But there are a few considerations that apply to businesses in regard to choosing with whom you should reciprocate with a follow.

The Electronic Holiday Card List

Some people suggest that you should follow anyone who follows you. Well, perhaps that works for some businesses. We're more cynical about such things, because we believe you should pay attention to only those you care about.

That doesn't mean "care about" in the sense of "I would invite them to Thanksgiving dinner" or "I would help him move into a new apartment." Your affection for them might last only as long as the time they spend in line for the cash register.

Truly large companies, as well as well-known celebrities, tend to take one of two approaches.

- Follow nearly everyone who follows them (**@yokoono** follows 760,000 people; as a more modest example, Portland Oregon's mayor Sam Adams, **@MayorSamAdams**, follows 42,000)
- Follow practically no one

The problem with adopting the former approach is that you won't be able to pay attention to the Twitter stream easily, which means you won't, which means you aren't listening. So why follow at all?

If you're a movie star or famous music artist, you can get away with following only 10 people because your followers are fans, and fans don't expect to be acknowledged. (They squee with pleasure when they are @Mentioned or Retweeted, however.)

FAIL WHALE

One reason not to adopt a "follow everybody" response is this: if you're not careful and auto-follow back people, you might be following a lot of spam bots. That lowers your company's credibility.

Neither the zero-followers nor all-followers should be your model. Instead, harken back to our advice about who to follow: Those you can learn from, those you can help, and those who interest you.

"Interest," in business terms, should not be automatically inclusive or automatically exclusive. In some cases, you might feel beholden to follow someone back because you believe he'll be miffed if you don't. It's rather like the motivations behind "If he sent me a Christmas card, I suppose I'd better send him one." (Shh, we won't tell: no one says you have to read his Tweets.)

In other cases, following back is a no-brainer for some marketing campaigns. Twitter accounts whose customer support role requires direct messages need to follow back just about everyone. Bank of America's help line (**@BofA_Help**), for instance, has 17,000 followers and follows back 15,000.

> **@BofA_Help @chenxiwang** Thank you for your messages and the info, I am researching now. I cannot send you a DM unless you follow me.^ss

In contrast, if you don't want someone to be able to send you direct messages, don't follow her. That's why many celebrities minimize the number of those they follow. Imagine how many annoying personal requests they would get if they had a different policy!

The Follower to Following Ratio

Prospective followers consider your willingness to engage with them before they click on the **Follow** button.

As one blogger wrote, "If you have 3,000 followers and only follow 50, then I consider you to be a Twitter snob. You like to be the center of attention, but don't like to acknowledge that other people have something valuable to say to you.

"On the other hand, if you follow 7,000 people and only 300 follow you back, that tells me that you're either using auto-follow software to rack up 'bragging numbers' or you follow everyone under the sun, but no one else finds your Tweets useful. If either of these are true, you need to seriously rethink why you are using Twitter."

Few Twitter users are so analytical about their response. However, the ratio between the number who follow you and the number you follow is a meaningful indication of your willingness to be social. And if you aren't willing to be social, what are you doing on Twitter?

Start following back real people who can potentially become brand advocates and customers. Social media has leveled the playing field between businesses and consumers, and consumers feel empowered. Acknowledge their presence; that's the easiest way to show appreciation.

Avoiding the Spam Approach

Someone must have convinced you that marketing using Twitter is a good idea, or you wouldn't have picked up this book. We're delighted that you did pick it up, of course, and we applaud such a wise decision. We like to think that by making an investment in learning to use Twitter well, your motivation is to create lasting relationships with the user community you serve, and the customers you hope to serve.

But not everyone thinks that way.

The Follow-Back Technique

A subset of "social media experts" insist that getting followers is the key metric to success. Instead of creating connections and encouraging a conversation, they exhort you to get as many followers as possible, and to follow only those who follow you back.

These folks maintain that your importance is judged only by the number of people who follow you—and you already know how little we believe that matters.

We work in the real world, however, not the happy-happy universe in which every business client or work colleague is as enlightened as you and we are. So while we plead with you not to adhere to the "get as many followers as possible" creed, we recognize that someone else may foist upon you such an unreasonable goal.

For example, one client of Esther's had as his sole social media metric "number of Twitter followers." It was wrong-headed of the client. It was also impossible to pry the misconception out of his head, despite the eloquence of her arguments and a private tantrum or two. With a choice between "Tell the client he's wrong and probably lose the account" and "Generate the statistics he wants to see immediately, then go back and do it right later on"—well, the kitties need their kibble.

In such a case, go ahead and use all the silly "how to get more followers" techniques possible to crank up the statistics and make your client happy. But then ignore those "followers" and build the traffic organically the right way.

At the very least, you should be aware how this is done, because inevitably someone will suggest it to you as a surefire way to success. We hereby arm you with an understanding of the technique so that you can explain why it's a really dumb idea. Tantrums optional.

FAIL WHALE

These instructions are meant for education only. Kids, don't try this at home. The "get followers quick" plans don't generate engagement, conversations, or business success. They only create a façade. If you have real business goals for using Twitter, using these techniques will disappoint you.

Push-Me Pull-You

You can get lots and lots of followers. But all the Twitter Follower Get-Rich-Quick schemes work on the assumption that you want to get more people to click on a link. They don't create someone who actually follows you. They don't find people who want to listen to you or engage with you.

The people who "follow you back" with these schemes are those who are interested only in broadcasting their own message; they aren't going to listen to yours. Or anyone else's for that matter.

One sign of a Twitter account that's just trying to get more followers: the use of hashtags such as #followback or #500aday, or the inclusion of these terms in the Twitter user's bio. Avoid following such people. Twitter is not a popularity contest. It's a conversation.

To get a lot of followers, you …

- Follow as many people as possible.
- Wait 24 hours, to allow your new "follow" to respond.
- Unfollow those who don't follow you back.
- Repeat.

Twitter limits the number of people you can follow per day. To begin with, you can follow 2,000 people. The limits are partially governed by the balance between those you follow and those who follow you.

Because of the ratio limits, this strategy depends on unfollowing the people who don't follow you back. If Twitter says you can only follow 2,500 users at a given time and 500 of those aren't following you, dumping them makes room for following a different 500 who might follow you back.

TWITTER TIP

This process might answer a minor mystery for your existing Twitter account, especially if you have relatively few followers and you cherish every one of them.

That is, you get a few new followers, cheer your popularity (They like me! They really like me!), and then discover your follower count is smaller the next day. (Sob.)

You were just the victim (well, victim might be too strong a word) of this "get new followers" plan. If you don't follow them back, they drop you. Don't worry about it. They were never really interested in you in the first place. Only in counting coup.

This process is tedious to do manually but is quite doable. In the last few years, however, several companies have sprung up to automate the process—though they don't tell you precisely what they're doing. These websites promise that, for a fee, you can obtain a specified number of followers. While the number of followers will in fact be achieved, you won't get anything substantial out of it.

Several websites that encourage you to purchase followers value each person at between 2¢ and 5¢. That sounds like a bargain, except you aren't assured of any further engagement or brand awareness. In fact, we'd be surprised if you got a single actual response from these robot-generated followers. They are not actual humans looking to interact; just other broadcasters looking for one-way conversations.

Other organizations have created formulas to place a value on a follower or Tweet. For example, a service called ad.ly allows brands to publish a Tweet out of a celebrity's feed—for a fee. According to E!, Kim Kardashian (**@KimKardashian**) gets $10,000 to Tweet ads, though her prices are at the top end.

What is the value of a fan, Tweet, or follower? The simple answer is: nothing. Your intent is, we trust, to build a community, not a popularity list.

The Least You Need to Know

- Build your follower list organically, based on offering value to the people who pay attention.
- Encourage people to Retweet and engage with you publicly, which extends your actual reach.
- Be aware of the shortcuts to gaining followers—and understand why they should be avoided.

Chapter 9

The Art of the Hashtag

In This Chapter

- Discovering how hashtags turn keywords into conversations
- Creating a hashtag-based chat
- Using hashtag tracking tools
- How Lexus used a Twitter chat to engage customers and enlighten executives

They are so simple—and so powerful.

A hashtag is just a word or phrase with a hashmark (#) in front of it. It can be anything.

Especially, it can be a path to better communication on Twitter. In this chapter, we show you how to make the most of them.

Hashtags in Depth

What makes hashtags special is that Twitter treats them differently from other text. Twitter automatically turns a hashtag into a hyperlink for searches of the tagged term.

For example, if you include #chocolate in a Tweet, then anyone who clicks on the tag in your Tweet is shown all other Tweets that use the tag #chocolate. Across Twitter. Around the world. Right now … with history that goes back for two full days.

> **@Fram_GuTierrez** Yum! #Chocolate! RT! Al que le gusta! (1 minute ago)
>
> **@babystylemag @collegeprepster @katespadeny** This may be your best color yet! #chocolate (2 minutes ago)
>
> **@laryycavalcante @GiovanaMadu** miinha sorvetiinha de #chocolate s2 (5 minutes ago)
>
> **@greenmissionmom** Earn money w/ #chocolate? #Win Dove Chocolate Discoveries Kit **@formulamom** #giveaway ENDS 10/14 wp.me/p1zrj0-1fy formulamom.com/review-dove-ch… (7 minutes ago)

Clicking the hashtag leads to searches for #chocolate (or #security or #moose), while people searching for chocolate (or security or moose) find the tagged terms as well as those same terms without tags.

Identifying Shared Interests

The idea behind hashtags is to get people to use the same one when talking about a specific topic. You will notice that Tweets tagged with the same hashtag all (or mostly) discuss the same topic. For instance, after the March 2011 earthquake and tsunami, there was plenty of discussion, but people used #prayforjapan most often.

Functionally, hashtags categorize Tweets so that they're part of a narrowed conversation and to make them easier to find in Twitter search. They are much like keywords in search engine optimization, or the tags you add to a Flickr photo. They give an additional context to someone reading a Tweet and, more often, they make it easy for people to find one particular Tweet.

There are no formal rules for hashtags. Nobody says, "This is the right way to do it." They are community-driven and often spontaneously generated by Twitter users, which means you can make up any hashtag you like.

Yet if you want to use hashtags to drive more business, it's wise to learn about the community conventions that have evolved.

The Latest Trend

To get to know hashtags, explore the hashtags in Twitter's trending topics.

If a word or expression is used by thousands of users simultaneously, it becomes what Twitter refers to as a "Trend." Twitter's *trending topics* list usually contains at least one hashtag.

DEFINITION

Twitter displays the **trending topics** in a sidebar on the Twitter home page, algorithmically identifying whatever is popular right at the moment. (Not what's popular on a daily basis or continues to be popular; otherwise "chocolate" would always be listed, at least in a just and fair world.)

As Twitter's Help pages explain, trending topics help people discover the "most breaking" news stories from across the world: "We think that trending topics which capture the hottest emerging trends and topics of discussion on Twitter are the most interesting," they write.

Trending topics generally highlight major news, events, major sporting events, TV programs, disaster relief, and political actions. Other times, trends are questions, jokes, or promotional memes.

Keep in mind that you can set your Twitter account to show only trending topics for a geographical area rather than worldwide. That's a boon for retailers and small businesses that care more about what's happening locally—and trying to get into trending topics themselves—than whatever is popular around the world.

Trends have become a heavily weighted metric in marketing. When a campaign #hashtag or phrase is trending, it means more eyeballs are drawn to it, multiplying the trending effect.

Tweeting with Hashtags

Hashtags mainly are helpful for expanding the reach of a Tweet or adding additional context. The most popular uses are these:

- To identify a keyword in your Tweet that might not be picked up by search
- To set the subject of a Tweet when the word isn't explicitly used
- To deliberately mark a Tweet as part of a larger conversation
- To offer insightful, humorous, or snarky commentary

The Descriptive Hashtag

Most hashtags are used as descriptors or keywords. People who care enough about the item you identified with a hashtag to click on the topic—such as in the preceding chocolate example—will find your Tweet among anything else by using that tag.

Throughout this book we've shown dozens of Tweet examples that incorporate hashtags, so we won't belabor the point. Either you use a hashtag as part of the body of the Tweet (sometimes more than one):

> **@avocados** Hosting a #tailgating party this weekend? Here are some great tips! http://ow.ly/6R5Bl
>
> **@LionBrandYarn** Heading to a spooky #Halloween party? These #crochet cat ears and paws whip up quickly. http://ow.ly/6QPaH #31patterns
>
> **@HP_SmallBiz** Exactly TWO WEEKS left to join our online scavenger hunt. Five #HP EliteBook 8460w notebooks & cash up for grabs! bit.ly/mZl112

… or you add a hashtag to better classify the topic:

> Study confirms genetic link to suicidal behavior bit.ly/hXHp8c #Science
>
> Turns out, we geeks REQUIRE innovation. It's in the brain chemistry, explains **@LisaVaas** http://bit.ly/ppxG6N #science #innovation

Descriptive hashtags put your thoughts into context. They let your followers and those browsing search results know that you want your Tweet to be associated with a specific subject.

You can spend way too much time agonizing over whether the hashtag should be at the end or in the body of the text. If it's tacked on at the end, the Tweet is easier to read, but the hashtag is likely to be chopped off in a Retweet. If it's in the Tweet, it's harder to read, but the Tweet is shorter.

> Vegetarian recipes: Raw Apple Vanilla Tart bit.ly/mWWCUW #vegetarian #recipes
>
> #Vegetarian #recipes: Raw Apple Vanilla Tart bit.ly/mWWCUW

Which of these is better? We don't know, either. But we'll think about it while munching on an apple tart.

Don't get worked up over this. We haven't found that it matters all that much. The only guideline is that it's vaguely rude to use more than three hashtags in a Tweet.

FAIL WHALE

Don't overdo it! Hashtags are frequently overused, used needlessly, and added to all proper nouns in a Twitter message, rendering them nearly unreadable. For example, this (sadly real) example from Maddaloni Jewelers demonstrates how little the company understands what it's doing. Is anyone going to search on "We"? "Buy"? "Sell"?

@maddalonijewel #We #Buy and #Sell #Gold #Silver #Diamonds

Similarly, don't include every variation; pick one. Not "I will be at the State Fair, #indy, #indianapolis, #indiana" but "I will be at the #Indiana state fair in #indy."

The Twitter Sidebar

Hashtags also denote personal commentary or opinion. This isn't quite as relevant to Twitter for dedicated marketing purposes as it is to putting personality into your Twitter stream. (Also, it's fun.)

In 2010, Susan Orlean (staff writer for *The New Yorker* and author of *The Orchid Thief*) wrote a *New Yorker* column, "Hash," describing the "mission creep" of hashtags. We excerpt the key bits to get her point across, and we also urge you to look up the entire column (it's very funny):

> *Frequently, [hashtags] are used to set apart a side commentary on Tweets, sort of like those little mice in the movie "Babe" who appear at the bottom of the frame and, in their squeaky little mouse voices, comment on what you've just seen and what you're about to see. A typical commentary-type hashtag might look like this:*
>
> *"Sarah Palin for President??!? #Iwouldratherhaveamoose"*
>
> *This usage totally subverts the original purpose of the hashtag, since the likelihood of anyone searching the term "Iwouldratherhaveamoose" is next to zero. But that isn't the point. This particular hashtaggery is weirdly amusing, because, for some reason, starting any phrase with a hashtag makes it look like it's being muttered into a handkerchief; when you read it you feel like you've had an intimate moment in which the writer leaned over and whispered "I would rather have a moose!" in your ear.*

We grant that most companies rarely have an opportunity to use hashtags this way. However, if yours is a small or solo business that strongly reflects your own personality, it's perfectly fine to Tweet something like this:

> Raspberries. Avoid them at all costs. #babysittingprotip
>
> dear skycaps: while your customer is in the restroom, do not leave their wheelchair and bags unattended. #thingsthatshouldgowithoutsaying

Similarly, as an individual or a very small business—wherein "who you are" doesn't interfere with the marketing message—you may also use the supremely social hashtags such as #FollowFriday (which we discuss in Chapter 5).

And as an individual (but perhaps not as a representative of a multinational brand) you can occasionally participate in what we can only call idle memes: the community telling jokes to itself. Among our favorites are these:

- #nicerfilmtitles represented "the kindler, gentler side of Twitter," and the Twitter community suggested such alternate movie titles as "The Bourne Diplomacy," "The Cheerful Bleating of the Lambs," and "Snacks On a Plane."
- #geekpickuplines is tacked onto Tweets like, "The moment I saw you my stack nearly overflowed" and "I can figure out the square root of any number in 10 seconds. Let's try it with your phone number."
- #bookswithalettermissing include "Lord of the Rigs: Frodo decides to go into truck driving," "The Handmaid's Ale—**@MargaretAtwood**'s best beer recipes," and "The Invisible Ma—Early polemic against single parent families."

The suitability of participation in such community Friday-afternoon-giggling is a matter left up to your own corporate culture. We hope yours permits it.

Engaging in Conversations

Hashtags aren't just search shortcuts. When a community of users shares a single hashtag, it enables the community's members to hold an ongoing conversation. This is most commonly used for Twitter chats and conference reporting, or Tweeting about a live event while virtually networking with attendees. (We'll get to those topics in a moment.)

But those are just the start. For instance, a hashtag can be a way to indicate that a Tweet is part of a branding message. One of Esther's clients uses a specific hashtag to indicate that the articles published on the client's site are part of a single campaign. Any Tweets with that hashtag appear on the publication's website (that took a tiny tweak to the website design), demonstrating to casual readers that others are engaged with the brand.

Hashtags can help you target an audience. A freelance web designer might tag Tweets that contain tips for fellow designers with #webdesigntip. This shows followers who she's writing for, labels her actions ("See! I share my experience!), and helps people sort through relevant Tweets by searching for that hashtag.

Joining a Cause

In one of the more heartwarming uses of Twitter, hashtags have helped to rally together people across the Internet to support both positive and controversial causes. The use of a common hashtag organizes the conversation.

Hacktivist group Anonymous, for example, used the tag #OpBart to keep track of conversation revolving around a peaceful (yet disruptive) protest conducted in San Francisco.

A more global "cause" hashtag was #EgyptUprising, in early 2011. Despite the Egyptian government's attempts to block Internet access, activists and protesters shared information about the events as they happened, so the world could track the events in Egypt in real time. The hashtag helped people identify the Tweets related to the ongoing events.

FAIL WHALE

It's certainly permissible for anyone—including a business—to participate in an ongoing movement. But we caution you to do so only after serious consideration, when you are certain that you are genuinely adding something to the conversation.

Some businesses imagine that if they string together a series of popular hashtags, they'll be picked up by search and gather more followers. Too often, the Tweet has nothing to do with the hashtags being used, and the useless Tweet only serves to dilute an otherwise helpful conversation. Remember the examples from Chapter 3, in which companies tried to leverage a news event for their own selfish ends. Don't be a hashtag hijacker!

Turning Hashtags into #MarketingWin

You can use hashtags just as anyone else on Twitter does and you'll probably get good results by doing so. Let's turn our attention, however, to a few ways that you can employ hashtags in your marketing campaigns.

Running Contests

If contests are a viable promotion for your business, consider crafting a hashtag to accompany it. By monitoring search results for contest entrants, the company can keep track of who is actively engaging with the brand and attract new participants.

For example, the first drink named with a tag (#VirginBull) won a #NextTopCocktail competition for **@VirginAmerica**. The drink's creator, **@DavidCruiseSF**, wrote in a blog comment, "I will freely admit that the power of Twitter (and other social media) with the use of the tag is what clearly drove the votes and our landslide victory. The #VirginBull earned 34 percent of the total vote; the next closest competitor was 13 percent. Is that a good way to use a tag? I would say Yes!"

Capturing Attention

Don't be afraid to ask your constituency to repeat your hashtag—especially if you give them a motivation to do so.

Hashtags can encourage participation, especially among an existing user community. Back in Chapter 2, we pointed out how the Arizona Diamondbacks frequently used hashtags, exhorting people at Chase Field to Tweet with a special-to-this-game hashtag (#BeatLA) and promising that their Tweets might show up on the scoreboard.

They aren't the only media-driven company to use hashtags. The Los Angeles Kings wanted hockey fans to get into gear with them for the 2011–2012 season. When the Kings and New York Rangers faced off in their opening game in Stockholm, Sweden, they held a "hashtag battle" during the game in support of the Children's Hospital of Los Angeles.

For every 5,000 Tweets using the hashtag #GoLAKings during the game, the Kings donated $1,000. The NHL team also incorporated a contest; those who Tweeted with the hashtag were also automatically entered into a drawing for airline vouchers from Delta Airlines. Rangers fans did the same with #GoNYRangers hashtags.

Hashtags During Conferences

Among techies, it was once common to live-blog an event such as a conference keynote address. Those who wanted to follow the latest announcements from, say, a Macworld conference would log on to an Apple news website to watch the reporter slowly type in what happened on stage. Usually this required users to stab at the browser refresh button as though it was a one-armed bandit and they had a pocketful of nickels.

Nowadays, hashtags have become the common way to share what's happening during events such as webinars, conferences, and seminars. Attendees share their responses in real time, engaging their own followers with their observations and speaker quotes, and ideally attracting more followers to the company and to the conference. It's as though everyone at the event is a live-news reporter broadcasting globally.

It's also a way for attendees and vendors to connect before the conference begins:

> Just arrived #bin2011, looking for other #mombloggers
>
> **@MidlifeRoadTrip** We'll be at #BlogWorld this week w/**@watchdotTV** ~Booth 321~ 2 LIVE MidLife Road Trip shows! Come say hi!
>
> **@startappdotcom** Who is going to be at #AnDevCon next week?

The hashtag is usually chosen before the conference. The organizer—which may be you!—establishes a hashtag and shares it with the audience (such as saying, "We'll use #ChocolateFTW as our hashtag" in the logistics section of conference announcements, and Tweeting it in the company's own Twitter feed).

FAIL WHALE

Pay attention to your hashtag! When you adopt a hashtag for an event or issue advocacy, ensure that the tag is not already in use for other topics. That's rarely a problem with a common abbreviation where it's your goal to participate in a larger conversation, such as #SmallBiz.

But it can be problematical for concise tags, such as #ACR rather than #AgileCodeReview. Before you tell everyone in the webinar to share their thoughts using the #ACR hashtag, make sure no one else is using it for, say, Tweets about "Assassin's Creed Revelations." That confuses everyone. (Not that we're admitting that something like that has ever happened to us.)

Participating in Twitter Chats

We can't all attend industry conferences. Heck, most of us can't even get to a monthly meeting of the local user group for our profession, whether that's a computer consultant's special interest group or a PR & Marketing association. Even though some of the presentations include bagels.

That's okay, because hashtags help communities of like-minded people create a regular gathering on Twitter. Chats let you network with real people who share your interests. These are largely for sharing information among professional colleagues (such as #PRChat or #JobChat) rather than marketing to customers—with notable exceptions.

A Twitter chat happens at a scheduled time, because it's a live event. (Though of course you can look at the archive later by searching for the hashtag; you just can't participate.) There are no categories, just people with usernames, like the AOL chat rooms of old. Using the same hashtag lets everyone follow each other as well as enables others to easily join in the conversation. (Bring your own bagels.)

Among the reasons to join a Twitter chat are these:

- To learn something new
- To share something you know
- To make new friends
- To be found by others
- To establish your personal branding

Hosting a Twitter Chat

Consider creating an industry chat to engage with other users and share information. If you have an audience who will listen, a Twitter chat can be another opportunity to attain thought leadership, grow your following, engage with social media users, and spread the word about your company. What's not to like?

This is as applicable to business-to-business marketing (for example, computer industry firm Forrester Research) as it is to consumer marketing (such as the Staples office supply company):

> **@forrester** Can enterprise suites like #CRM or #ERP empower customers? forr.com/qo3upx. Join our Tweet jam, 9/8 @ 11 am ET. #BPF11
>
> **@Staples** Looks like someone's taking a coffee break. Care to join? You're invited to our #CoffeeSocial tomorrow! See you there. pic.twitter.com/JDczpogb

While you can promote these on Twitter, you should also advertise the Twitter chat using your other outreach media such as email newsletters. Be sure to ...

- Set a date and time (including time zone information).
- Be clear about what you plan to discuss.
- Tell people how to participate. Don't assume the participant is more than a Twitter novice.

Don't expect miracles from your Twitter chats. Aim for engagement rather than huge participant numbers.

For example, BBC Radio 1 held a live Twitter chat with its interactive editor Ben Chapman, enabling listeners to post questions for him as part of Internet Week Europe. Although the BBC has over 60,000 followers, only six questions were asked.

Jem Stone, executive producer for social media at BBC Radio and Music, admitted to Business Zone editor Dan Martin that the Twitter chat was fairly quiet. "This was an experimental event as part of a business/corporate-related week very much targeted at industry themes. The promotion was fairly limited on our part and I wasn't that surprised at having so few questions. We certainly weren't arrogant enough to assume that a large audience was a given."

Tracking Hashtags

You can track hashtags with brute force, such as a general Twitter search (and thus a saved search) or monitter.com. But most people turn to a Twitter client for ongoing tracking. Any self-respecting Twitter client application lets you create a column in which to show all relevant searches—including hashtags.

Yet there are a few tools specific to hashtags worth exploring.

Hashtags.org

Hashtags.org's simple interface helps you search for hashtags as well as their trending popularity.

For example, searching on the hashtag #business graphically displays the times of day and days of the week when the #business hashtag is most popular. Below the graph, you also see the latest Tweets that include that hashtag. When a hashtag takes off due to a news event, the graph is remarkable.

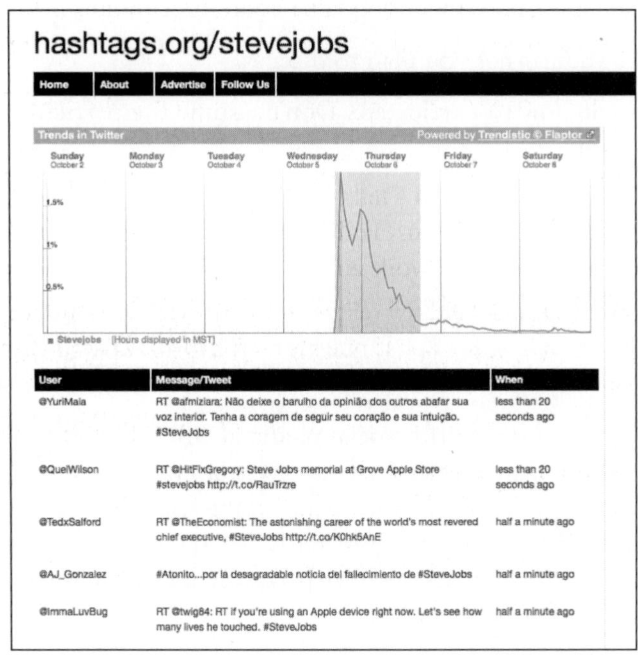

Hashtags.org graphs hashtag popularity over time.

Twubs.com

Twubs.com lets Twitter users form groups around popular hashtags and connects the dots, so you can learn that people in a group about open government are also interested in economics. You can see which hashtags are popular by categories including books, conferences, the Internet, science, news, and much more.

Because Twubs groups hashtags into categories, it's an excellent place to find other Twitter users with similar interests. Because it's meant to bring people together—with hashtags as the connector—it also shares items of interest to a "twub," such as reminding people of #agchat, a "weekly streaming agriculture & farm conversation" every Tuesday from 8 to 10 P.M. Eastern time.

What the Trend

Some of those hashtags are mighty obscure. What the Trend (WhatTheTrend.com) shares user-defined explanations of Twitter's trending topics, with constantly updating, crowdsourced definitions, and explanations for why the topic is trending.

It also includes an application programmer interface, so your web developers can program your website to tap into the latest trends.

In September 2011, HootSuite acquired What the Trend "to help define and understand trending Twitter topics."

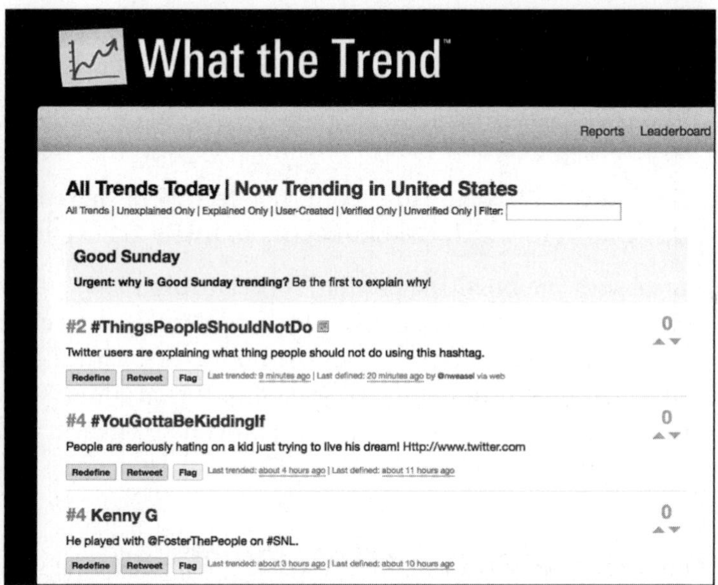

What the Trend identifies trending topics and crowdsources their explanations.

Lexus: Driving Personality into a Twitter Conversation

Need evidence that Twitter chats can be useful? Start your engines.

People love their cars. They love to talk about them, complain about them, and share stories of the first car they owned. (A 1975 VW Bug that had 14 inches of play in the steering wheel and a heater that wouldn't turn off. Just sayin'.)

But consumers don't tend to put a human face on the businesses they purchase their cars from. Lexus aimed to change that—and to put a face to the car company's brand.

Reflecting Corporate Values

Beginning in October 2010, Lexus began scheduling Twitter chats that accompany a live, in-person dinner, one every two or three months. An executive from the automaker comes to a customer's house, a renowned chef cooks dinner, and Nancy Hubbell, the Lexus Prestige Communications Manager, Tweets about it on the company's Twitter feed.

"It's an opportunity to infuse more human elements into our brand," she says. "Putting a face and person behind the Twitter feed is really beneficial. It's more meaningful than 'Check out our latest product.'"

With the Lexus dinners, she wants to encourage a feeling of shared experience and demonstrate the lengths to which the brand goes to listen to customers.

As odd as "dinner with the boss" may sound, this campaign had a direct connection for Lexus. "There's a Lexus covenant that says we will treat every customer as a guest in our home," Hubbell explains. Thus the notion of treating customers as the company's guests in their homes (with several of the customer's friends) was consistent with the company's values. And, she points out, Lexus has always been about customer service.

Program Goals: Everybody Learns Something

Lexus executives were supportive of the plan from the beginning. They understood Hubbell's intent to give unique access to the executives through social media channels, and the opportunity for the executives to learn directly from customers.

The engagement goals certainly have been met, in Lexus' eyes, because everyone gained better understanding of customer issues—especially with an emotional connection. For example, Hubbell says, her boss was amazed at the problems customers shared about their other cars. "It's like having a bad boyfriend," a customer told him. "They treat you terribly, but they look so good!"

"I think that was a real eye-opener for him," Hubbell says. The conversation the general manager had with the customer underscored Lexus' renewed emphasis on design. "It is absolutely a focus group—but among friends with great food and a fair amount of wine."

Bon Appetweet!

During the dinner, Hubbell says, she sends about 50 Tweets. (She does apologize in advance to followers that she may be clogging their Twitter feeds.) "I pick and choose the things to Tweet about that I think people will find interesting. I identify key points people can relate to. And I post pictures of really cool food."

The event generates a few hundred Tweets. But, she points out, she isn't posting during a high-traffic time; these events often happen on a Friday night. "The most I've had is five Tweets at the dinner," Hubbell says.

> **@lexusofportland** Join **@Lexus** Friday night as GM Mark Templin dines with one of their customers and their friends. We'll be eating & Tweeting. #LexusDinner
>
> **@Lexus** Templin asks what everyone's favorite car and why. His was a Triumph T6 from his college days. #LexusDinner ^NH
>
> **@Americanluxury** RT **@lexus** Car salesman told a woman to come back with her son so he could help her. Ouch! #NotALexusDealer #LexusDinner ^NH <— HAHA!
>
> **@ColumWood @Lexus** Just got home after a long drive from Detroit to Toronto, read the entire stream of #LexusDinner Tweets. Very entertaining.

"This is all about connecting with the customers and getting info from them," she explains. "[The executive] gets reams of data."

The customers certainly don't mind it, either. "People are enthused about their cars," says Hubbell. And they are talking about their cars even if the manufacturer isn't part of the conversation.

She's been somewhat surprised by the detail people pay attention to. They Retweet what's been posted, and they ask questions. "It sparks a conversation separate from the dinner as well," she adds.

Social Media Lessons

When Lexus began its social media campaigns, the team worried whether they would have enough content to keep it alive and meaningful. "Now every department is begging and pleading to get on the calendar," Hubbell says.

Her rule for information shared on Twitter: it must pass the test of being something followers will enjoy.

"Don't think about what you want to share," she advises. "Instead, think about, 'What do our followers want to know?' Put the focus on them." Try a variety of things. See what they respond to. Gear your messages to resonate with your audience.

"We have really learned as much from our followers as we have shared," says Hubbell.

"It used to be that you would buy an ad, place an ad, and if people showed up, great. Now we get instant feedback. You can't get any better tool than that," she says. "You know what works. You can better reach your audience in a way that is meaningful to them. And that's the key to good marketing."

The Least You Need to Know

- Use hashtags to organize and categorize your Tweets, and make them easier for Twitter users to find.
- Using relevant hashtags puts your Tweets in front of an interested audience, which naturally leads to more Retweets and more engagement.
- The more targeted and accurate your hashtags, the more targeted followers you're likely to accumulate.
- Use hashtags to participate in conversations during conferences or Twitter chats.

Twitter Marketing Campaigns

Part

3

Without a marketing strategy, Twitter is just typing. A successful Twitter marketing campaign begins exactly the same as any marketing plan: defining your target audience and then setting specific objectives that can be measured.

If you ever took a "Marketing 101" class, you probably had someone drum into your head the acronym AIDA: Awareness, Interest, Desire, and Action. This rudimentary sales and marketing funnel is just as relevant to social media marketing efforts as it is to the business niche with which you're comfortable. We show you how to create a marketing plan and put it into practice, from setting business goals to implementing the project workflow. Without raising the ire of your corporate overlords.

If your customer gets great service, she may tell all her friends. If another customer has a lousy experience, he will Tweet about it, too. Consider the response of one Houston-area restaurant (@DownHouseHTX) when a customer wrote a negative Tweet as she was dining. In this case, reported the *Houston Press*, the customer was kicked out.

> *Matsu [the customer] has achieved mild, local notoriety for her late-night Tweets, even recently winning a Houston Press Web Award for that very activity. Down House, for its part, has achieved a reputation in the short time since its opening for having capricious service. The two collided in a Twitter-fueled episode that resulted in general manager Forrest DeSpain calling the bar, speaking directly with Matsu, and asking her to be ejected from his establishment.*
>
> *"She called him a twerp," DeSpain said by phone, referring to a bartender. DeSpain runs the Twitter account for Down House and was irritated that someone would bully his bartender, as he saw it, and took action despite not being at the restaurant that night. "I immediately called up here and talked to her in a polite manner and asked her if she had any kinder words." She didn't, DeSpain said, so he asked her to leave.*

Matsu responded with several negative Tweets, most of which would make any business owner cringe. It's one thing to deal with problem customers one on one—and even more of a problem when they have a large Twitter following.

It's All Local

Many other businesses want Twitter users to pick up the phone, to visit an e-commerce site, or just to have warm, fuzzy thoughts about the company (that is, branding). For retail businesses, the ultimate goal is to get people off their butts and physically make a trip into the store. That's different, but it's also a plus, because your followers can take direct action.

It's easy for businesses to adopt the mindset that Twitter is a global tool, not a local tool. However, several features are suited to doing business locally.

First, Twitter searches can be made based on area code or [illegible] data.

Designing a Successful Twitter Campaign

Chapter

10

In This Chapter

- Learning why you need to plan a social media campaign
- Mapping out your Twitter strategy
- Designing a workflow to ensure that stakeholders are engaged
- Identifying the steps to take before you start Tweeting

"If you build it, they will come" is a great movie quote, but a poor strategy for a business hoping to get attention from Twitter. With over 50 million Tweets sent per day, and an average of 460,000 new Twitter accounts set up daily, you have to work to get your company noticed.

But before you can implement any Twitter marketing effort, you need to know where you're headed, you need to decide who's responsible for each role required, and you need to establish the company ground rules.

Any marketing strategy that includes social media marketing needs a more specific goal than, "Let's use Twitter." Twitter is just another communication medium, like TV or radio or print ads. It has its unique challenges and advantages, and you're reading this book to learn what they are. But before we dive into them, recognize that your existing marketing skills and company goals should inform the decisions you make in implementing your Twitter strategy.

If you have a clear marketing plan in place, in which you've identified target customers and planned how to present your company to them, the Twitter plan is relatively easy: it's an extension of your brand's existing personality. If your brewery empire has been a success because you appeal (and market) to macho men between the ages of

25 and 35, your Twitter strategy most likely will target the same audience. It doesn't have to—some companies have used Twitter to break new ground—but most businesses do treat Twitter as an extension of existing marketing efforts.

Larger businesses have staff to debate the merits of market strategies, but if you're a small shop who (rightly) sees Twitter as an affordable way to reach prospective customers and create community loyalty, you may want to take a tiny step back to consider your overall marketing goals. Who do you want to reach? With what message? For what actions? (You might spend some time with *The Complete Idiot's Guide to Marketing* by Sarah White if you need help with the marketing basics.)

Creating a Twitter Marketing Plan

"Because everyone else is doing it" is a terrible reason to create a social media campaign, including Twitter. You have to know why you're using social media to reach people—otherwise, don't bother.

Like any marketing campaign, you will have overall goals ("get more business") and specific marketing projects ("attract a new market of younger users"). One is overarching, while the other is a tactical plan. Without a strategic plan in place, however, any energy you put into marketing your business will be haphazard and disorganized.

Setting Goals

Here are just a few of the reasons you might turn to Twitter:

- Build better customer relationships
- Create a community for your fans
- Find out what your customers are saying about you
- Give your company a human voice
- Use external perceptions to help the business make internal decisions
- Establish yourself as an expert voice in your community
- Establish or underscore your brand
- Generate sales leads

There is no one right or wrong answer. Twitter can serve all these needs, and more—though rarely all of them at the same time.

Don't try to accomplish every goal with Twitter to begin with. Work on one project at a time—even if we give you more ideas than you can possibly tackle at once.

Even if your Twitter campaign goal is crystal clear, such as "I want to get more people to my restaurant," you also need to figure out how you will measure progress. What does success look like? How will you know if your efforts have been effective? How will you learn from mistakes?

The point is, you must have specific goals for your Twitter involvement. And you must stick to them.

Oh, sure. Stick to the goals. That's easy for us to say. We don't have to cope with your office politics. But if your office status meetings resemble a wrestling match, it's even more important to spend time to get everyone on the same page.

A Team Effort—Even If You Are In Charge

If you're in a business with more than a few people, defining your social media strategy should involve people from outside the marketing department.

Make sure everyone understands the goals. If the Sales VP imagines that the Twitter account exists to line up more prospective customers, while you're streamlining the process for branding or customer service, someone is going to be disappointed. And disappointment tends to make people cranky.

Worse, you'll be setting yourself up for internal politics when the Sales VP declares the social media strategy to be a waste of time, because he didn't get what he wanted (but may never have expressed aloud).

TWITTER TIP

Ideally, get the boss to make an edict about using Twitter. Social media is not a light, frivolous thing for a business to do, any more than is any other marketing strategy. Although it can be a bit more fun than most.

As with other changes in company directions, the effort is far more successful when the direction comes from the top. If the CEO has set social media as a key marketing strategy, you will encounter less resistance, especially from people whose jobs are unrelated to marketing.

Budgeting Time for Twitter

Some of the things you might want to do with Twitter may require that you work with other departments. If you plan to Tweet blog posts from the company founder, the founder has to actually write those blog posts, and the website content editor has to ensure those posts are online. If you plan a contest for Twitter followers to submit photos (and perhaps win a trip to company headquarters as a grand prize), someone outside Marketing probably has to cope with a lot of logistics.

Social media takes time—more time than you and your boss might budget for—and that's time not spent on other marketing efforts. That's especially true when you're just starting out. Things that will come naturally to you in just a few weeks take careful, deliberate thought today. You probably don't mind personally, because Twitter is more fun than, say, editing yet another press release, but the people in other departments may see it as a distraction from their real jobs. Unless, that is, the directive comes from the executive office.

So before you go any further, make a list of your goals for using Twitter. Get input from other stakeholders in the company. Find out what their expectations are.

TWITTER TIP

Ordinarily you might not ask people from outside Marketing and PR for ideas about how the company can use a communication medium. Twitter is a happy exception. Many of your colleagues are using social media themselves, even if it's just as an individual Tweeting about personal hobbies. You're likely to get more suggestions than you can handle.

Then prioritize the list. You may be able to accomplish more than one goal, but you probably can't tackle more than a few of them at once. Make sure everyone is on board.

Creating a Campaign Checklist

Armed with a clear marketing goal, you may be anxious to get started. You want to attract followers, to start Tweeting, to include your social media activity on your website and elsewhere …

But wait. There's more work to be done first.

A successful social media strategy isn't simply about the message the company puts out. Your Tweets have to come from somewhere. Plus, because Twitter is about conversation, you're bound to learn new things about customers, the community, the marketplace. (If you don't learn something, you're probably using Twitter incorrectly.) Someone must be responsible for disseminating the new knowledge within the company and ensuring that, when appropriate, the right person responds in a timely manner.

Approach the project in stages:

- Listen
- Organize
- Document
- Measure

In this chapter, we discuss creating a listening program, engaging stakeholders, and establishing a social media workflow.

These stages apply to both your overall marketing efforts on Twitter ("get new customers!") and specific projects you might focus on along the way ("get more business from vegans because we have such wonderful tofu pizza toppings"). It's an iterative process.

The Information Gathering Phase

You wouldn't show up at a business meeting where you don't know anyone and just start talking, would you? You might introduce yourself, then quietly listen to other people to learn the organization's culture, discover who the leaders are, and figure out what you might contribute.

Twitter is a community, and it follows the same rules as do other human communities. So before you start blithely Tweeting whatever comes to mind, spend some time getting comfortable with it—before what you do "matters." Join Twitter with a personal ID, perhaps one you plan to throw away later. Use it to get comfortable with Twitter as an individual. It will take you that long to get used to writing messages that are only 140 characters long.

Don't Tweet about what you had for lunch. Don't follow your friends with this ID. (Well, okay, do, because you care what they're up to, but that's not your primary goal here.) Instead, use this opportunity to learn what you can about what your competition is doing with Twitter, which of your suppliers and customers are using it, and what they're doing right and wrong. Identify the people who may be influencers. In short, snoop.

Follow competitors, customers, influencers. Follow the hashtags that you believe may be relevant to your business area to see if they bring up the sort of info you expect. Search for the questions your prospective customers are asking. Watch how companies lauded for their "best practices" manage Twitter, especially if they're using it in the same role you intend to (such as customer service).

TWITTER TIP

As part of your "listening" phase, you can indulge yourself a little bit in your personal hobbies, such as people—and especially brands—in the beer-brewing or racecar communities. You can learn, too, from what other types of businesses do. Thus you can tell yourself you're working while you're reading about the latest developments in hop growing. Now *that's* a fun day at the office.

This is also a good time to "play with" the tools you might use during the Twitter marketing campaign. You can use different Twitter clients to see which might serve your needs, or set up a trial for a Twitter metrics application to watch competitors' Twitter streams. Learn what each of the tools can do while you get familiar with the ways companies communicate online.

After a week or two of acclimating yourself, and reading the case studies and other suggestions in this book, sit down and brainstorm. What could you do with Twitter? Make a list. Expect to start simple and add more projects gradually. But this is a good time to imagine what you might be able to do … eventually. Prioritize and ask what is feasible now and what should wait until later?

The Organization Phase

Once you gain a measure of confidence, define your specific objectives, define your initial tactics, and tie those objectives to metrics.

That is, if you aim to use Twitter to draw more customers to your online musical instrument store, you might decide you'll use coupons and will also highlight company blog posts about the history of stringed instruments. Coupons can be measured by telling Twitter users to use a "secret code," but how will you identify sales leads that come through Twitter?

Using Personas to Identify Target Audiences

One way to get organized is to define "personas" for the type of person you intend to reach, based on what you already know about your customer base as well as the information collected from social media listening and direct engagement.

You often have more than one persona. For example, a bed and breakfast might have a "persona" for a leisure traveler and a business traveler, each of whom has different criteria for choosing a place to stay. The same B&B might also develop a persona for other influencers, such as the chamber of commerce or other organizations that might direct people to the business.

In contrast, a manufacturing company that aims to use Twitter to beef up its customer support reputation might develop personas for the different kinds of users and their needs. A historical mystery book author should think about the different people she wants to attract: readers, certainly (in which case she might begin to consider whether posting articles about the historical time frame of her novels might attract a new audience), but also bookstores, reviewers, and publishers.

Create a chart for each persona. What information does that person need? How is he comfortable communicating? What is his background? Who influences her? What sort of media does she prefer? What drives him: price, convenience, features?

Don't stop there. Does he create, share, curate, or lurk? Does she behave differently on different social channels?

Prioritizing Who to Target First

Often you find you have more personae than you can handle, as each persona needs something different. If that's the case, identify which audiences matter the most to your marketing plan right now. You don't have to do this all at once. Start small, and grow gradually.

You don't want to start with your most important target audience immediately. You're bound to stumble in your first Twitter campaign—yes, even with our help—or at least you are bound to lack confidence. Pick a smaller target that's nonetheless relevant to your overall goals, and begin with that.

By the end of this stage, you should be able to identify your goals, in stages.

Documenting the Campaign

Once you've chosen your destination, it's much easier to manage the logistics of your Twitter marketing plan, and to communicate them to other people in the company.

This is the point at which you really need buy-in from stakeholders. You got their input and agreement on the company's goals for using Twitter. Now you need their participation when it comes to meeting those goals.

Setting Expectations

Be careful to set expectations realistically. In our experience, company executives (particularly those who aren't tech savvy or who have no personal experience with online communities) imagine that Twitter will be an overnight success, and that your company will gain 2,000 followers in a week.

They may pressure you to "deliver" in an unreasonable amount of time; if you fail to do so, they'll jettison the plan. If you don't make it clear that this is a marketing program and not a get-rich-quick scheme, you will be tempted to take dangerous shortcuts that easily can backfire on the company's reputation.

As part of this process, ensure that you budget time and resources for Twitter—for yourself and for anyone who is tagged to participate. The scope of your project may require cash outlay for an enterprise tool, such as one to monitor social media traffic. You don't want the CFO to be surprised when you show up with the purchase-order form.

In the simplest form, your time-and-resources plan may be, "I will spend an hour a day on Twitter marketing."

Don't underestimate scheduling issues. You don't want the Marketing Director to assume that managing the Twitter account can be added to your responsibilities without affecting your other tasks. If the CEO says, "Sure, I'd love to Tweet!" then make sure she schedules time to really do so.

Taking the Stakeholders to Lunch

The time requirements are more than your own. If your project requires integration with other departments (such as adding Twitter features to the company website), the website developers need to put that project on their own schedule. If you expect other employees to Tweet, budget training time for the staff to learn Twitter basics and any tools on which the company standardizes.

When you meet with other stakeholders, you'll learn which of your brainstorm ideas are doable. They may help you identify amplification opportunities, for example, or tell you about an entire cache of "How to use our product to do groovy things" documents that would be perfect for one of your target audiences.

Lawyers Get Scared

In larger companies, you also need to meet with the Legal department to learn about constraints due to industry regulations or other criteria. These may not be reasonable, but you probably have to live with them.

For example, at one multinational business, the Legal department decided it couldn't display a Twitter stream on any of the company's web pages, even if it was simply a stream of any mention of its products (e.g., "I sure love my BigCompany Gizmo!"). The Legal department feared that the company would be sued by a Twitter user who was offended that the Tweet sounded like he endorsed the product. "But if you get the Twitter person's explicit permission," Legal said cheerfully, "that would be okay!" Uh, no. Not likely. But it was important to know about that (foolish) limitation before the IT department began designing the website Twitter integration.

MARKETING WIN

Never ask your Legal department, "Can I do this?" The answer will always be no. They are professional worry-warts; lawyers are paid to think about every possible risk to the company. Instead, tell Legal, "This is what I'm doing. Protect me." You won't always get your way, but it helps.

This is the time, too, to ensure that your company has its own Twitter rules of engagement. Everyone who Tweets on behalf of the company needs to adhere to the corporate guidelines. Of course, that means you have to first create those social media policies.

Designing Social Media Workflow

It's rare for only one person in a company to manage Twitter and other social media efforts. Even in a small business, you need to ensure that other people take action, whether it's to respond to a customer issue or to integrate market intelligence with product design. In other words, think about workflow and your business's communication process.

Ensure that those who create the content you will Tweet have that information ready. If your plan assumes that you'll Tweet company blog posts, someone has to write those posts. Someone—likely you—must ensure the content is timely, relevant, unique, and valuable. Once the content is published, it has to be properly optimized, syndicated, and promoted to your target audiences. That's a lot of to-do items for a single individual, or at least for a mere mortal who imagines she'll get something else done that day.

TWITTER TIP

Go back to your list of target personae and what sort of information they want to discover, such as "interesting places to visit" or "how to improve my swimming skills." Who in your company can supply that information? What does that person need to create it or ensure that you have it to disseminate? How long will it take? Answering that question will determine your workflow.

The workflow consideration can be a significant one, especially in larger firms. For instance, one of your Twitter campaign goals may be to establish the company as a business with impeccable customer support. If by using Twitter you discover a disgruntled user (Hurrah! The plan is working!), you need to connect her with the customer service department to get to the bottom of the problem. You need to ensure the user's complaint is resolved, because the only thing worse than a broken gizmo is a tech support department that leaves you hanging.

And once it is resolved (say, by sending the customer a new unit), you need to take advantage of the marketing activity because, well, that's part of the goal. The person running the Twitter feed needs to communicate with the formerly disgruntled user to ever-so-gently encourage her to crow about your laudatory customer service so you can then Retweet this to all your other followers. It's great that you've made the single user happy, but it's far better if the world knows you have happy customers.

Sounds simple enough. However, think of how many departments have to work together to ensure that single customer turns into a testimonial. Now multiply it by hundreds.

To achieve that, you need a system by which the customer service department lets you know that the particular miracle has been solved. Under ordinary circumstances, after all, you have no reason to know about a specific trouble ticket's status.

If everything happens just the way we described it above, you're on a path to success. But if the customer support staff have no idea you're even on Twitter, and they don't recognize this customer's problem as a PR opportunity (as opposed to a run-of-the-mill support query), they may drag their feet. Since you're sending in the support request in a nonusual manner (such as an email message to the department VP rather than the user's problem report entered via the company website), the usual bug-reporting workflow might fall apart. And then you'll be in a worse place then when you started.

In a small company, this usually isn't a big problem. Interoffice communication can be accomplished by standing on your desk and shouting really loud. (Not that you would do this, I suspect. It might squash your sandwich. But you could.) Even so, part of the reason you need the rest of the staff to be on board with the Twitter plan is so they understand that while they may have work to do, many Twitter users are even more impatient than you are.

Your metrics and listening efforts should uncover customer service issues, sales opportunities, recruiting, and media opportunities. With a clear workflow in place, appropriate departments will be aware how they are involved and can take action.

Identifying the Front-Line Communicators

We devote an entire chapter to social media roles, and who ought to be in charge. For now, note that there are several roles and ensure that someone is signed up to do the following:

- Manage the Twitter stream (post Tweets)
- Gather information (data mining)
- Identify opportunities (who should we follow?)
- Track performance (monitoring and metrics)

If you're a solo shop or a small business, it's likely that you personally are responsible for each of these roles. In larger businesses, the complexity is magnified.

Engage!

Finally, you're ready to begin communicating and engaging with your customers! If you did the legwork outlined previously, this part of the process will be blissfully easy.

Choose Your Basic Tools

With other business software, selecting application software is a big deal. Once you enter all your data into an accounting application, you're fairly well tied to it. And adopting a customer-relationship management application is a serious commitment.

Happily, that isn't the case with Twitter, at least in your initial phases. You can do everything you need with the web-based Twitter client—though most people running a marketing campaign quickly outgrow it. Almost every Twitter client has a free version, with additional features available once you pay for a premium version. By the time you need more, you'll know why you need it.

Even better, if you don't like one Twitter client, you can easily shift to another one. In most cases, you'll still have access to all the data tracking you put in place.

If you auditioned Twitter tools back in the first information-gathering phase, you probably have a good sense of the tools you like, by now. If not, look through the chapter describing what you get from each tool, pick one, and dive right in.

Establishing the Company Twitter Accounts

The goals you defined should have helped you determine who will be the "face of the company," a corporate account, a company executive, a support department, and an expert voice who represents the firm's innovation.

Whether that is one account or more, it's time to set it up, including defining the biography text, choosing a Twitter background, and picking a Twitter ID.

Fire up the keyboard and start typing!

TWITTER TIP

After all this, are you unsure of what to actually say? Refer to Chapter 6, where we give you plenty of guidance.

Measuring the Results

If you have been in business for more than 10 minutes, you already know that you can't judge the success of a marketing program without some way to recognize what success looks like.

We go into detail later about how to monitor and measure your Twitter marketing campaign. At this point in the process, the important checklist item is to align the metrics with the campaign goals. For every goal you set in the first place, ask yourself, "How will I know if we're achieving that? How can I know if I'm getting better or worse at it?"

To begin with, measurement doesn't need to be elaborate. You can manage Twitter success with four basic numbers:

- How many Tweets did we do?
- How many followers do we have?
- How many people Retweeted us?
- What is the total audience reached by all of our Retweets?

Each of those is more important than the last. Eventually, you can get more sophisticated. But if people who have a lot of followers are Retweeting your company, it's a good sign that you're saying interesting stuff.

MARKETING WIN

Remember the support of the executive office? Make sure you pay them back by keeping them in the loop. Figure out what motivates the folks upstairs and give them reports that answer those needs. Use reporting to close the feedback loop with community managers and customer-facing staff so they see the social media effect of their efforts.

Don't collect metrics only to create pretty charts to show off to the CEO when you talk about the Twitter campaign. These measurements should help you know whether you're achieving your goals, identify when it's time to take it to the next phase, and enable you to integrate what you learn to improve the business.

The Least You Need to Know

- Identify your marketing goals with the input of company stakeholders.
- Establish an ongoing listening program.
- Put a social media workflow in place to ensure that you can meet your objectives.

Chapter 11

Logistics of Your Twitter Campaign

In This Chapter

- Considering your staffing needs
- Ensuring steady Tweets with an editorial calendar
- Determining how frequently to post

By now, you've established the ground rules for your Twitter marketing campaign. You know where you're headed and you have identified the steps to reach that goal.

But there's a big step between "Let's do this!" and a carefully mapped-out set of to-do items. In this chapter, we help you grasp the logistics necessary to bring your marketing plan to fruition. Here's what needs to happen behind the scenes and how to establish your day-to-day approach.

Defining the Campaign Scope

Every campaign and brand is different. The loftier the goal, the more complex and labor-intensive your campaign. No window of time guarantees success.

Some campaigns might revolve around a specific event, which are confined to a smaller period of time and require fewer resources. For example, consider a live event such as a conference, where the goal is to get attendees to share on-site experiences. In this case, signs prompting individuals to Tweet with a specific hashtag or to follow the event's Twitter handle would be a likely campaign component.

Other campaigns might not be as straightforward. In a political campaign, the media and public constantly scrutinize the candidate's Twitter stream. Every Tweet has to be carefully crafted and must support the candidate's platform. The duration could last months, with many components to deploy and track: Twitter Q&A chats, sponsored Tweets, one-on-one engagement, and monitoring opponents' accounts, just to name a few.

Regardless of the scope of your campaign, you need all the resources in place to ensure success. Primary among them, of course, is the team that brings the plan to fruition.

Budgeting Time for Engagement

One of the biggest mistakes businesses make is underestimating how labor-intensive Twitter can be. Properly monitoring your brand and responding regularly and frequently requires someone's time and attention—plenty of it. Between posting Tweets, ensuring that there is something to Tweet about, responding to followers, and monitoring brand Mentions, half the day disappears.

And that doesn't count the amount of time you spend really engaging with people on Twitter and reading what they Tweet, responding to their comments, and finding out what they view as important. Somehow this always requires watching a cute kitty video (you have to; it's work-related!) or following a half-dozen links to articles that are only vaguely relevant to the business. After all, if you expect people to be attracted to what you post on Twitter, don't you expect to be attracted to what they post, too?

Creating a Project Manager Role

The larger your brand and the more frequent the engagement, the more resources you need to invest. In significant Twitter marketing efforts, a dedicated staff member typically is assigned to Tweet on behalf of the brand. This person may be responsible for other social channels as well, such as Facebook marketing, but however wide the scope, the individual needs full ownership over the asset.

That social media role may be taken on by someone in the Public Relations or Marketing department, or in an agency that serves those functions for your business. For businesses that have the budget to support a full-time hire, the role of Social Media Manager or Community Manager is a common title. This is a relatively new profession in the marketing world, but it's an important one.

Many small businesses simply rely on their existing staff. This might require some training up front, and it's time that isn't spent on other critical business tasks, but don't be in a hurry to outsource this task. Nobody knows your business better than you, and nobody you pay cares as passionately about it.

TWITTER TIP

Don't make Twitter a chore. It's never a good situation when Twitter is additional work for a staff member who doesn't want the responsibility. Instead, ask your existing staff if anyone has an interest or proficiency in using Twitter. This requires less training, rewards staff initiative, and produces better results.

The other option is to outsource your Tweets through a third party, either an individual or a dedicated agency. If you choose this path, you still have to work with the outside resource to understand your business and marketing messages.

Establishing a Listening Program

A thoughtful and strategic listening program ensures that your brand is being mentioned in a positive context—and that you respond appropriately when it's not. By listening (on Twitter and, hey, in the real world, too), you ought to be able to gain insight and knowledge from the general public, fans, and foes. Listening programs are also useful in preventing (or coping with) crisis communication scenarios. And of course, it's a way to get a pulse on competitors' brand perceptions. (Hopefully, just so you can say to yourself, "Nyah, nyah! We're cooler than they are!")

Use Twitter's search features to your advantage. Regularly monitor relevant keywords, such as industry topics, individuals, competitors, and brand Mentions.

Brand Mentions include the names of your products, services, and key public individuals (such as your company executives). **@Apple** might regularly identify all Twitter Mentions of Apple, Mac, iPod, iPad, and MacBook. SmartBear Software (**@smartbear**) might look for anyone mentioning the company name or its products, such as "AQtime" or "TestComplete." Include common misspellings.

A variation on brand Mentions are customer-centric references, which are brand Mentions that relate to people's needs or emotional responses. Domino's Pizza (**@dominos**) could (and probably does) pay attention to phrases like, "Craving Dominos," "Dominos in St. Louis," or "Where can I get Domino's?" As part of your listening program, these help you identify your biggest fans—and why they feel that way.

Your listening program should also support customer acquisition. What kinds of questions do prospective customers ask? What might they Tweet about, which your company has a solution for? **@smartbear** could search for "quality assurance," "programming tools," or relevant hashtags like #SQA (a common abbreviation for software quality assurance). The Clorox Company (**@Clorox**) would look for "cleaning," "whiten," or "bleach."

MARKETING WIN

Use your target audience's language instead of your own jargon. As with search-engine optimization for your company website, it doesn't matter what you consider an important or relevant term; it matters only how customers describe the concept—especially the marketing "pain."

For instance, marketers imagine that people want to hear about "best practices" and indeed they do. But the only people who Tweet the term "best practices" are in marketing and PR. Ordinary people write things like, "I wish I had learned …." This can help you Tweet a link to your blog post, "5 Things Master Woodworkers Wish They Knew When They Started" rather than "Best Practices in Woodworking." Same blog post, different keywords.

Domain registrar **@namecheap** regularly listens for Tweets mentioning words related to domains and hosting services. By recognizing the language that their prospective customers used, they can word their Tweets in a manner that most resonate with the intended audience. By understanding what topics mattered in domain registrar choice, **@namecheap** launched its Twitter account in January 2009 and ran weekly Twitter contests that gave away one-year domain registrations. The result was a 20 percent increase in sales.

You already pay attention to your competitors' successes and failures through other media. Twitter gives you an excellent way to keep tabs on them and to compare your and their marketing. Monitor their brand Mentions along with your own. Snoop on their Twitter feed to keep track of their coupons, engagement, and noteworthy news.

Automating the Listening Process

This doesn't need to be an arduous manual process. You can save searches that you perform frequently. Note the "Save search" at the top right of the following figure. Thereafter, clicking in the Search bar at the top of your Twitter page brings up the most recent Tweets with that keyword.

Saving a search.

A small business can afford to wade through the search results manually; there won't be that many relevant Mentions. Larger businesses might drown in a tide of product-name Tweets. If you have the budget, consider the purchase of tools that promise to track the sentiment of social media Mentions. For example, after a successful advertising campaign, you can watch the trend change from "that pizza is awful!" to "best pizza in town."

A slew of social media monitoring, publishing, and analytics platforms include custom searches as just one of their features. These dashboards can be instrumental in helping you listen on Twitter, and also help you manage your workflow within teams and other departments.

Getting Tactical About Workflow

Enough with the listening, already! When you are ready to begin engaging in online conversations, you need to establish a *workflow* to ensure everyone in your company gets the information he needs and schedules tasks. Especially you.

DEFINITION

Workflow describes the order of a set of tasks—performed by humans or software—to complete a given procedure within an organization.

This isn't only about Tweeting. When listening efforts uncover customer service issues, sales opportunities, recruiting, or media opportunities, someone has to liaise with appropriate departments.

Here are some of the to-do items to consider as you prepare for launch. (We offer guidance on many of these issues in other chapters.) You won't need to do every item on this checklist, but they help identify the tasks and resources required.

- ❒ Do you need to coordinate who responds to online conversations? How should you schedule company representatives' time or segregate topics?
- ❒ How will you ensure that team members don't duplicate responses?
- ❒ Where and how will you disclose who is participating on behalf of the brand?
- ❒ Who defines the company "voice"? What will you do to ensure consistency across conversations?
- ❒ What does the ordinary posting schedule look like? Does the team post weekends? Does the weekend workflow differ from weekdays?
- ❒ Are domain experts assigned to engage with specific individuals, such as media relations or more-than-trivial customer complaints? How are they brought in (and out) of the conversation? How will you triage conversations for different response types?
- ❒ What will you use to record conversations? What manual method or tools let you store and search past correspondence?
- ❒ How will you report on what you learn?
- ❒ What do managers need to see about metrics and your engagement, measured against your marketing objectives? How do you deliver that information? Who delivers it? How often? Who reviews it and makes recommendations?
- ❒ Can a set of standard Q&As frame your responses to common issues? Where does this information come from? Where is it stored? How is it updated, and by whom?
- ❒ What are your guidelines for responding to Tweets?
- ❒ What process will your team follow when they encounter an issue for which they don't currently have an answer?
- ❒ Does the team use individual accounts or one corporate account? Who takes care of registering them?

- ❒ Should your team use their own personal accounts?
- ❒ What is the company's social media policy? How do you get interested parties to sign off on it (literally and figuratively)?
- ❒ How will you approach the influencers in your market? Who'll do that?

Create an Editorial Calendar

No matter how you define your Twitter marketing campaign, you should have plenty of data to share with your followers. It might be company blog posts, or videos captured at conferences, or infographics put together by an outside agency. Whatever the nature of your content, messages have to be relevant and timely.

How can you ensure that you have something to post? The same way any magazine does. Schedule the content, from task assignment to production.

The best way to manage your Tweets is to keep a master editorial calendar that incorporates key dates, promotions, reminders, and other content you can plan ahead for. In devising the timeline, consider the following:

- If you are working with other agencies, have you worked their content into your content timelines?
- How often will you Tweet original content?
- How will you divide up content creation?
- Who will write it, tape it, edit it?

For example, Moda Fabrics (**@ModaFabrics**) entices quilters and other sewing enthusiasts to consider the many ways they can use the company's fabric designs. The manufacturer sells almost exclusively to fabric stores, but they know that retail store customers often come into the shop with a specific fabric in mind—and Moda certainly would like it to be theirs.

Thus Moda set up Moda Bake Shop (**@ModaBakeShop**), a website with online recipes that use their precut fabrics. A Twitter account lets followers know about new instructions posted, such as this:

> **@ModaBakeShop** Looking for a cool boy's quilt? Look no further than "Robot Love" **@ModaBakeShop** today! bit.ly/o3zL8w

Before that Tweet can be posted, though, someone has to orchestrate its creation: designing and creating the quilt, photographing it, writing the how-to instructions on the website, and giving the URL to the company's social media team. Each of those takes time. And if the company wants to keep a regular stream of those posts to keep customers engaged, they need to ensure that the designer, quilter, blog author, and website designer each deliver their pieces by a specific time. How long will it take each person to do her bit?

Consider repurposing or leveraging your existing content. If your team already puts out video content and digital articles, why not share links to those assets on Twitter? Don't create unnecessary work for yourself if you can avoid it.

Twitter Tag Team

Although your brand should have one unified voice on Twitter, your account can be managed by multiple individuals. This type of setup is ideal for popular brands with a high volume of Mentions because responsibilities can be shared across your team.

Some brands post links, comments, and questions under an anonymous brand voice, but "sign" all @replies. In other words, if you ask a question to the business Twitter account, you get a reply from an individual.

MARKETING WIN

Even when multiple people contribute to a company's Twitter feed, let the human side show. Bringing out individual personality adds a nice touch to your Tweets and reminds followers that real live people are standing by to help and inform. When it comes to customer loyalty or customer service, everyone loves that personal touch.

An easy example of a Twitter feed managed by several people is the domain registrar GoDaddy (**@GoDaddy**). Four individuals Tweet; they end each Tweet with an initial to signify who responded. The standard way to sign a Tweet is to use the ^ symbol followed by initials, or some variation thereof—as long as you're consistent.

> **@GoDaddy @PeterHing** I'd certainly like to try. Could you follow me and send a DM with the domain name on the hosting account? ^A
>
> **@GoDaddy @Mami2Mommy** Thanks for letting us know. I forwarded your Tweet to his sup. Stay Awesome! ^Jr

> **@GoDaddy @chrisrbanker** Christopher, better safe than sorry on the notices. You can stop them by canceling or renewing that domain. ^Jr

Apart from splitting the responsibilities, the benefits of setting up your team this way tie into accountability. If someone misinforms a customer, the source of information can always be attributed to the right individual.

Managing Multiple Accounts

For larger or more diverse businesses, it might make sense to manage multiple accounts on Twitter. Each business unit has its own goals and potentially has separate audiences. Separate Twitter accounts make it easier to service the needs of the department, manage staff, and drill into the interests of the customer or user of the single identity.

It might make sense to divide the accounts by product line or category. Instead—or in addition, for a very big business—you might set up separate Twitter accounts for customer support versus sales. If an enterprise organization maintains separate accounts, the purpose of the accounts can be conveyed clearly. It's easier for the general public (and especially the target customer) to know why a Twitter account exists and how it might be relevant. For the business, it's a strategic move that alleviates management and staffing headaches that could arise when one too many teams try to manage a single account.

For some businesses, managing multiple accounts can cause more harm than good. This is true especially in cases of a lack of Twitter proficiency across the organization—aw, heck, let's just say, "When people don't have a clue."

Even when there is a strong strategic lead or project manager—that would be you—multiple accounts can cause heartache. Marketing often leads the creation of Twitter accounts because the "how to communicate with the public" expertise is in the department (or at least they believe so). The Marketing team is equipped to staff the account and can think through the various campaign components outlined in this chapter.

For other teams in the organization, this might not come as naturally. If the rest of the business is not committed to the effort (such as a tech-support department that's ho-hum about responding to Twitter and puts answering phone calls higher in its priority), the effort may lend itself to failure. You've seen the evidence yourself: countless abandoned Twitter accounts and individuals Tweeting as employees without a clear strategy. Before encouraging multiple Twitter accounts, have a clear game plan in place for all employees or teams to follow. Also account for having the right tools in place to manage multiple accounts.

Transparency of Your Twitter Team

It's a best practice to disclose up front who is Tweeting on the account. Is it a PR and corporate communications team? Is it a team of community managers? Or maybe it's a combination of both and customer support? Whatever the mix, you can use your Twitter background and/or bio to let users know.

This ties back into issues of accountability. When you deliver information to users, it's helpful to trace it back to the individual source. You can also credit team members who go above and beyond to respond or provide help on Twitter.

Helping Followers Find the Right Account

If a lot of people at the company Tweet—or only a few—then a random Twitter follower has no idea how to find the "right" person. You probably have one overarching brand account, but if you also have one for customer support or a particular product line, how will random users learn who they are? That's as frustrating as calling a company help-line on the telephone and being bounced from one department to another.

Therefore, create a company page or other easy-to-Google resource where web searchers easily can discover your social media presence and the right department.

Both the Albuquerque City Government and the University of North Carolina Kenan-Flagler business school make it easy for users to find their digital footprint. Each has accounts representing various groups within the larger organization. Kenan-Flagler shows its various degree programs, departments, the dean, and the faculty.

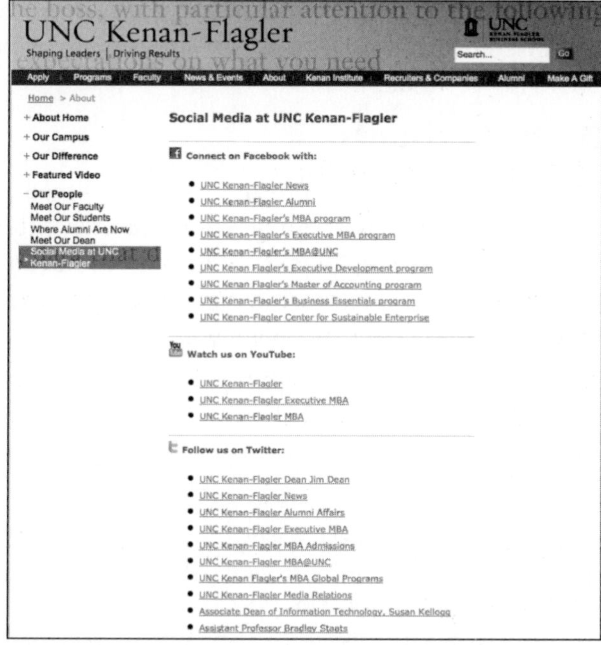

The University of North Carolina's social media contacts

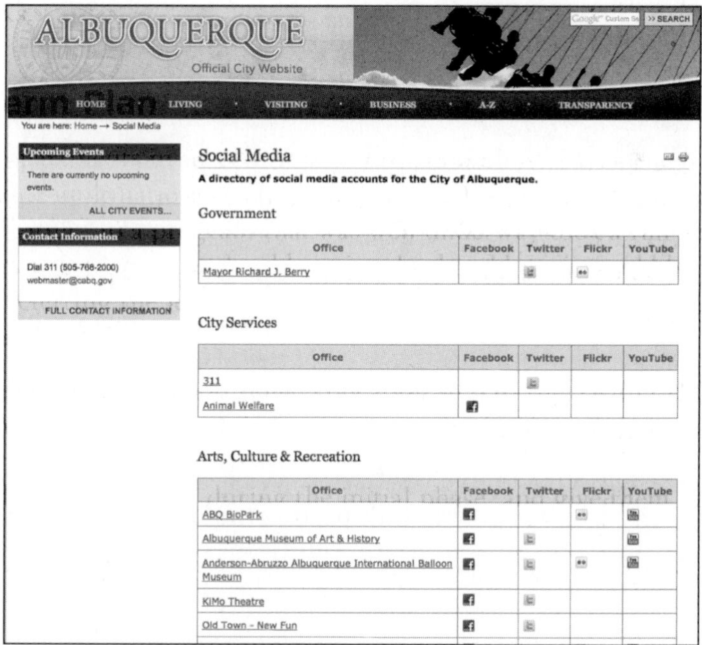

The Albuquerque City Government's social media page

The Albuquerque City Government helps its constituents find the right resource, whether that's the Museum of Art & History or Mayor Richard Berry.

Monitoring Multiple Accounts

We have stressed the importance of monitoring your social media campaign, simply because you can't judge success without some sort of metrics. Multiple accounts offer several advantages, but they also add greater complexity—not the least of which is requiring you to put more effort into monitoring the results. If three people contribute to a customer service account, someone has to judge who's getting the most success so others can learn from her techniques. If the company manages a dozen accounts based on product line or company representative, someone needs to minimize duplication and contradictions.

Monitoring tools enable businesses to manage multiple Twitter accounts from a single dashboard; they also include other features such as scheduling Tweets. For businesses that have more than one individual managing a Twitter account, picking the right tool helps teams coordinate their workflow.

In Chapter 13, we go into some detail about what to look for in monitoring Twitter accounts, and keeping track of who Tweeted what on behalf of the company. If you have a larger-than-one social media team, note that your choice of tools will be framed by these requirements.

When to Tweet

You want to engage your followers. You want to whisper in their ears at the time they are most open to hearing from you, when they are actively reading their Twitter stream—and ready to both take action ("I must follow that link!") and click on the **Retweet** button.

You don't want to inundate followers with information, yelling in their ear so often that they unfollow you. On the other hand, you don't want to be so invisible that they forget about you or, worse, imagine that your silence means you don't care—or perhaps are no longer in business.

In other words, how often should you Tweet? What's the best time of day, the best day of the week? Can you get away with posting the same content occasionally … or ever?

MARKETING WIN

Remember our analogy of Twitter as radio? Your radio station—your Twitter account—has to take into consideration when your target audience is "listening to the station." Traditional marketing mavens learned long ago that "drive time" is the best time to capture the attention of hungry people stuck in their cars during rush hour—and radio stations charged higher rates for that in-demand drive-time. Give some thought to the time of day or day of week when your audience is paying attention. A restaurant that Tweets a 10-percent-off coupon for lunch today at 11 A.M. might get the attention of office workers whose tummies are getting rumbly.

How Often to Tweet

Capturing your follower's attention has less to do with the frequency at which you post than with writing compelling content. Anyone who Tweets too frequently without something the reader wants to hear gets unfollowed very quickly; if a follower can rely on you to never waste her time, she will put up with a heavy stream of information—among which, of course, are your deliberate marketing messages.

Some businesses Tweet three times an hour. Others Tweet once a day. Don't look for a magic Tweet frequency. Instead, focus on consistency.

As a general rule, a business should Tweet at least twice a day. Even if you feel you have little that is unique to offer, a twice-daily rhythm lets you deliver information about yourself, your followers, and your shared interests.

Twice a day is a bare minimum; ten times a day is reasonable. Imagine if a newspaper or magazine only published an issue "whenever they felt like it." You want to demonstrate that your account is active, and that means showing you have a heartbeat.

MARKETING WIN

If anything, Tweet a little more often than you think is appropriate. Most businesses suffer from not Tweeting enough; we rarely see any Tweeting too much.

Tweet often enough that your name stays in front of your audience. Take into consideration that your followers probably follow hundreds, if not thousands, of others. Many of those people are Tweeting at the same time you are and distracting your followers from your Tweets. Don't get lost in the shuffle.

Don't take "two to ten times a day" as a rule. These numbers are just-getting-started guidelines. Your main concern should be providing valuable content. Think about why a user should follow you in the first place. Are you interesting, funny, helpful, or conversational?

What you are Tweeting is far more important than how often you are Tweeting it. Besides, if you get engaged with people on Twitter, you will soon stop paying attention to your frequency and instead pay more attention to your message. Which is as it should be.

Using Tools to Schedule Posts

Timing can be everything on Twitter. You want to maintain a visible presence without inundating your followers with a barrage of Tweets. Just because you schedule your personal "Twitter time" for 8 A.M. to 9 A.M. doesn't mean that your followers want to receive 20 Tweets from you in that hour. If indeed they are actually listening; perhaps it's breakfast time for them, in their time zone.

To avoid Twitter saturation, schedule your Tweets strategically. Twitter clients such as CoTweet and HootSuite help you choose when the Tweets appear. In Chapter 14, we cover specific tools.

Pick and choose times of day when you can engage at a high volume. This might be during a Twitter chat or perhaps within a specific block of time every day. You can't be online all the time, but to some degree you can appear to be.

Using tools to automate their posting, space out your Tweets. Rather than seeing your Tweets in batches, you maintain visibility in followers' Timelines throughout the course of the day. For international brands, it means a constant Twitter presence across time zones.

TWITTER TIP

For some businesses, time of day is important. Make it clear to your followers what they can expect from you and when they can expect it. If your account is designed to promote daily deals, do it at a specific time of day and stick to that schedule.

Reposting Tweets

In general, you never want to copy and paste Tweets and publish them multiple times, because it looks lazy. People will think, "Don't you have anything else to say?"

However, it's completely acceptable to send similar messages spread out over time. For example, an online retailer making a big push for a "back to school" sale can Tweet countdowns to when the promotion launches.

This is modified somewhat if you post frequently and have developed a loyal following and a significant reach. You can repost items throughout the day, assuming that your audience checks into Twitter regularly, and account for users in various time zones.

Guy Kawasaki (**@kawasaki**) is a tech-industry celebrity (he was part of the original Apple Macintosh team) and a venture capitalist. Every day he posts three to four items per hour, around the clock, to nearly 400,000 followers. Most of these Tweets point to one of his own sites (such as Alltop, which he runs). Kawasaki Tweets every item three or four times, scheduling them at different times of day. His audience tunes in to Twitter at different times during the day; the follower who read a Tweet at 8 A.M. (her time) is unlikely to see the duplicate at 2 A.M. (her time).

With that many Tweets, repetition isn't an irritation. As with other marketing efforts, such as TV ads, it takes repeated messages to get noticed. Kawasaki found that four was the optimal number to convert people reading his posts into traffic back to his website.

Obviously you can't repost the same Tweet very often if you have a relatively moribund Twitter stream and relatively few followers (especially in a small geographical area). If you Tweet 10 times a day, a single repost is 20 percent of your message. Anyone scanning your stream to see if you're worth paying attention to is apt to be unimpressed. However, if you post a lot, it's easy for someone to miss your brilliant post or link, and thus it's okay to repost—sometimes.

There's a lot of content on Twitter and your original Tweets might be missed. It doesn't hurt to re-send later in the day so long as you modify the text a bit.

Timing Your Posts for Best Response

Social media analysts like Hubspot's Dan Zarella have attempted to develop a science of when best to Tweet. His analysis shows that Retweets are more common during the day, with a higher volume of Tweets as the week progresses and a peak on Friday afternoons.

If you use a service like Rowfeeder to analyze your Tweets, you might start to see patterns as to when your Twitter followers engage. Tools like Tweetstats.com analyze your Twitter activity and show you when you received the most Mentions and Retweets.

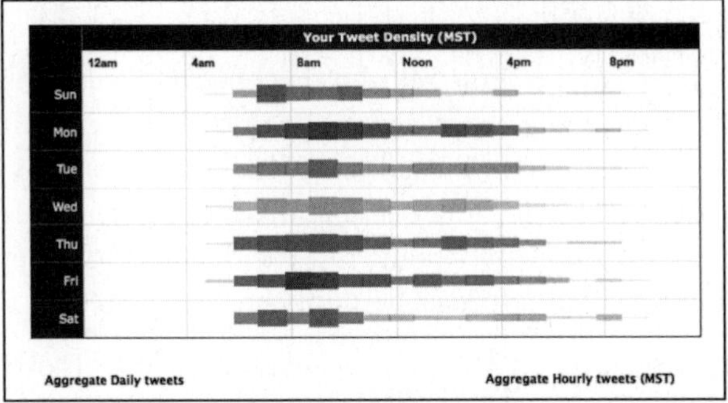

Tweetstats can graph when you post most of your Tweets.

That said, don't get too hung up on the time of day or day of the week. Providing relevant, timely content on a daily basis will produce the results you want to see.

The Least You Need to Know

- Consider project workflow and the time commitments required by everyone who contributes—directly or indirectly.
- Don't underestimate how labor-intensive Twitter can be; staff accordingly.
- Pay attention to the days and times when your Tweets get the most response.
- Maintain an editorial calendar of Tweets that ladder up to your larger marketing plan.

Chapter 12

Your Social Media Team and Policies

In This Chapter

- Deciding on the responsible party for your company's social media programs
- Creating a cross-department team to ensure that information is shared and communicated
- Identifying what should be in the company's social media guidelines
- Separating employee roles

Conducting a marketing program using Twitter implies that the Marketing department holds sole responsibility for the success of the social media program. Well, maybe.

If your business is very small, then one person may be in charge of social media marketing. The same person may be responsible for delivering technical expertise, invoicing clients, and taking out the trash, too. Larger businesses, at least those big enough where "department" means more than "at Molly's desk," usually subdivide roles and responsibilities with a lot more granularity.

And as you'll learn in this chapter, with a lot more friction, too.

Who Owns the Twitter Campaign?

In the best of organizations, different departments genuinely collaborate on the company's goals, strategies, and tactics vis-à-vis Twitter marketing (and probably on lots of other things as well, such as the best place for the company picnic).

Even when that's the case, however, one person sits at the head of the table. There is one person all heads turn to when the group cannot easily reach consensus. Whether it's the CEO who says, "I've decided; let's do xyz" or the project manager for the new product line, someone has to be in charge. While who that someone is might seem "obvious" to you, let us stress, this can be a big political battle.

FAIL WHALE

Ownership of the social media marketing plan may be a political bone fought over by every big dog in your organization. It's a fun, high-profile position, making it appear to be a way to get executive attention. And because it's a new area with no established rules for "this is the way everyone does it," everybody's opinions are valid for who should be in charge.

You've already seen how many ways Twitter can be used for business communication: for sales, for branding, for customer support, etc. It's a megaphone, and you can use it to broadcast just about anything you want to say.

If you're in Marketing, you probably believe that the Marketing department obviously should "own" the Twitter channel. Someone in public relations will feel just as passionately that the ultimate responsibility belongs to PR. Community managers may argue that it ought to belong to them. And now there is a whole new business specialty: social media managers.

There is no one answer for every company. The "right department" to be in charge depends on the nature of your business, its short- and long-term goals for social media marketing, and, realistically, who wants to be in charge.

Table 12.1 helps you sort out the trade-offs.

Table 12.1 Ownership of the Twitter Marketing Campaign

Department	Advantages	Disadvantages
Marketing	Understands the steps that move customer from "prospect" to "a closed sale"	Thinks primarily in terms of sales, which may be too heavy-handed for a conversational medium
Public Relations	Understands the notion of branding and creating relationships	Are trained to "control the message," thus may have a hard time adjusting to Twitter's interactivity and transparency
Community Manager	Understands how to engage with users, whether cautious tire-kickers or disgruntled customers	May be so in tune with the community that the marketing issues are back-burnered
Social Media Manager	Knows the Twitter tools and techniques	May not know the company products and services

Who Gets the Megaphone?

Marketing people see Twitter as a driver for sales, usually in a very direct manner. Their goal is, "Get people into the store buying stuff." They are especially good at thinking up promotions, whether that's online contests or integrating a Twitter account with the company's website. They are good at ensuring that there are breadcrumbs along the path for a casual Twitter follower to be carefully led to an e-commerce "buy now" form.

That's not a bad thing, but marketing is apt to see Twitter in regard to sales leads rather than branding or "conversational marketing." An emphasis on closing sales can turn your Twitter stream into exhortations to "Buy now, buy now!" rather than real engagement with live humans.

FAIL WHALE

In our experience, social media campaigns driven by a not-with-it marketing person are the most likely to fail. Marketing people, especially those driven by quarterly sales quotas, often demand immediate results. And "results" mean a sales chart that looks like a hockey stick.

PR people see Twitter as their province because so much of what you do online is for the purposes of branding and other issues of company reputation. They are right. Twitter is about how the company presents itself in public in the most direct way.

But traditional PR professionals think in terms of controlling communication. They want to "sell the company message," which is more about talking than it is about listening.

In most companies, the political struggle for "Who owns Twitter" is between Marketing and PR. We have seen some mighty corporate wrestling matches that make the Battle for Helm's Deep in *Lord of the Rings* look like a tea party, with scones and clotted cream.

But you may have another person on staff who is uniquely qualified for dialogue, for instance a community manager. That person may work in technical support, developer relations (which is often under the Marketing department), or another area where a soothing and understanding online bedside manner is a job prerequisite.

The Community Manager (who usually has far less of a voice in these decisions) sees Twitter as connecting with people—definitely her area. But converting Twitter followers from conversations to taking action? Maybe not so much.

MARKETING WIN

One community manager, Ross Turk, explained why he's in charge of his non-profit's Twitter account:

"Social media really isn't a marketing concern alone. It also involves customer support (helping people); sales (qualifying leads); investor, public, and analyst relations; research and development (gathering new product ideas); and legal. It's a company-wide thing, just like community management. That's one reason why it fits."

"It also fits because the goal of any company's social media strategist should be to encourage others to participate, aligning everyone's message just enough but not too much. So in many ways, it's just like managing an internal corporate community."

New Kid on the Block: The Social Media Manager

As you've already learned, there are a lot of steps in the day-to-day execution of a Twitter campaign, and they are time-consuming. Doing them well requires some expertise.

A social media manager aims to combine all the roles above—marketing, PR, community management—or at least to act on behalf of all of them. Social media managers are hired to build the brand's social properties, moderate them, look for new opportunities, etc. He's there to promote and interact. Some companies hire an outside agency to manage social media for similar reasons, to let an expert do it.

However, unless the social media manager is really savvy about the business, that can translate into "dilute what all the stakeholders want." A social media manager may know more about Twitter than about what the company sells.

That's especially a problem because this very important role—the public face of the company—is often given to an entry-level staffer. In businesses that are not wholly committed to social media, we've seen job descriptions for "social media manager" where the position description is basically that of an intern.

FAIL WHALE

No one feels more strongly about this point than Peter Shankman, a well-regarded PR pro who created HelpAReporterOut.com, a very cool site that connects subject-matter experts with journalists. In early 2011, Shankman wrote that social media "experts" might know the tools but they don't know what should be said, or why, or to whom. And especially, they can't write with any brevity (like, say, 140 characters to get a message across). "You know what the majority of people calling themselves social media experts can't do, among other things? THEY CAN'T WRITE. The number of 'experts' out there who can't string a simple sentence together astounds me."

What's Best for You?

So who should you pick to lead the campaign?

Realistically, the answer may be you. You're reading this book. That means you're the most personally engaged with the effort. You care. You think it's fun to chat with customers, or you are motivated to figure out why your existing social media efforts fell flat, or someone forced you to read the book because you lost a bar bet.

As with so many other jobs, the person who is best for it is the person who is already doing that job, especially if she is doing it on her own as a volunteer.

The choice of the "best person" should be aligned with the company's social media goals. If you want to use Twitter primarily for branding, for instance, then the PR people are the pros. If it's largely a customer support role, see if you already have a community manager in-house.

Despite all that, in most companies the Marketing or PR department directs Tweeting and other online posting activities. What's most important is that the individual in charge is well versed in the company (read: understands the company like the back of his hand) and has the proper internal connections to get answers to questions and resolve issues in a timely manner.

The Social Media Task Force

No matter who is "in charge," this is a group effort. Your Marketing department may manage all the social media accounts, with different leads responsible for each. However, all departments will convene regularly to brainstorm and to maximize efficiencies across the platforms.

If you're Tweeting for the brand (especially if the Twitter account itself is your company's name), it's going to be cross-functional, regardless. One reason that Marketing so often runs the show is because they are in a good place organizationally to handle this. Marketing already interfaces with Technology, Product, PR, Sales, and Support. But Twitter marketing always bridges departments and functions.

To figure out who ought to be at the table, consider the different tasks that are involved and who might be the best resource.

Employee Roles

We all wear many hats. Even in a sole proprietorship, a business owner knows that she is sometimes the company treasurer, sometimes the marketing department, sometimes the subject-matter expert who sells her advice.

It's no less so in a larger business. Even when you are given a narrow responsibility, you have several roles.

So while we list many Twitter roles, many of them can be done by a single person. All of them can be done by a single person, in fact, which is why Twitter has been so successful for small businesses.

The Person Who Tweets, But Tweets What?

Before you can Tweet, you have to have something to say. For some of us, it's no trouble to generate witty banter. We make pithy observations about the state of the universe, whether it's related to our brand, a relevant news item, a business partner's activities, or how the day is going.

Yet this is what stops so many people from using Twitter, or what keeps them from using it well. They have no idea what to talk about. And they imagine it all needs to fit in 140 characters, without taking into account that with links and photos, your business can connect followers to information with a lot of depth.

Content generation. The first role, then, is ensuring that someone in the company is generating something to Tweet. That doesn't mean just fun cat photos to share (though neither of us will ever object to that). You have plenty of knowledge inside the company or you wouldn't be in business. Someone needs to be responsible for soliciting input, finding out that HR has a job requisition to share, setting up data feeds from other departments, or encouraging employees to blog. All of those are items to be Tweeted.

MARKETING WIN

Allocate resources for content creation guided by a social editorial schedule. Whether you direct Twitter followers to employee blogs or how-to videos, ensure that there is a regular and steady supply of content.

Information dissemination. Because this is a book about marketing with Twitter, we sort of ignore your other social media efforts.

You shouldn't, though. Most companies engage with the world in multiple ways, so it's important to ensure that someone thinks about coordination between social channels. Working together, message distribution and reach can be amplified significantly. Consider how the Twitter team can integrate with the company's blogging efforts, crowdsourcing and voting, discussion boards, events, staffing, photo-sharing, podcasting, presentation-sharing, social media releases, fan pages, sponsorships, and virtual worlds.

For instance, enterprise consulting company Cap Gemini has technology experts in, as they cheerfully point out, 40 countries. Many of their employees give presentations at technology conferences. One of the best ways to improve the company's branding is to share that expertise with the thousands of people who follow them.

> **@Capgemini** Bright talk summit ea and innovation dlvr.it/gtSfz

In this case, Cap Gemini shared a PowerPoint presentation about enterprise architecture through SlideShare. We might argue with the wording here—it really doesn't tell you anything, does it? But the point is that someone at the consulting firm was aware that the presentation was made, that it was posted to SlideShare, and it was available to be Tweeted.

MARKETING WIN

The communication goes in both directions. If the Cap Gemini Twitter team discovered that this Tweet was Retweeted hundreds of times, that's information that should be communicated in the other direction: People like this. Do more of it.

Respond and engage. Listening to and learning from customers involves interaction. Whether you aim to uncover sales opportunities, offer superlative customer service, or just make the business seem all warm and fuzzy (encouraging your followers to think, "These are the folks I want to do business with"), the best Twitter success stories involved engagement.

This shouldn't be too difficult, because you care about what your organization does, and the people it affects. So respond!

> **@Rick_Bayless** a little tart, a little sweet, complex, slightly vegetal RT **@JenWorstell** What do ground cherries taste like?

Don't just answer questions. Ask for opinions!

> **@RailLife** U have an opinion on proposed bus route changes? Give 'em your .02. fb.me/IV65vnSl

> **@Chevrolet** You can fit up to 8 of your friends in your #Traverse. What's the best feature on your #Chevy?

Create a human face and personal touch. Whoever manages the Twitter stream mustn't forget that this is a communication medium, not simply broadcast (like radio or TV). The individual needs permission from the company to act like a human and express her own opinions.

@OdellBrewing Wish we were there! RT **@beerbloggers** There is a bit of CO representation! **@carnie_nbb** of **@newbelgium** **@HerzMuses** of **@craftbeerdotcom** @ #BBC11

TWITTER TIP

The "personal touch" is still done with a measure of enlightened self-interest. While we are sure the person Tweeting for the Odell Brewing company sincerely wished he or she could attend the BBC food-and-beer event (well, who wouldn't?), all the people and companies listed in that Tweet will see a Mention in their Timelines, and, at the very least, become aware of the Odell Twitter account. Since all those people and companies obviously share an interest in beer, they may well become new followers.

The Twitter Team Back-Office Staff

All those roles previously discussed are communicators—someone representing the company who actually says something.

The person who manages the Twitter account may get the glory, but in most businesses, plenty of other stakeholders contribute. These may include the people who write the blog posts you share, the in-house technical experts who give you answers to the Twitter community's questions, Human Resource's job listings, customer support's FAQs, and other documents. Your IT department will probably get involved as you brainstorm new ways to integrate your Twitter activity in the company's other online efforts. You may need to call upon the public relations and Legal departments to manage risk while adapting to an environment with less control. These people may not be involved on a day-to-day basis, but when you need them, they must be ready to help.

Here are some of the roles to consider, most of which are discussed in depth in other chapters:

- **Amplification**—Getting the Twitter account noticed
- **Monitoring results**—Gathering statistics and human analysis
- **Outreach**—Finding people on Twitter who need your help
- **Reporting**—Summarizing results to management or other stakeholders

- **Legal**—Getting in the way or, less cynically, ensuring that nothing is said that can cause the company harm
- **Oversight**—Making sure the account's Tweets stay in line with the corporate goals and this specific campaign's plan, and encouraging people to remember to laugh

Just How Big a Team Is This?

That's a lot of roles—maybe a scary number. Just how many people should be involved in this effort?

As with so many other business issues, it depends. Most businesses can afford to start small, even if the company is relatively large. You'll learn from experience when and where you need to add staff or other resources.

Larger businesses may need to staff up sooner. If you work at a company that's a "household name," especially one that generates strong customer opinions (positive and negative), you could be inundated by the response. And as a new Twitter presence, it's even more important to respond to all (or at least most) of them.

For instance, at AT&T (**@ATT**), two PR people began tracking customer complaints on their own. Despite their best efforts, two people couldn't direct all the issues they discovered to the right contacts, and it was really overwhelming.

That turned what was originally a PR function into a customer service role. As of 2010, the company had 13 customer service reps devoted to Twitter and was actively hiring more personnel. None of them are idle, either; **@ATT** has nearly 100,000 followers.

TWITTER TIP

When your company needs several people to work on a Twitter account or set of accounts, be sure to budget resources for staying in sync with one another and smoothing the workflow. Some of these are easily addressed—it's become commonplace to see an individual's initials at the end of a team member's Tweet ("Glad we could help! ^GM") to track contributions—but other solutions may take more effort.

Who Tweets?

Anybody can Tweet, of course. If you are a sole proprietorship or a very small company, there's no question about who will have fingers on the keyboard, because it's you.

But when Twitter is part of a company marketing strategy, the "who Tweets" becomes a business decision—even in the smallest of businesses.

Appropriate Roles for Standalone Accounts

Marketing or PR may be the people with their hands on the brand's account, but not always. Many companies, even small ones, have several accounts, many of which are operated independently.

Here's an overview of who might post:

- The "face of the company." The CEO or other key person associated with the business. For Dell computers, that's **@MichaelDell**. For Craigslist, it's **@craignewmark**.
- CEOs and other executives. Sometimes these are the same as the face of the company—sometimes not.
- Tech Support. Customer service departments often have their own accounts, such as Bank of America's **@BofA_Help** or Foursquare's **@4sqSupport**.
- Your experts. This might be the "talent" such as the techies who built the software you sell, the sport's team players who fans come to see, or a well-known musician.

Independent Voices

It's easy to forget about another category of people who may be Tweeting "for" the company: people who represent you, temporarily or otherwise, but are not part of the business. Your responsibility for these Twitter accounts is muddy at best.

For instance, if your business hires an outside consultant to redesign its website, it's feasible that the consultant could Tweet something about what she learned. In most cases, that will be benign or even positive ("Wow, **@YourCompany** has even more books to include in its e-commerce catalog than I realized!") or it may be clearly negative ("Annoying: Found all sorts of security vulnerabilities in **@YourCompany**'s existing website").

It's hard to give guidelines here because these independent voices are largely outside your control. Sometimes their influence is debatable.

For example, comedian Gilbert Gottfried was fired by his employer, insurance company Aflac, for whom he was a spokesperson. He made at least two jokes about the tragic earthquake in Japan. Aflac is the top foreign insurance company in Japan and gets 75 percent of its revenue from that market; naturally the insurance company was concerned about courtesy in public communication. But Gottfried wasn't Tweeting as an Aflac representative; those were his own words and he isn't the most self-effacing individual to begin with.

Social media policies may affect the legal agreements you draw up with contractors. You don't want an advertising agency to post a video of its ex-client being an idiot.

We can't tell you how to or when to "control" independent voices. All we can do is advise you to consider what your own policies are, and be sure to track their Tweets.

Defining Your Social Media Policies

With that many people on the playing field, the game needs rules everyone can adhere to. On the one hand, you want to encourage your experts to participate on Twitter because you want to show off your company's brain trust; on the other hand, you don't want them saying anything stupid.

The idea is to establish a governance model that doesn't stifle employee freedom. We hope that didn't make you snort in derision.

Why You Need a Formal Policy

Too many companies count on the good sense of employees to make sure that the company's important intellectual property doesn't wind up in the wrong hands. That was the result of a survey of 1,225 enterprises worldwide conducted by Applied Research on behalf of Symantec.

Wrote Michael Vizard at ITBusinessEdge, "As social media becomes more commonly used across the business world, it's only a matter of time before we see the number of fines and other penalties associated with social media breaches start to ratchet up. In fact, the survey finds that typical IT organizations have to deal with, on average, *nine social media-related breaches a year*." (Emphasis ours.)

FAIL WHALE

If you don't want your company to end up as an example in the next edition's "When Twitter Goes Wrong" chapter, you must ensure that employees understand and agree to the company rules.

Yet how can they agree to rules you never enumerated? A June 2010 report from Forrester Research, the "CIO's Guide to Creating a Social Media Policy," found that 43 percent of respondents' organizations had no social media policy; 11 percent were unsure if a policy existed.

The same people you most want to participate on Twitter—the business experts and opinion leaders—also pose a danger of over-sharing company activities. Slapping a phrase, "I work at Company Name, but my words are my own" on a Twitter bio does not necessarily prevent your representatives from sharing, especially out of pride. If an employee gets excited about something the company is working on, he wants to tell everyone.

"Maybe you work for a drug company that's on the verge of developing the cure for cancer. Maybe the company is developing a new car that runs on curbside trash—in other words, something everyone will want," Bill Brenner warned at CSO.com. "By sharing too much about your employer's intellectual property on social networks, you threaten to put it out of business by tipping off a competitor who could then find a way to duplicate the effort or find a way to spoil what they can't have by hiring a hacker to penetrate the network or by sneaking a spy into the building."

What to Include

The best social media policies are tailored to your organization's culture, workforce, and level of literacy with the Internet and social media.

Internal communications in small companies are relatively easy. Your social media policy might go something like this: "Don't do anything that causes awkward, tense meetings to happen the next morning, unless it's for the greater good."

It's natural to write the social media policy from the company's point of view, but if you want buy-in, make it a collaborative effort. None of your employees wants to screw up. They just want to know where the lines are before they inadvertently trip up. At IBM, the employees created the guidelines; managers merely provided input alongside.

MARKETING WIN

Guidelines for social media can be incorporated into existing media-related policies, in which you treat social media like any other form of media. Don't assume that you're done—those media policies are usually written for executives and PR, but it's a head start.

When a company dictates policy on social tools without social input by the employees, you risk the employees finding ways to skirt around the rules. Let them argue it out. Should "No swearing online" include the word "bloody"?

In practice, we've found that business's social media policies reflect a company's culture—for good or ill. If the business is clamped down in its internal communication, it might require every Tweet (every Tweet!) to be blessed by Legal and PR for approval. (Yes, this is a real example.) That this misses the point of Twitter is almost irrelevant; in the real world, you can't change company mindsets with a single document.

As you create your own, keep the following in mind:

- The policy should be positive. Rather than telling employees what they *can't* do, focus on what they *can* do. That makes them feel empowered rather than hindered or restricted by the rules.
- Keep people accountable. If you are willing to bend the rules, then those who are granted exceptions need to be responsible for their actions.
- Consider your policy a work in progress. As you learn more about social media, the policies should evolve. Set a time after putting the policy in place—maybe four to six months—when you evaluate what's working and what might need to be tweaked. Gather feedback from stakeholders and employees to implement changes.

MARKETING WIN

Sample guidelines can help you draw up your own policies. Search for "social media policy examples." Top on the list is Chris Boudreaux's website, with over 150 policies for perusal: http://socialmediagovernance.com/policies.php.

What Can Be Said

Most social media policies reflect management concerns about employees who might Tweet about their personal beliefs, such as politics, religion, or culture. Some of these expressions have the potential to negatively impact partners or customers in other regions or cultures. What's the definitive line between work and personal?

No, we don't always know, either. But the policy of right-and-wrong issues can be much less obvious than the usual "flame bait."

We all want to cheer the achievements of our co-workers, and for most employees there's no question that a "Yay! My buddy got a promotion!" is a more-than-acceptable Tweet. That is, unless the promotion is a matter of public record that ought to be under the control of the PR department.

For instance, a minor league player baseball player Tweeted, "Congratulations to **@otherteamguy** for being called up to the majors!" Nice sentiment. The "congrats" message was Retweeted everywhere, within hours. It's wonderful to say "Good news buddy!"—except the team hadn't announced the move yet. Oops.

This is as benign an example as we can imagine, at least for the baseball fan who's glad her favorite team got more firepower in its pitching staff. It's a problem, though, for the team's PR department, who are supposed to control when and how to announce the call-up. (What if the rumor the team player Tweeted was wrong?)

It's one thing to say, "Don't do this on Twitter," but what do you do when it does happen? The breach isn't always a firing offense, as with the baseball example. Yet the policies need to make the consequences clear.

The Least You Need to Know

- Marketing and PR are usually in charge of the Twitter marketing campaign, but they are not always the only appropriate choices.
- In most companies, the social media team orchestrates contributions from many other departments.
- Many companies have more than one corporate Twitter account and more than one "voice." Consider what works for your firm.
- Your social media policies have to spell out what can be Tweeted online and what happens when the rules are broken.

Monitoring and Analyzing Your Twitter Campaigns

Chapter 13

In This Chapter

- What data to collect and how to analyze it
- Metrics and their use in improving your marketing campaign
- Measuring social media influence considerations

You might have a great Twitter program in place. You have plenty of feedback, you're attracting new business, and people say nice things about you online. Groovy. But if you don't find a way to track and measure your success, you cannot take the marketing program to the next level.

Back in the planning stages, you set goals for your marketing program. Here we help you learn what's important to monitor and how to analyze the results, so you can make better business decisions.

Monitoring Your Brand

We like to think that you instinctively know why it's important to collect metrics on your social media marketing plan. Without some kind of measurement, how do you know if you're reaching your goals? How do you know if one plan is effective and another is not?

Unfortunately, in the hectic effort to share information on Twitter, sometimes it's easy for analysis to get shunted to the back burner. You know you should look at the data so that you can make better decisions and use your time better. But daily demands—not the least of which are publishing Tweets—put such analysis tasks on the "I'll get to it sometime soon" list along with "clean out the refrigerator" and "update my 401(k)."

It's necessary, though. And if you do it well, it can save you time and help you work smarter.

Identifying What's Important

Whether you spend a half-hour a week on it, or you dedicate staff to the task full time, there are three parts to the monitoring and analytics effort:

- Deciding what to track
- Analyzing the data you collect
- Turning that data into actions that improve your marketing prowess

In other words, you monitor Twitter to collect information, which you then measure and analyze into an "Oh hey, that helps!" moment. You'll encounter several terms for this process, such as *social media monitoring* and even buzz monitoring. It's the process of listening to, observing, and recording online conversations that are relevant to your business and its brand.

DEFINITION

Social media monitoring is the use of (usually automated) tools to process online discourse. It typically looks at thousands (or even millions) of conversations to track the effect of campaign activities.

Monitoring can be passive, such as listening to people to find out what interests them. Or it can be active, searching for specific references to the product, marketing campaign, and the brand.

Social media campaign measurement usually encompasses more than Twitter, though naturally that's where we put most of our attention. It's likely that your monitoring efforts also track the effects of campaign activities on other social networks, as well as blogs, video- and photo-sharing websites, and discussion forums. Your attention is usually on all user-generated content that touches your products or industry.

Collect Data That Helps You Make Decisions

In this chapter, we deliberately underplay the role of tools to collect Twitter metrics. The next chapter introduces you to software you can use to slice and dice the data (from free to oh-my-gosh price points), but we minimize attention on tools and focus instead on gathering data that helps you make decisions.

It's tempting to track dozens of metrics. Some of the tools make it easy to do so. However, you can drown yourself in information. Monitoring data is only valuable if the metrics relevant to your company are tracked, analyzed, and then applied to your strategy. If a data set doesn't help you improve your marketing program, then don't bother collecting that data.

Look first to the goals of your marketing program, and then figure out what information helps you learn if those goals are being met. Think back to the answer you gave early on, when you answered, "What does success look like? How will we know if we achieve it?" Consider the information you need to measure the achievement. Those metrics may vary based on your current stage in the marketing plan.

Make sure the goals are really appropriate for a campaign. For example, reaching the largest number of people may be less important than reaching specific people.

There are four types of social media monitoring:

- Brand monitoring focuses on tracking and analyzing the conversation about your brand, its products, and your competitors.
- Campaign measurement analyzes a specific social media campaign's performance for reach, participation, and engagement.
- Contests and promotions use hashtags or coded links to track entries in a Twitter contest.
- Market research metrics are used to analyze the conversation for specific topics or markets.

Many businesses initially look at the company and its products compared to its competitors, within the context of its market and its current social media efforts. That is, where are we now?

Once a Twitter marketing campaign is underway, ongoing monitoring can identify opportunities to engage with target audiences such as existing customers or a specific set of potential customers. Ongoing monitoring should lead to specific actionable recommendations that feed back into the creation of strategic content.

MARKETING WIN

Companies need to monitor word of mouth more than ever. According to Nielsen Research, consumer recommendations are now the most powerful form of advertising: 78 percent of people trust customer reviews.

Your Analytics Team

Your Twitter marketing team might be you, solo, or it might be an entire department. An individual can handle the simplest of monitoring roles, but if your project is large and complex, consider bringing in a specialist.

With a small company, reporting is pretty straightforward. However, in large or complex organizations, decisions need to be made as to whether reporting is segmented for specific business units, divisions, or even departments. As with analytics for web properties, it helps to have a specialist to make sense of the data. The expense might not seem likely at the start, but larger organizations should plan to bring on an expert once the program gains momentum.

Because of the complexities and technologies involved, you may be tempted to outsource the entire monitoring effort. Yet, as Susan Etlinger, an analyst with Altimeter Group, explained during a panel discussion at the Web 2.0 conference, "If you outsource, you really have to think it through," reported InformationWeek. An advertising or marketing agency is likely to produce glowing reports showing its efforts are boosting your company's online reputation. Agencies also see social media analytics through the lens of marketing automation, she said. They may miss other signals that ought to flow to the business's customer service or product development teams.

Most of all, outsourcing runs counter to the realization that organizations need to be more analytical to thrive in the world of new media. When you outsource, "You're slowing down that organizational learning," Etlinger said to the panel attendees, reported InformationWeek.

In other words, outsourcing may promise useful benefits, not the least of which is expertise that you don't have to develop in-house. But that leads to a long-term problem: you don't develop the expertise in-house.

What to Monitor and Track

You can track just a few items—or dozens.

These are the guiding questions to ask: What information should I look at? How can it help me make better decisions?

The Minimum Data Set

We will shortly list all the things you can monitor. But please keep in mind that you don't have to track all of these. Small businesses and those who are starting out can keep things simple and use growth trends to ascertain that they are making progress. As long as you're getting more attention, it's a good thing.

In other words, some of this information you *need* to have; other bits are *nice* to have.

The primary metrics are also the easiest to acquire:

- **Followers:** How many people have elected to follow you, and how many people you're following.
- **@Mentions:** The number of people who mention your Twitter handle.
- **Retweets:** How often people repeat what you wrote.
- **@Replies:** The number of users who reply to you.

Although we urge you to minimize the importance you give to follower count, that number does provide some useful information—especially if it's growing organically. Consider your follower numbers as a measure of how interesting others consider your company … and not more than that. (The radio may be turned on, but that doesn't mean anyone is in the room.)

Far more important are the number of people who engage with you. Someone who takes the time to respond to you or share your Tweets with her own followers is a far stronger sign that you're reaching someone and that you matter to her.

Why Followers Don't Matter

The most obvious number to look at is the number of followers you have. After all, you might have a brilliant content plan, but if nobody is listening to your voice, all the effort is wasted.

As a result, most people care passionately about how many followers they have, based on the assumption that "more is better." Sure, it's great to have a lot of followers, but they are valuable only to the degree they pay attention to your Tweets, are influenced by them, and, ideally, take action on them.

Certainly, the difference between 1,000 and 500,000 followers is substantial, but it only indicates that a lot of people once decided to click on the **Follow** button.

Follower numbers are too easy to game. Even without truly slimy techniques, you can follow a bunch of people to see if some will follow you back. You could give away a really big prize to new followers, even if those new followers don't care about your updates. Be choosy instead.

The worst thing about emphasizing your follower count is that it gives you the wrong focus. Your goal is not to get as many followers as possible. It's to reach more people who are drawn to your products and services. Setting up the right incentives for your business is critical for achieving your goals.

Twitter Metrics Checklist

Here we detail a handful of useful metrics. You can track plenty more—often with good reason. Don't feel that you must use all of these; apply them only when the data can help you make a better decision.

Track how many users have added you to lists. If someone adds your account to one of his lists, it means that he cares enough about your Tweets to want to organize them in a group of related and respected experts. You influence *that* person, if nobody else. (Sure, you could be listed under "Bozos I read only to amuse myself," but we like to think this is rare.)

You might think of the number of lists on which you appear as a *respect ratio.* Divide your follower count by the number of lists on which you appear. So if you have 7,300 followers and are on 74 lists, your respect ratio is 7,300 ÷ 74, or about 99. As long as that respect ratio increases, you're doing fine.

MARKETING WIN

Look, too, at the other people on those lists. Ideally you are in good company, alongside well-known people in your industry. If so, you're likely to be more respected and are more likely to gain more visibility. A list of "people with a first name of Esther" . . . not so much.

Track the number of times people contact you directly (direct messages). Like @Mentions and Retweets, this number can measure how well you connect with people and indicate some level of conversation. The value varies based on the type of account you have. A Twitter account with a strong emphasis on customer service (requiring people to send account numbers privately) has far different numbers than a branding-centric account.

Count brand Mentions. Track the number of people who mention your business name in their posts. An upward trend probably means good things—unless you're trying to cope with a PR meltdown.

Count competitors' brand Mentions. As a separate category of brand Mentions, include competitors. Monitor competing company social participation for comparison and for opportunity.

Track clickthroughs. If your business frequently runs promotions or regularly links to its own site (such as to lead followers to blog posts), then it's worthwhile to code them separately and track the number of clicks you receive. Watch for consistencies in what is shared and commented on. That tells you what kind of information your audience wants to get from you.

Watch your conversion rate. It's not always easy to track the number of followers who become customers. Look for conversions to sales or other marketing actions, such as those who sign up for a webinar. This makes the most sense when you use different landing pages for each campaign or each targeted link in a Tweet.

MARKETING WIN

Temper the tracking with a larger context. The science of attribution is still pretty darned weak. A tracking cookie may show what link a user clicked, but it doesn't show all the other influences that caused her to do so, such as TV advertisements or offline conversations with friends.

Record your followers' time zones. Knowing when your followers are awake may help you time your Tweets to ensure they are in front of the most eyeballs.

Making Sense of the Data

The aim of collecting all that information—either manually or using a dedicated tool—is to identify what's working and what isn't. The data should help you gain confidence in your approach: what to change to make a technique work or to discard it. Identify what *is* working and then scale up that approach.

Looking Beyond the Numbers

Don't generalize your results too much. You likely identified more than one target audience. Ultimately, you want to know whether your Tweets are positioned and delivered effectively for each of those specific target audiences.

Divide monitoring parameters by major conversation themes and marketing messages. This helps you focus on organized, actionable data. You don't need to care about every John Doe or spambot that mentioned your new product. You do need to turn a wild social media jungle into key findings that lead to specific strategic recommendations.

Step back from all the statistics-gathering to measure brand-centric concepts (including sentiment, which we address in the next chapter). Look for customer-centric measures such as their personal needs (irrespective of brand) and the types of questions prospective customers are asking.

Also correlate your results with the time of day, type of Tweet (a link to a blog post versus a link to a sales promotion), and tone (snarky, factual, chirpy-friendly).

Putting the Data to Work

What you do with your social media monitoring is as important, if not more important, than getting the monitoring in place. The end of all this data analysis should be a set of actions to take. Ask the data what's working. Gather the information, analyze it, and then change how you act.

Remind yourself occasionally that measuring followers, Retweets, and all the rest of the monitoring process is an activity—not necessarily a result. Ideally, you want to be able to post a slide showing that the cost of handling a customer inquiry online is 10¢, whereas handling the same inquiry over the phone costs $6 including infrastructure and labor costs. Eventually, you may determine a custom social media metric, such as percentage of inquiries resolved outside the call center.

If you focus on observation rather than data collection, you can get a real and valuable source of insight. Analysis lets you learn how people talk about you, the language they use, and how they compare you to competitors.

In the end, analytics are just a barometer of how well you're doing. The true measure of your success is always conversions and any activity that can somehow be directly or indirectly monetized.

Taking Action on Monitoring

Using the terms people choose to discuss your products or its business category helps you refine your search strategy, so that you adopt relevant language and expressions in your marketing and PR activities.

When you first begin monitoring brand Mentions, you may be overwhelmed with the number of times your company is mentioned or the business category is discussed.

You will be tempted to respond to every one: to counteract every negative comment, to answer and spread every positive experience, and to resolve every question. It's a natural response, because you care passionately about your brand.

But often the best approach is not to respond. If you have nothing to add, don't say anything. If your response will only inflame a situation, stay out of it.

There are two very clear cases where a brand should always step in:

- Where an actual customer service complaint is being expressed. Help people reach the support channel.
- Where incorrect things are being said about your company. Correct the incorrect messaging that is being spread and answer any questions.

The Value of Social Media Influence

Not all followers are created equal. You know instinctually that quality is better than quantity, and that it's better to be followed by the 100 most important people in your business than by 10,000 strangers. You need to know how influential your network is to truly understand what your followers mean.

The problem is, no one can confidently measure how important one person is compared to another. That's true in the "real world" and also within social media.

For instance, it'd be great for your small business to be written up in *USA Today.* Thus a journalist who writes for *USA Today* is more influential to your company than is a blogger of a Me and My Dog site. Right? Obviously.

Unless, that is, your company sells gourmet dog food and the blogger has a million followers who hang on his every word.

It's difficult to accurately determine which followers can positively affect your company. And that's why services have sprung up to measure social media influence.

The New Field of Social Media Influence

There are two metrics that all this data tries to approach: engagement and influence. We've already discussed engagement (at length) as the degree to which people genuinely connect with you.

The other issue is influence: how much your followers value what you say and their likelihood to share your Tweets. It's kind of like digital name-dropping—how many times has your name been mentioned, and by whom?

A related term is reach. Reach measures how many Twitter users receive your Tweets directly (your followers) and indirectly (your followers' followers). The further your Tweets spread, the more impact you and your brand potentially have.

Engagement, influence, and reach are similar to one another, but not quite the same. They are pieces of the same puzzle, however, and shouldn't be viewed in isolation.

The New SAT Score

Remember when you started college, and every freshman asked each other, "What was your SAT score?" The answer didn't matter, you knew. What *did* matter was that the school had accepted you, whether it was because you had a perfect score on the college entrance exam or because you wrote an entry admission essay that blew away the college admissions board. Starting on the first day of school, the only thing that would make a difference was your own performance; the SAT score had no further relevance.

But still you asked, because you knew it measured *something*, even if no one was sure what it was.

Thus it is with social media influence. Several sites aim to measure it even though we all know that no score is a true measure of our worthiness as human beings or as business entities.

Currently, at least three companies specialize in social media influence measurements: Klout, PeerIndex, Kred, and PROskore. By the time you read this, there may be more. Each of these services tries to measure how influential you are among your followers on Twitter.

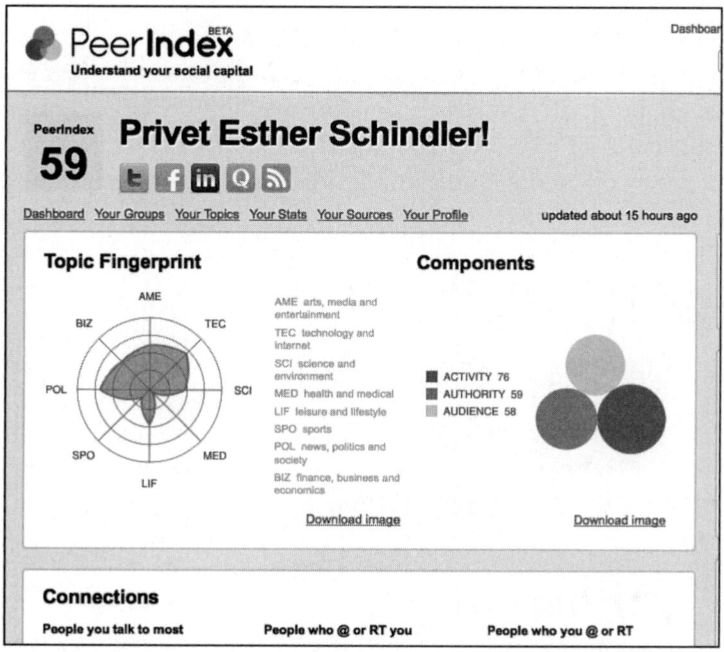

Peer Index shows the areas in which you're most influential.

Klout defines itself as "The Standard for Online and Internet Influence," and rates your social influence score based on reach, user engagement, and the size of your following. Typically, Klout is used as an analytics tool to help you better engage and grow your following by discovering where you succeed, and where there is opportunity for improvement.

Klout evaluates users' behavior with complex ranking algorithms and semantic content analysis to measure the influence of individuals on social networks. On Twitter, Klout's influence score is based on a user's ability to drive action through Tweets,

Retweets, and more. The free site also factors in Facebook fans as well as connections on LinkedIn, FourSquare, and other social media services.

Social media influence services usually give you a general score on a 1-to-100 scale. Most celebrities have Klout scores over 70, with Justin Bieber at 100 and Lady Gaga at 93.

The more interesting stats are more refined. Klout's True Reach, for instance, tells you how many of your followers are really engaging with your Tweets; it also shows amplification probability, network influence, and the topics the individual or business Tweets on most frequently.

You aren't limited to looking at your own data; the free service lets you look at any Twitter user's Klout score. Nor does someone need to deliberately sign up in order to get a Klout score. The service crawls Twitter and ranks members automatically. If you want to grow your score, you can log in and give it a bunch of information about your online activities.

Klout shows the topics on which Yoda has the most influence (or at least Tweets most often), including Jedi.

Is Your Score Big Enough?

Whether or not you like the notion of social media influence, others are using it.

For example, when Bal Harbour Shops hosted a VIP lounge at its Fashion's Night Out party in Florida, it required guests to have a Klout score of 40 or higher.

It isn't just ritzy joints that use "influence" as an acceptance measure. The U.S. Federal Trade Commission (FTC) gave its approval to a new startup that runs social media background checks on potential employees. The firm, Social Intelligence, can scan through Facebook updates, photos, videos, and groups, plus anything people contributed on Twitter, LinkedIn, and YouTube.

Plus, if your own career touches on social media—such as working as a public relations professional—expect your social media behavior to be part of the criteria your employers and clients use.

For example, in my (Esther's) role as online magazine editor-in-chief, I look at a prospective writer's Klout score. I look at lots of other things, too, but because it's so important for the articles I publish to be noticed, I generally give "extra credit" to authors who have successfully amplified their work. That is, I hire their megaphone as much as their skill at research and writing.

What "Influence" Measures—and What It Doesn't

Anything that assigns a number to our value is nervous-making, and these scoring systems are no exception.

"Mechanically measuring someone's influence using an algorithm is going to be imprecise and quirky," pointed out Gary Schirr in a blog post called "Why Klout is Dangerous." He asked, "Does anyone really believe that Justin Bieber is the most influential living being? or even the most influential online American?" Justin Bieber has a much higher score than Marc Andreessen, who invented the web browser, cofounded Netscape, and has a long list of achievements. Who is more important?

"Klout's bigger flaw is that its scoring system is tied to membership," wrote longtime journalist Paul Gillin. "The more you tell Klout about you, the higher your score is likely to be. This linkage fundamentally undermines the quality of the service. In effect, Klout pays you to endorse its service by rewarding you with a higher rank. If Google did that, Congress would be holding hearings."

Because we tend to "get" what we measure, tools that measure social media influence worry some people—including us, sometimes. Because "Klout" has value, people will be motivated to "earn points" rather than to behave in a manner that is appropriate to the community. That motivation may include cheating or gaming the system, in much the same way that search engine optimization has been affected by "content farms."

The Least You Need to Know

- At a minimum, monitor the trends in your follower counts, Retweets, and Mentions.
- Collect data only insofar as it helps you improve your marketing program and your company's ability to deliver quality products.
- Social media influence is important even if the services to measure your influence are still imperfect.

Tools to Tweet and Monitor Campaigns

Chapter 14

In This Chapter

- Understanding the criteria for choosing Twitter tools
- Differentiating between monitoring tools and management tools
- Peeking at the features in widely used Twitter tools and platforms

While you can track what happens on Twitter manually, using just the Twitter web client, it's a lot easier to use tools designed expressly for the purpose. You have plenty of options, too, for everything from a better way to post Tweets to enterprise-class suites that report trends across several social media campaigns. And with price ranges from free to "Oh my, they want how much for that?!"

Monitoring your marketing efforts makes sense for many reasons. You can ...

- Identify what people say about your brand in real time.
- Keep track of your competitors' activities.
- Watch industry trends based on conversations and reactions.

Twitter changes fast, and so do the tools that support it. Our intent throughout this book is to share advice that helps you use Twitter for many years, but we recognize that this chapter on tools is apt to go stale. We show you what can be accomplished with the current versions so you have a sense of what's available, but new software versions are sure to be released and new products announced. However, we emphasize the criteria you should consider in tool choice—criteria that apply to any Twitter tool you may adopt.

Understanding Tool Categories

If you can imagine doing something with Twitter, there's probably a standalone tool to help you accomplish it. Probably more like three.

Whether you want a tool to help you find and manage followers, a service that connects your Twitter account to your Google calendar (TwitterCal), or a way to send payments via Twitter (TwitterPay), your biggest problem is apt to be choosing the best solution rather than finding or building your own tool.

We mention relevant tools throughout the book in the appropriate context, such as tools to find people to follow. In this chapter, however, we do a deep dive on two important categories: Twitter clients and monitoring software.

These have a surprising amount of overlap, largely because several Twitter clients include basic monitoring and tracking features. The keyword is basic. A full-on social media management tool does more than just monitor and publish on Twitter. For one thing, the serious management suites usually encompass other sites, such as Facebook and LinkedIn.

These checklists help differentiate between these two types of tools.

Standalone Twitter clients do the following:

- Emphasize content publishing
- Help manage conversations across multiple usernames
- Sometimes work outside the web browser, running as standalone desktop applications
- Include built-in URL shortening
- Use tabs or columns to separate streams from different accounts, contributors, hashtags, and lists

Dedicated monitoring systems place more emphasis on analysis rather than publishing. Their features generally include these:

- Advanced analysis of social media engagement
- Sentiment analysis
- Tools to make it easier for teams to contribute to business Twitter accounts
- Tracking across multiple social media networks

Criteria for Evaluating Tools

Every purchase involves multiple decisions. You need to balance features and complexity, price and support, bells and whistles with training time. So it is with these tools.

If you were looking to purchase a new cell phone, you might evaluate features such as email integration, sound quality, keyboard styles, and app availability before even considering price and providers. The same is true of Twitter and social media monitoring tools. While each tool has its benefits and demerits, you need to start with a shopping list, and understand why you want (or don't want) a particular feature.

The following are among the criteria to consider:

Posting features. Some Twitter clients are particular to Twitter. Others—sometimes referred to as social media dashboards, which sounds a little classier—let you post to Twitter, Facebook, and LinkedIn from the same user interface. You can schedule Tweets to post at specific times of day, enabling you to spread out the content without having to hover over the computer.

Monitoring capabilities. How much data do you need to track? At the most basic level, you can save searches or receive alerts for a handful of keywords. At the other end of the spectrum, monitoring can include tracking a large set of keywords across Twitter as well as other social networks like Facebook, and even blogs and forums.

Workflow. Some platforms permit you to authorize multiple individuals to access an account. Sometimes they let you assign messages, log notes, and assign different levels of access.

Analytics. If your success metrics are number-driven, you may need tools with strong analytics features. For basic statistics on audience growth and engagement (the number of @replies, direct messages, and Mentions) a number of free platforms may satisfy. However, as you get into analytics around large volumes of Mentions, sentiment, and trends, you need a more sophisticated platform.

Ease of use. If a feature-rich tool is too complex for you to understand, you won't use it. The user experience can make or break a platform, and user-experience beauty lies in the eye of the beholder.

Mobility. Some Twitter clients are streamlined to make it easy to post from a smartphone. They integrate with the phone's camera and simplify the user interface. Few are optimized for business use, but if your Twitter team is on the road often, you may need to consider mobile features.

Price. Many of the free tools do everything you need. When your requirements expand, your budget needs to expand, too.

For most businesses, tool choice boils down to cost. Smaller businesses can't justify spending thousands of dollars a year on monitoring software, and the "enterprise" tools are priced for big budgets.

The larger the brand, the greater the volume of conversations. For a Fortune 500 company, expensive monitoring software is completely justifiable, as brand management is a full-time job with many balls to keep in the air. Major holding companies, like Proctor & Gamble and Pepsico, have large teams responsible for monitoring the social web.

Twitter Clients

You could spend an entire week trying out Twitter clients. There's no single dominant platform that "everyone uses"; entrepreneurs keep finding new ways to present and organize Twitter information. It's all a matter of preference. Some people like Tweeting from their web browsers, and others prefer standalone desktop clients.

Currently the most popular Twitter clients are CoTweet, HootSuite, and TweetDeck. Each is updated frequently (sometimes we think too frequently) and they continue to impress us with new features.

Most Twitter clients share the same basic functionality, including the ability to manage multiple Twitter IDs from a single dashboard. They differ most in their interface, treatment of team workflow, and integration with other social media sites. Over the next few pages, we give you a sample of their features and UI to help you get a sense of what to expect.

CoTweet

CoTweeting is when more than one individual shares the responsibility of Tweeting on an account. The application CoTweet aims to help fulfill that mission: to help teams share responsibility.

One of the biggest challenges when sharing a Twitter account is knowing who is Tweeting, when they're Tweeting, and how to coordinate responses. With the CoTweet dashboard, multiple Twitter accounts are displayed neatly in the left sidebar. To give a new individual access, simply enter his email address; the new team member gets a notification that you've granted him permission to use the account.

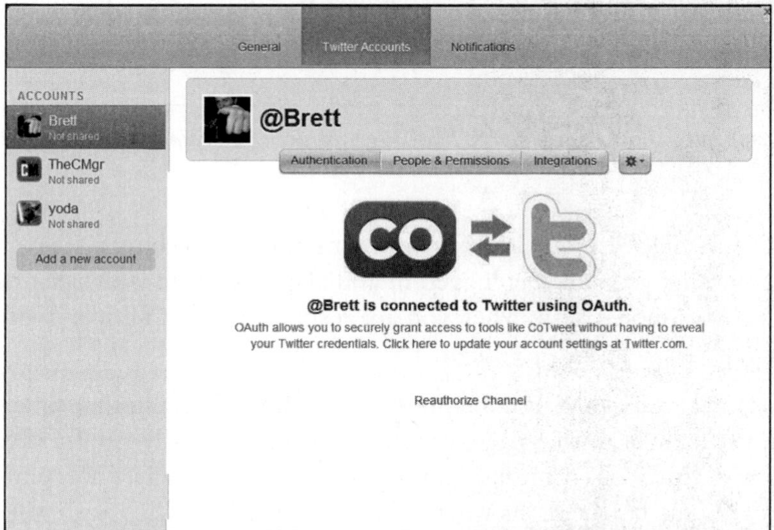

CoTweet uses Twitter OAuth service to confirm the ownership of an account.

Like most Twitter clients, you can publish a status update right away or schedule it for later. And it has a built-in URL shortener. All Tweets appear in the right panel under the Sent and Scheduled tabs.

Most teams that share Twitter responsibilities sign their Tweets in some way. CoTweet lets each contributor choose a short signature, such as his initials with a carat or tilde.

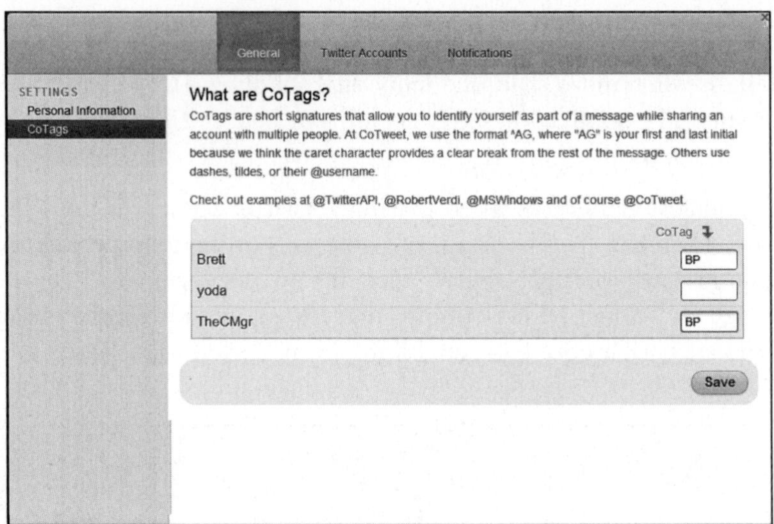

When Brett Tweets on behalf of ***@TheCMgr****, he adds his initials to identify that he posted the Tweet.*

Twitter clients like CoTweet let you post from multiple accounts. If you Tweet on behalf of a brand, you can stay logged in and also post from your personal Twitter handle. It's even more useful when you are responsible for multiple Twitter accounts at a company.

With CoTweet, you can assign members as "on duty." During that time, all account notifications are sent to that person's inbox. That's especially helpful if you manage an account in shifts, as is common for customer service Twitter accounts. Team members only see notifications when they're the person tasked with responding to an item.

But what about instances where you're not in a position to respond? Sometimes another team member is better equipped to answer a question; perhaps your shift is ending and you want to make sure the next person addresses a Tweet. CoTweet's solution is to create assignments for team members. For every Tweet that comes through in your stream—whether it's a public Tweet, an @Mention, or a direct message—you can assign a specific follow-up.

For example, an airline representative might see a customer Tweet about a delayed flight, and respond to that individual with an apology about the delay. She might then assign a team member to follow up a half hour later, via direct message or a public Tweet, to say "Hope you have a safe flight!" before the plane takes off.

Other features include …

- Saved searches. You can keep a dashboard of multiple searches, organized into their own separate columns.
- Built-in Klout score display.
- General profile display. Click on a username to see the account profile in the right sidebar.
- Log notes about a specific user.

Like many web applications, CoTweet operates on a "freemium" model. You get a certain amount of functionality for free; when you need more, you pay for it. For some, CoTweet's Standard edition of the platform suffices. However, medium to large organizations might find that they need CoTweet Enterprise, which supports both Twitter and Facebook management. According to CoTweet, "As a growing number of employees contribute to the social conversation on behalf of their brands, Enterprise easily scales to support an unlimited number of users, advanced workflow (with workgroups for account control), more analytics, third-party integrations (including Salesforce.com), productivity tools (such as advanced scheduling), unlimited conversation history for deeper customer relationships, a mobile app, rich profiles of fans and followers, and much more."

HootSuite

HootSuite is another popular browser-based tool that helps teams collaborate on Twitter. Like CoTweet, HootSuite also offers two versions, Pro and Enterprise.

One HootSuite distinction is its integration with many social media sites. The platform lets you manage Twitter, Facebook, LinkedIn, Google+, Ping.fm, WordPress blogs, MySpace, Foursquare, and Mixi from a single dashboard.

The free version of HootSuite works fine as a personal social media dashboard, with topic search and keyword tracking, columns based on searches, message drafts, and separate tabs for each social media network. Team collaboration is charged monthly, based on the number of individual users.

The HootSuite user interface is column-based. You can show accounts, lists, keywords you're monitoring, and lots more. Team collaboration features let you track responses, assign messages to team members, and schedule updates. Its built-in URL shortener, Ow.ly, helps your links fit in 140 characters; HootSuite collects metrics based on Ow.ly clickthroughs.

HootSuite presents Twitter streams in column format.

Among the best-loved attributes of HootSuite is its analytics capabilities. You can automate and customize reports that keep team members up to speed on scheduled updates and campaign results. HootSuite's social analytics consist of over 30 individual report "modules" accessible through a redesigned launch bar. Users can select from a variety of modules in any combination to build custom reports; or for quick reporting, choose from a selection of premade report templates.

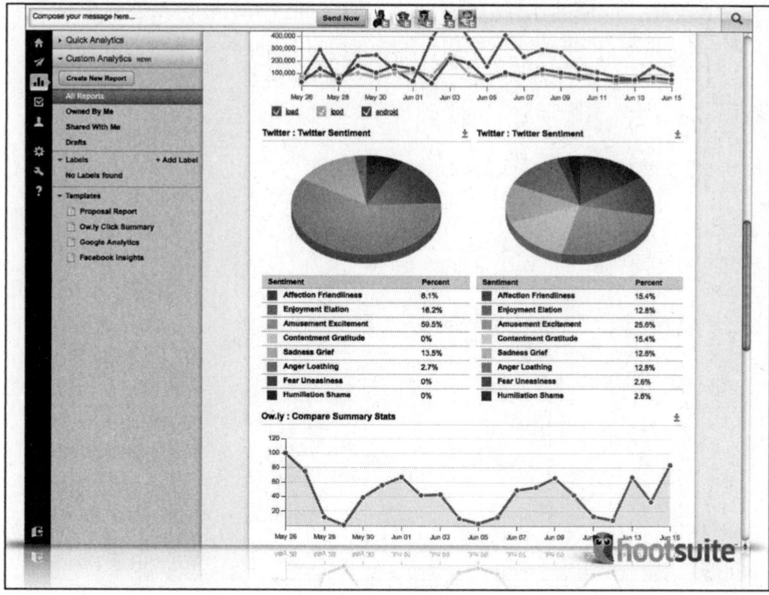

HootSuite's analytics dashboard lets you track progress against company metrics.
(Image courtesy of HootSuite)

TweetDeck

TweetDeck was one of the first desktop Twitter clients, released in 2008; it has since been acquired by Twitter. The desktop version, based on Adobe AIR, has been supplemented by a mobile and browser version. The TweetDeck desktop client includes pop-up notifications to alert you to new @Mentions, direct messages, and other customizable updates.

TweetDeck is also column-based. By default, it shows your Twitter stream, @Mentions, and direct messages. You can add columns for saved searches, hashtags, Twitter lists, and its own lists. You can record, share, and watch video clips within TweetDeck, upload photos from within TweetDeck, and preview short URLs before linking to them.

TweetDeck lets you organize Twitter streams in columns.

It also supports several social networks, including Facebook and LinkedIn, so you can post to more than one at the same time.

TweetDeck, which is built on open-source software, emphasizes publishing rather than analytics. Its website describes TweetDeck as "air traffic control for Twitter," and its feature set is built for the individual power user. Because it runs as a stand-alone application, the Twitter feed doesn't get lost in yet another web browser tab.

Those are just three of the dozens of Twitter clients available. If you're looking for platforms that put an emphasis on publishing, you should also consider these other alternatives:

- Seesmic
- Whirl
- Tweetie
- Digsby

Dedicated Monitoring Tools

Tweeting an appropriate message is one thing. But as with any other media campaign, you can't improve what you cannot measure. Tools make the task of marketing more efficient and effective, and with so many businesses turning to Twitter, the number of "solutions" is vast. These tools can help with everything from source network connections to social content management to engagement measurement.

Monitoring tools can be free or they can cost more than a few hundred dollars a month. The more sophisticated the technology, the more expensive it usually is. In our experience, no single platform gets the job done on its own. They all require a keen eye to sift through the data and put it into context.

Some platforms monitor more than just Twitter. They contain richer feature sets that get into volume, sentiment, trends, and influence. Pricing is usually contingent upon the number of queries or keywords you track. For large companies, these become necessities. Smaller businesses with a more localized customer base may find them to be overkill.

MARKETING WIN

When we say there are a lot of social media monitoring tools, we aren't kidding. In 2009, Ken Burbary (**@kenburbary**) and Adam Cohen (**@adamcohen**) created an open directory of social media monitoring tools (http://wiki.kenburbary.com/contributors); today it contains more than 200 entries of platforms that help businesses better manage the social web.

Our favorite resource for finding Twitter add-ons and applications is oneforty.com (**@oneforty**). After you identify the items on your shopping list, you should probably start at oneforty to look at its most recent tools and product summaries.

Usually, you can request a free trial; the enterprise-class tools have dedicated sales staff who are happy to give a custom demonstration.

Remember back when you drew up your metrics for the social media marketing campaign? Your monitoring application should help you capture and report most of these items, so that you can see where you're getting the most success and the best bang for your buck. Among the metrics to look for are these:

- Quantity and quality of commentary about your brand/business
- Follower numbers

- Leads generated, with the help of tracking IDs or different landing pages for different campaigns
- Quantity and quality of incoming links

When evaluating product features, look at how each platform treats notifications and how thoroughly and accurately it picks up on Mentions. Monitoring for Mentions can be really hit or miss depending on the brand or keyword. For a brand like "Dove" or "Tide," differentiating the brand versus the word is a complicated challenge. Sophisticated monitoring tools emphasize their ability to make sense of Mentions across the web and to contextualize them in searches.

Another thing to look for is *sentiment analysis*. For some brands, it's not enough to know when conversations are happening about your brand, but to know the context in which they appear.

Are people saying good things about your products or services, or are they making complaints? Some tools can parse out sentiment in searches and decipher whether the volume of conversations is primarily positive or negative.

DEFINITION

Sentiment analysis analyzes text to discover, extract, and analyze sentiment, opinions, passions, and emotions. While it's easy to discern the differences between some opinions ("This coffee maker is great!" versus "This coffee maker stinks!") the gray areas are harder to identify—much less count. Sentiment analysis looks for more than plus, minus, and neutral; businesses want to know why, with a high degree of granularity. This is becoming a common way for brands to gauge customer opinion of their companies and products.

These are other questions to investigate when evaluating enterprise monitoring solutions:

- Does this integrate with my current CRM solution? Some integrate with email and customer relationship management systems like Salesforce.com.
- Can multiple individuals access the account, or do I have to pay per user?
- Does the monitoring application only crawl social networks? Or can it also search for web Mentions on blogs, websites, and discussion forums?

Monitoring for Free

You don't have to spend a lot of money; some free or inexpensive tools can help you with monitoring basics.

The most basic option for monitoring is Twitter's native search function, and saving searches for your most important keywords.

Regularly search for brand, competitor, and keyword Mentions. A university might search for school name, prominent deans and faculty, competing schools, and general education trends or news. Harvard might monitor Harvard, Harvard University, MIT, Ivy League, Higher Education, and Professor X (though that might bring up Mentions of the *X-Men* movies—perhaps they might use an actual professor's name instead). With Twitter Advanced search, you can get surprisingly specific.

In addition to Twitter's native search, consider using some of these other free applications in your monitoring efforts:

- Monitter.com is a browser-based dashboard that shows a never-ending stream of keywords and phrases. Each search term can have its own column, so you can see what's being discussed in one easy-to-read panel.

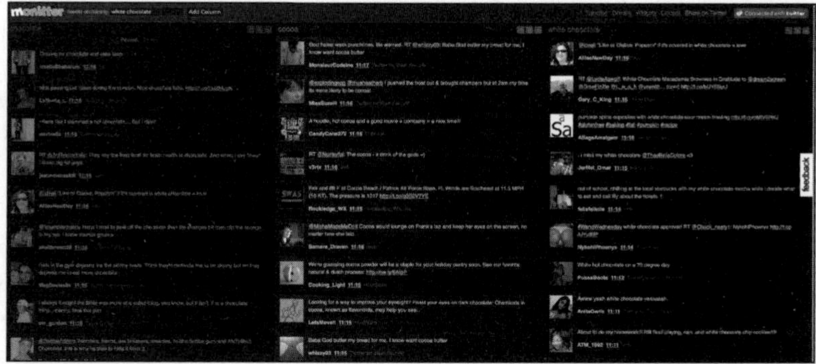

The free Monitter lets you peek at keywords and phrases used across Twitter.

- Socialmention.com and Twazzup.com enable you to pull Mentions across the web (not just Twitter), see which links were shared the most, and identify the top influencers who Tweeted.
- Tweetbeep.com is a subscription service that sends you a digest or email alert whenever someone mentions a specific keyword or phrase. It works similarly to Google alerts, but specifically tracks Twitter.

- Contaxio.com enables you to manage your Twitter account by assessing who your followers are. You can keep track of reciprocal relationships as well as the rate of growth of your account and see if specific Tweets trigger unfollows.
- Twitterfall.com and Tweetchat.com are helpful tools for monitoring Twitter chats or real-time events. For example, if you organize or participate in a Twitter chat (such as #prchat, #edchat, etc.) you can easily follow the conversation by monitoring the hashtag. This also comes in handy during conferences or global events such as the Super Bowl and award shows.

Business-Class Monitoring Tools

With a lot of data to gather and evaluate, established brands need tools to help them understand and gain insights about their social media performance including detailed metrics, sentiment analysis, and analytics reporting. Several of these tools don't just collect data for listening programs, or track and monitor responses. They also provide advice on how to use social media and offer staff training.

Some services cater to small businesses that want to handle monitoring analysis internally. Others are tuned for global corporations needing access to expert analysts in addition to a robust suite of social tools that plug into business processes.

At a minimum, these provide a snapshot view of your business and its performance on the social web. Most do much more.

There are several competitors in this space. Among them are these:

Radian 6. Radian 6 is focused on conversation engagement on the real-time web. It can aggregate all the conversations taking place about your brand—on Twitter as well as Facebook, blogs, and video-sharing sites—and analyze those conversations with suggestions of how to respond. A web-based dashboard lets you set up topics, track metrics, and link to workflow tools to help you assign tasks to staff, recording who's engaging with whom.

You might be swayed initially by Radian 6's monitoring dashboard, which tracks Mentions on over 100 million social media sites. But once you lay your hands on Radian 6's engagement console, which helps businesses coordinate your internal responses to external activity, it becomes apparent why Radian 6 has become the go-to tool for some of the biggest corporations. (That's not their marketing speak. That's our experience.)

Argyle Social. Argyle offers all the by-now-standard tracking tools. What sets them apart is their emphasis on showing how social efforts influence the bottom line (or fail to). With conversion analytics, the company promises to help businesses close the loop between social media marketing and a website purchase or action.

Argyle integrates with a business website using code embeds. That gives the business visibility into things that happen on the site, such as email signups, sales conversions, and other meaningful business outcomes. It helps you determine which content works, and how to optimize Twitter use so you can make smarter business decisions. More than tracking Twitter Mentions, Argyle aims to ensure that social media workflow and monitoring are ringing the cash register.

Argyle Social.

Sprout Social. This cloud-based software integrates with Twitter, Facebook Pages, LinkedIn, FourSquare, Gowalla, and other networks. In addition to the standard complement of tracking tools, Sprout Social offers contact management and competitive insight.

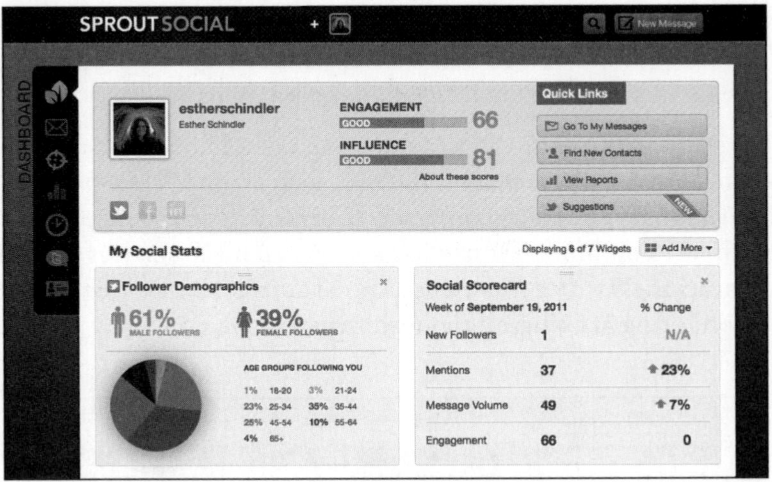

Sprout Social.

That's just a sample. You might also want to investigate these:

- Lithium
- Sysmos Heartbeat
- Alterian SM2
- Crimson Hexagon
- ScoutLabs
- Collective Intellect
- Sprinklr

The world of Twitter tools is vast, but if you understand what features you care about most, then your most difficult decision is which of the many applications best suits your needs.

The Least You Need to Know

- Twitter clients emphasize publishing to social media sites, whereas monitoring tools are focused more on listening and analytics.
- Know your criteria for evaluating tools before starting your search. More features aren't always better.
- TweetDeck is the client for the power user, whereas HootSuite and CoTweet cater to team collaboration.
- While expensive monitoring solutions might sound appealing, you can mix and match a number of free products to get the job done.

Tailoring Twitter to Your Business Needs

Part 4

Most of the "rules" of making Twitter work for business apply to everyone: communicate, respect others, don't act like a jerk. Using social media to connect, engage, market, and sell your product or message is applicable to any business, nonprofit, government agency, or freelancer.

Yet Twitter can serve some businesses or company roles uniquely. Public relations professionals want to use Twitter to score big media coverage and build relationships with key influencers. Small businesses want to leverage local opportunities to draw Twitter users into their stores. Customer support departments enable the business to connect with the people who buy their products, both to offer technical help and to amplify customer success. In this part, we highlight opportunities and tools that make Twitter an excellent vehicle for your particular niche.

How Small Businesses Can Use Twitter

Chapter

15

In This Chapter

- Understanding the advantages of Tweeting for your small shop
- Paying attention to building a personal brand
- Dedicating time for Twitter
- Connecting with sales outlets

Twitter offers unique advantages to small businesses and a few extra challenges, as well. Mostly, it's a win for small businesses, because Twitter levels the playing field. Online, your voice is equally loud whether yours is a one-person business or whether you work for a mega-corporation.

In this chapter, you learn how many of the principles of Twitter marketing are the same as for larger businesses, though your tactics may be modified based on resource availability.

What's Different About Twitter for Small Businesses?

Throughout this book, we use examples from big companies whose names you recognize, whose reputations precede them, and who generally find it easy to get attention. That's intentional, because it's reassuring to know that even the "big guys" struggle with the same goals you do.

Some of their struggles are a bit different than those of a small company. Unsurprisingly, large businesses have quite a few advantages when it comes to marketing—not the least of which is a marketing department. And money to fund it.

However, small businesses can and do achieve wonderful things with Twitter simply because Twitter is open to everyone. It's as easy to get noticed as a tiny business—someone who hung up her own shingle—as it is for a "household word" company. You are limited only by your personal skill.

Finding Influencers Just an @Mention Away

For example, small businesses can exploit the power of word of mouth by interacting with authenticity and personal warmth. Most small businesses get their customers through personal recommendations, and Twitter is their digital manifestation.

For example, in 2008, Brian Simpson was working as the social media manager for the Roger Smith Hotel in New York City. He set up the account **@rshotel** and used his personal account (**@bsimi**) to connect with digital influencers and bloggers.

Because of the transparent nature of Twitter, Simpson could identify when trend-setters were coming to town for a conference or event. He'd personally reach out to bloggers who had large followings and traveled often—personalities like Chris Brogan (**@chrisbrogan**) and C. C. Chapman (**@cc_chapman**)—and offer them discounts. In turn, they'd Tweet about their stay at the hotel, their great experiences with Brian and other staff members, and sometimes they would write glowing reviews on their blogs.

In less than a year, the Roger Smith Hotel became the Twitter Mecca of Manhattan.

It's a prime example of how a small business can leverage personal outreach to drive significant word of mouth.

The Solo Business Difference

The best and worst features of running a solo business include these:

- You are the face of the business. Or in marketing terms: you are the brand.
- It can be difficult to keep your personal life separate from your work life.
- You do everything yourself. You have to do everything yourself. You're responsible for everything from delivering services to marketing to paying the bills. And don't forget to take out the trash.
- Nobody is looking over your shoulder, telling you what to do.

The resolutions to many of these challenges are outside the scope of this book, such as learning how to avoid procrastination, and teaching yourself the difference between work-time and personal time. However, each has a direct impact on how you use Twitter ... for good and ill. Let's take a look at how these attributes and challenges affect your Twitter marketing.

The Nimble Small Business

Small businesses drive the economy. Whether your company employs 5 people, 50, or 250, it can generate products and services of value, create a healthy work/life balance, and keep quality controllable.

Small businesses, too, have their plusses and minuses that affect their Twitter use:

- Budgets are small.
- Decisions can be made quickly, but wrong decisions can be deadly.
- Many consumers prefer to deal with small, local businesses.
- Getting visibility can be difficult, especially in an industry with many similar competitors.

By now, you've figured out that Twitter helps you address all of these because it can be done on a shoestring budget, it emphasizes the personal touch that makes small businesses unique and special, and your "reach" is a measure only of your skill in connecting with the right people—all of whom are accessible online.

Taking Advantage of Small Business Strengths

Small businesses usually are nimble. They—by which we mean you—can change "corporate direction" overnight. "Getting buy-in" is accomplished in a single meeting during which all the stakeholders can share a single pizza, rather than six months of tedious arguments.

And the business advantages for small businesses are manifold.

Building a Personal Brand

"Personal brand" is among the terms bandied about by the chic intelligentsia who are ever so buzzword compliant. For most small businesses, the phrase is meaningless. Except it does mean something; you just may not speak of the phenomenon in the same terms.

In a small business, especially a tiny company such as a sole proprietorship, you sell your personal expertise. The team who develops the "solution" is probably also the person who does payroll and sorts through the postal mail. Even in larger small businesses, the company culture is driven by one or two people who set expectations for staff, customers, and anyone else you do business with.

In particular, when customers or clients deal with your company, it's your authority as a trustworthy subject matter expert that causes them to choose you. The company image is you: your behavior, your public persona, your expertise.

So a fiction author who wants to get her novels noticed can, and should, incorporate her personality and her interests in her timeline. We've seen some novelists "marketing" their books only by trying to sell them, and other solo craftspeople do nothing more than link to an etsy.com listing. The most successful are those who intersperse self-promotional Tweets (such as book signings and other reminders that, yes, you're in business), with Tweets that show who you are, what you care about, and who matters to you.

> **@JStevenYork** Got galleys for upcoming anthology "Westward Weird" today w/my "Clockwork Cowboy" story in it! #steampunk
>
> **@JStevenYork** My motto: "Fire and forget." RT **@robholts @JStevenYork** lesson 1 Look in mirror & reject your own query until it no longer hurts to hear it.
>
> **@CleoCoyle** Two more views on my book trailer and we are at 5,600. Thx, everyone! http://youtu.be/CmgZXq8Gqjs
>
> **@CleoCoyle** My Buttermilk Apple Snack Cake recipe: Click link for a keeper PDF: goo.gl/r4aTJ Enjoy! #baking #cake in #NYC #newjersey #longisland

The result is this: existing fans connect to you, as well as to your books. New people think you're cool, and seek out your books.

The sense of "personal brand" presents special opportunities for small businesses on Twitter. It's easy for you to interact and share one on one because really, who else is going to do it? You aren't afraid to let the company exhibit a personality and you aren't nervous about its effect on the corporate image; you are the image. You are whoever you present yourself to be.

This is a strength. Most people easily empathize with other people rather than "brands." It's a smaller step for someone to engage with a person than it is to leave a comment for a logo. It's easier to agree (or disagree) with a person than it is with a faceless company.

And it's your key to success.

The Personal Touch

When you have a great experience in a small boutique store, chatting with the owner, or getting focused attention from the salesperson, doesn't it make all the difference? We are all grateful for the service of a Mom-and-Pop store rather than a major retailer or department store: a warm greeting, their memory of the last time you visited, their in-depth knowledge, and the sense that they sincerely appreciate your custom.

It's those personal touches that make or break a business. On Twitter, use this to your advantage!

The most successful "solopreneurs" on Twitter do three things well:

- They have a distinct personal voice and point of view.
- They aren't afraid to engage.
- They understand the needs of their audience.

In Seth Godin's book *Tribes*, he emphasizes the connection between individuals and leaders in order to effect change. As a solo business owner, you have a unique opportunity to create a tribe: a group of individuals who feel connected to you, your ideas, and your business. Twitter helps you create a platform to showcase your expertise, grow your network, and ultimately, drive business results.

For example, Laura Fitton (**@pistachio**) engaged with individuals in passionate one-to-one dialogue. She created a loyal "tribe" of followers: people who actively sought her out, booked her for speaking engagements, and sent clients her way. Today, she's employed by Hubspot, an online-marketing company that acquired her startup, oneforty.com, in 2011.

Personal engagement is a wonderful thing, but it can be a pain to keep your personal life and your business life separate. For many small business owners, their personal life and business life are hopelessly intertwined.

Often this is to their benefit—a chance discussion at a hobby store that leads to your designing the store's website—but it can be especially problematical on Twitter. It's wonderful to display your personality on Twitter and to share who you are and what you care about, but what's too far? We've seen people Tweeting things that are far from business-oriented and thus inappropriate.

FAIL WHALE

One weakness for solo shops is matters of personal privacy. Pay attention to how much you say about your personal life, especially if you make yourself very accessible.

It's one thing for an employee of a small business to Tweet that she's going on vacation. But it's another thing for someone who regularly Tweets about working at home to say she's going to Cancun—because it's advertising that she's leaving the house empty.

It's All on Your Shoulders

In small businesses, especially very small ones, everyone is responsible for multiple roles, with wide-ranging responsibilities. And of course, any solo entrepreneur functions as a one-person team.

That's an advantage and a disadvantage, especially when it comes to marketing.

As the only person managing your Twitter account, you don't have to go through approval processes, coordinate with team members, or worry about being "on-message." The reality is, everything you say is a reflection on your business.

Ideally it's a positive reflection on the business, and in most cases we are sure it will be. First, by reading this book, you are learning how to participate in the conversation online (not to mention demonstrating evidence of your fine judgment when it comes to book choice). Even if you didn't read the book cover to cover, however, small businesses run on personality and personal service—and that's something that can't be matched by the big chains you often compete with. You understand "engagement" natively, when it seems like big corporations need to get a smile approved by management.

The freedom from oversight means that your only social media corporate guidelines are those you develop yourself. Nobody tells you what to do! You don't have to comply with a corporate policy about what may or may not be said on Twitter. You can write about your children, congratulate an employee on his bowling trophy, issue laudatory Tweets about your favorite burger joint, and comment about your creative process ("Spent a half-hour trying to find the bug in this code ... ah, GOTCHA!"). It's all to your business's benefit, because no one doubts that there is a live, breathing, caring human who is intimately involved with ensuring the company delivers quality.

FAIL WHALE

Without someone to set the ground rules, you can get caught up in the heat of the moment and make dumb mistakes. Nobody tells you when you just said something really stupid.

Remember the pizza restaurant, back in Chapter 3, in which the proprietor called a customer a dumbass? Sometimes, it's a good idea to have a rulebook, and to comply with it.

Plus, when you have to do *everything*, you may not do all of it extremely well. Especially when it isn't your core function.

Twitter: The Savior for the Marketing-Inept

Some people are entrepreneurial by nature. They love to schmooze, they know how to make deals, and one-on-one networking comes easily to them. Whether they work for themselves or operate a business of 100 employees, for these people, promoting their companies is as natural as breathing.

For many small businesses, though, especially startups, it's quite the opposite. The entrepreneur went into business for herself because she loves to write software, or she is passionate about making pottery. Marketing and PR are immodest or awkward, accounting is confusing, and any time spent on activities that don't involve programming or clay are just, well, wrong.

Even if they're perfectly willing to do marketing, many solo shops and small businesses aren't very good at self-promotion. These same people can speak passionately about their area of expertise (in fact, it's hard to get them to shut up), but marketing? They go silent. They have no idea what to say in order to sell their products and services, so they resort to "Buy my stuff!" or "Look at our great deals!"

This is one reason that Twitter is such a boon to small businesses. You don't need to be a marketing genius. Twitter lets you be yourself. Tweet about the things that matter to you, to your customers, and to your industry … just as you would (and probably do) talk with other people who share the same passions you do. If, every so often (perhaps 1 in 10 Tweets), you say something actively self-promotional, it works.

MARKETING WIN

Fiction authors are instructed, "Show, don't tell." The same advice applies to marketing, especially in a small business. Don't try to convince people you're wonderful. Don't beat your chest with outrageous claims.

Instead, simply show your expertise. Followers will draw their own conclusion, based on your willingness to share, the topics you talk about, and the information you impart.

Consumers using Twitter might use it to opine about sports or the latest TV show, which are personal passions. If you run or market a small business, then we trust you are crazy about what you do, whether it's pool care or high-tech seeds. All you need to do is share those passions and your target customers will respond to them, and to you.

For example, Latham Hi-Tech Seeds (**@LathamSeeds**) absolutely is marketing in these two Tweets:

> **@LathamSeeds** In 12 short hours, I'll be helping set up 4 Franklin County IA's inaugural #harvesttour. Looking forward 2 star gazing tonight w/ my family!
>
> **@LathamSeeds** Effective rootworm mgt may include insecticides, crop rotation & planting hybrids w/ multiple traits for RW resistance: bit.ly/qUBjHZ

The first Tweet shows that the family-owned, independent seed company is active in its community, and is run by real people (who apparently like stargazing). The second, which links to a blog post about agricultural issues, demonstrates that they know about raising crops. If you're in their target audience, you can only be impressed.

Conversing Is Easier Than Marketing

Even when small businesses care about marketing, often they're inconsistent about its use. Many tiny companies, especially, operate on feast or famine. They market and communicate when they're hungry for work, and they put their heads down to concentrate on delivering when they're busy.

That can be bad news for a Twitter feed. If you only Tweet when you're idle, you look absent when you're busy. If you're busy for a long time (say, *cough* writing a book), would-be customers might think you're gone.

Yet we all know that people want to hire others (especially service workers such as consultants) who are high in demand. More than one client has commented to us, "Do you have time to take this on? You said on your Twitter feed that you're overloaded." (The obvious answer is, of course, "I always have time for you!")

The lesson is, keep communicating even when you're busy with a project. If you adopt a conversational style of marketing—sharing the items that interest you, responding to others' Tweets—it can cover up the fact that you've no time to blog or do larger-scale marketing activities. Plus, it's okay to talk about what it is you're working on, in a general way (see that Tweet about bug-stomping); that shows you're busy instead of idle—and again, you're demonstrating your expertise.

If you know you are headed into a busy period, such as an accountant bearing down on tax season, plan ahead. Schedule a few Tweets a day. Check in once a day for a few minutes, and schedule a couple of Retweets. That keeps your stream active, even when your attention is focused on a deadline.

And even when you're slammed with work, you want to use Twitter just to stay in touch with colleagues, your industry, and the rest of the world.

Managing Your Time

Consider the challenges of working effectively and efficiently. Automating Tweets, scheduling them, and a strong monitoring plan can make your workflow easier to manage. Learn to plan your workday, wherein you Tweet in blocks of time.

Because nobody is looking over your shoulder, it's easy to get distracted by the cool stuff you find online. Be careful that you don't get caught in the weeds. It can be addicting and a tremendous time-suck if you don't manage yourself properly. (Not that we are speaking personally, you understand.)

One of the great things about working for or owning a small business is that you can operate independently. But it has its downside: nobody jiggles your elbow to remind you how much you intended to accomplish today. If you're just goofing around online, you're forgetting the point of using Twitter for marketing. All of us can do this once in a while, and sometimes we should, when we discover a cache of useful information that helps us with our work. (For small business owners especially, this is the only "on-the-job training" we get.) But it's very easy to lose the whole morning by following links to frivolous things or reading everybody's activities while ignoring your own responsibilities.

To avoid Twitter addiction, set clear metrics. Constantly ask yourself these questions:

- Am I connecting with people who I otherwise would not be connected to?
- Have I received any PR or referrals from Twitter in the last month?
- Is my audience growing?
- Am I learning from my network?

If you can answer the majority of these questions with a resounding yes, then consider your time on Twitter worthwhile. If that's not happening for you, revisit your Twitter goals so that the time spent is an investment in your business rather than a clever way to procrastinate. (But first, let us show you this great kitty video.)

Finding Suppliers and Customers

Whether you're a solo business or a small one, Twitter can be a great channel for sourcing suppliers and customers. A local business can reach a national audience by being personal, establishing thought leadership, and listening to the needs of others.

Twitter lets small businesses find suppliers and customers in totally new ways. One case study illuminates the resources available to even the tiniest company.

A Fashionable Example

New York City–based Black and Denim (**@blackanddenim**) is an eight-person apparel company that has turned to social media in a big way—with big results.

In a matter of weeks, Black and Denim got three new stores to carry its clothing after the apparel company followed the stores on Twitter.

They aren't looking only for new retail outlets. "If a follower really likes the product, he becomes a brand ambassador," says brand manager Roberto Torres. "He will go to his local independent boutique and request the owners to take a look at our line."

By interacting with the people who wear the clothes—not just the stores that already carry the brand—Black and Denim creates active free representatives for the brand who truly believe in the product.

But it's not just sales:

- Via Twitter, they network with other apparel companies, especially those who share a sense of importance about being made in America. They compare notes on streamlining operations, understanding conflicts, and sharing ideas.
- They've found designers and other service suppliers. "We have discovered a ton of up-and-coming artists (photographers, designers, fashion moguls, and new media artists) that have found inspiration in Black & Denim, and vice versa," says Torres.
- Press response has been even better than sales, Torres says. "We have been featured in two national brand blogs," he crows—one in Miami, the other nationwide. "We went from 300 followers to over 2,600—in less than 21 days."

No PR, Just Outreach

Plenty of small businesses aim for the same goals, but few are as deliberate in their efforts. "We don't Tweet stuff like, 'OMG, This is the best brand and you are going to make tons of money,'" says Torres.

The company knows who they want to reach and they go after them directly. Armed with a list of 2,000 clothing boutiques, they narrowed their search to find stores with an online presence. "If they have Facebook and Twitter, we approach them like that. Some stores are active; some are not," Torres explains.

When **@blackanddenim** follows one of those boutiques, the store gets a notification that they have a new follower. "They get the opportunity to decide whether they want to follow us or not. We do custom Tweets about them and their store location, and we ask them questions."

Black and Denim uses Twitter as an introduction; they don't expect to get a new store from a single Tweet. "We ask them for traffic, location, clients, price points. We share tips on how to make their store better. We try to show how our business model aligns with theirs. That we have a sellable product," Torres says. "The network expands and reciprocates as much as you put into it."

Their outreach program doesn't stop with existing industry lists. They used tweepi.com to find men's blogs that gained national notoriety (that is, industry insiders). "We then looked at who those are following. From who they follow, we divided the categories into fashion, tech, sports, etc. We tailor our Tweets for that day based on who we just followed," says Torres.

"Twitter allows us the opportunity to get the party started," he says. "It bridges time and space (distance). Since they can answer at their own leisure, we don't have to be in the same city to talk to them."

Could a big business have done all that? Possibly. Is that success story tailor-made for a small business? Absolutely.

The Least You Need to Know

- Small businesses have the freedom to communicate with more personality—which usually comes naturally.
- Twitter is ideal for small businesses that are uncomfortable with marketing, because it isn't "marketing." It's just being yourself and demonstrating your passion and knowledge.
- Don't be shy of personal outreach. A small business's ability to respond swiftly is an important advantage in connecting with customers and influencers.

How to Use Twitter in a Retail Environment

Chapter **16**

In This Chapter

- The unique challenges retail stores face online
- Identifying Twitter users at the hyper-local level
- The importance of location-based marketing
- Using coupons, contests, and other promotions

Retail businesspeople work hard. You're on your feet all day, you have a never-ending parade of impatient people demanding immediate attention, and, if the retail business is also a small company trying to survive in a big-box world and fighting for attention among online vendors, the competition is relentless and fierce. Yet marketing budgets are slim to none.

Happily, Twitter is an astonishing resource that addresses many of these challenges (except the sore feet). Going digital is among the best approaches a retail business can adopt for optimal exposure. In this chapter, we show you how to apply your existing hands-on skills to Twitter, and teach you about unique services to attract more attention.

What Makes Retail Different?

Traditional marketing is a passive, one-way experience. You advertise products and services—on the radio, in the newspaper, on websites—and then you cross your fingers and hope people will respond. You scatter seeds in well-prepared ground, and then wait for the business to grow.

However, retail businesses have always been the opposite; they are inherently social and dynamic. In retail environments, every interaction can produce direct business value with a lasting result, because the customers are positioned (quite literally) to return to the store if they are treated well.

A salesperson in a boutique store can influence your buying decision with a recommendation. You might visit a new gift shop at the mall because you heard about it from a neighbor. You return to a corner coffee shop because every time you go in, the proprietor knows exactly how you like your latte.

For instance, we met a salesperson in a dress department. She kept files on favorite clients and called them when new dresses arrived that she knew they would like. Twitter allows you to do that on a larger scale by sharing photos of new arrivals and even sending @replies directed to your best clients.

Personal Service Is in Retail's DNA

With any retail business, personal service is expected. Unless your business has nothing but self-service kiosks, your unique selling points are the knowledge of your staff, their empathy with the customer, and a sense of community.

That puts you ahead of many other businesses that attempt social media marketing. You know community and personality. They struggle to adopt it.

On Twitter, you can go above and beyond—publicly. And maybe get some extra attention as a result.

For example, PR and social media pro Peter Shankman (**@petershankman**) is a frequent diner at Morton's Steakhouse (**@Mortons**), the sort of customer who demonstrates why retail loyalty programs are so effective. Morton's knows Shankman by name based on his mobile phone number, no matter which city he calls from to make a reservation. If anyone has earned special attention from the restaurant, it's Shankman—not to mention the business's awareness of his 100,000+ Twitter followers.

Nonetheless, before he boarded a plane from Tampa to Newark, Shankman jokingly asked Morton's Steakhouse via Twitter if they could meet him with a porterhouse steak when he landed. Lo and behold, they did.

Shankman blogged:

> *Looking for my driver, I saw my name, waved to him, and started walking to the door of EWR, like I'd done hundreds of times before.*
>
> *"Um, Mr. Shankman," he said.*
>
> *I turned around.*
>
> *"There's a surprise for you here."*
>
> *I turned to see that the driver was standing next to someone else, who I just assumed was another driver he was talking to. Then I noticed the "someone else" was in a tuxedo.*
>
> *And he was carrying a Morton's bag.*

Needless to say, the incident earned the restaurant a lot of positive attention and, consequently, many more followers.

MARKETING WIN

Do your best to know your local influencers and most loyal customers as well as which of them use Twitter. Focus your efforts on how you can engage with them to provide superlative service—and perhaps have them share their experience.

Retail Depends on Local Word of Mouth

It's wonderful that your staff's behavior can generate public acclaim and better awareness. But be aware that public response can backfire, too.

Restaurants are among the most visible businesses on Twitter because their customers want to interact and respond. They share reviews and photos of dishes with their friends, use location services like Foursquare to announce where they are, and—this is where it gets dangerous—they call out establishments that disappoint them.

"The way you show you're enjoying [your meal] is that you Tweet about it," Paula Murphy told the *Houston Press.* Murphy's firm, Patterson & Murphy, handles PR for a number of Houston restaurants. "But just as quickly as they could say something positive, they could say something offensive and negative."

If your customer gets great service, she may tell all her friends. If another customer has a lousy experience, he will Tweet about it, too. Consider the response of one Houston-area restaurateur (**@DownHouseHTX**) when a customer wrote a negative Tweet as she was dining. In this case, reported the *Houston Press*, the customer was kicked out.

> *Matsu [the customer] has achieved mild, local notoriety for her late-night Tweets, even recently winning a Houston Press Web Award for that very activity. Down House, for its part, has achieved a reputation in the short time that it's been open for having capricious service. The two collided in a Twitter-fueled spectacle that resulted in general manager Forrest DeSpain calling the bar, speaking shortly with Matsu, and asking her to be ejected from his establishment.*
>
> *"She called him a twerp," DeSpain said by phone yesterday afternoon. DeSpain runs the Twitter account for Down House and was agitated that someone would bully his bartender, as he saw it, and took action despite not being at the restaurant that night. "I immediately called up here and talked to her for a few minutes and asked her if she had any kinder words." She didn't, DeSpain said, so he asked her to leave.*

Matsu responded with several negative Tweets, most of which would make any business owner cringe. It's one thing to deal with problem customers one on one—and even more of a problem when they have a large Twitter following.

It's All Local

Many other businesses want Twitter users to pick up the phone, to visit an e-commerce site, or just to have warm, fuzzy thoughts about the company (that is, branding). For retail businesses, the ultimate goal is to get people off their butts and physically make a trip into the store. That's different, but it's also a plus, because your followers can take direct action.

It's easy for businesses to adopt the mindset that Twitter is a global tool, not a local tool. However, several features are tuned to doing business locally.

First, Twitter searches can be made based on area code or other location data.

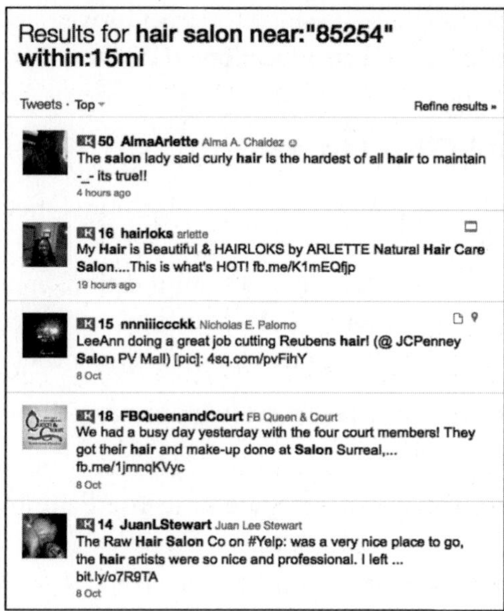

Twitter's Advanced Search lets you find Tweets published down to the zip code.

Several Twitter add-ons (most of them free) expand on this functionality, including Twellow.com, localtweeps.com, and localchirps.com.

A savvy retailer can look for local people Tweeting about his business area. A restaurateur might search for Tweets using keywords like "hungry" or "where to eat" and send an @Mention offering a free dessert as an incentive. A hair salon owner might answer questions about hair styles for curly hair. It's always good to communicate with prospective customers—and even more so when they're in driving distance.

When Brett was traveling to a Long Island vineyard, he Tweeted that he was headed to the North fork of Long Island. A few wineries Tweeted invitations to visit. Whether your business is in the tourism or hospitality business or a hard goods retailer, you can get new customers simply by Tweeting at the right place and the right time. When they are thinking about buying, be the company that comes to mind.

Think competitively, too, especially if you're the up-and-coming business that has to woo people from an entrenched alternative. For example, look for tweets about visits to competitors' locations and offer a discount to try yours next time:

> Them: Having wings at BDW's … love the hot sauce
>
> You: Since you love wings, we would love you to try ours. Download this coupon and save 10%.

The advantage? Other people will see your Tweet as well, and may download the coupon, too. It's a great way to introduce lots of clients to your product.

A-Fordable One-on-One Marketing

"While we provide full customer support via traditional means, we have also taken our efforts online in order to provide an even easier way for customers to engage with us," says Zach Bello, the marketing and communications manager for Lebanon Ford, a Ford dealership in Lebanon, Ohio. "We're using social media to interact with our customers on a level that they might not have yet at another car dealer."

> **@lebanonford @jamesdefelice** How did everything turn out w/ the F-150? Hope all is well :) ^JC

> **@lebanonford** Top 5 Ugliest State #License Plate Designs bit.ly/q45qi0 ^JC

Don't expect customers to flock to your Twitter feed. "It's more about going out and finding the customer rather than them coming out and seeking us," says Bello. "We use Twitter as a way to listen rather than sell."

Bello customized Twitter searches around the dealership's geographical location within 50 miles, targeting keywords like "car" and "auto." He adds, "In addition to picking up anyone near us who is talking about their car, we also search for people who are talking about our competitors. This way, when we notice someone has had a bad experience somewhere else, we can jump in and offer a solution."

One of Bello's Twitter searches found someone complaining about his unhappiness with Toyota Customer Service; he had gotten the runaround with his local Toyota dealership. "He Tweeted, asking why Toyota Customer care wasn't listening to him, and we responded, 'While they might not be listening, *we* are,'" says Bello. The customer brought his Toyota to the Lebanon Ford dealership for the repair.

MARKETING WIN

Retailers shouldn't worry much about dispassionate metrics. Even though you want to measure your efforts, the hardest thing is tracking ROI—and that may be nearly impossible. Says Bello, "When it comes to Twitter, the ability to find that conversion isn't always there. It's very hard, if not impossible, to see that 'Tweet A caused this person to purchase B.' This is why some companies don't even bother with [Twitter], because they can't see the ROI behind it. Twitter, and social media in general, is really more about connecting and engaging with the customer."

"Businesses need to get away from seeing the different social media avenues as a way to sell their product," Bello advises. "It helps to build a relationship that will ultimately build trust with them, which in turn can result in a sale. But going into social media with the mindset of just selling more product isn't the way to get started."

One demonstration of the car dealership's commitment is 24/7 customer engagement from the two people staffing the social media channels. "If we get a Mention at 2 A.M., our phones will go off and we will respond. While the likelihood of that happening isn't very high, customers like to know that it's available to them," he says.

Twitter is a great way to sort of "humanize" your brand, he asserts. "Speak as a human, rather than as the brand or company as a whole," says Bello. "This makes it more personal and allows for a more natural and comfortable conversation."

Tips for Retailers

Other categories of business, such as computer consulting or household goods manufacturers, rely on branding and indirect methods of convincing people that, really, you are the coolest folks in the world to deal with. Retailers have more options.

Give Customers a Reason to Come In

For retailers, Twitter isn't an opportunity to change the way business is done. Rather, it's a great way to leverage personal relationships, word of mouth, and simple one-to-one gestures. These are things you already do—now you have a new venue in which to do them, reaching new customers and building loyalty among your fans.

MARKETING WIN

We might argue that retail was the original social media, since local businesses have long understood the value of knowing their customers and creating a personal connection.

Rather than being intimidated by Twitter, think of it as an attempt to recreate the retail experience from a time when a store knew who you were and what your likes and dislikes were.

Retailers think obsessively about what it takes to bring someone into the store. Whether you're used to advertising in the local newspaper circular or you donate time to the local Chamber of Commerce to develop others' awareness of your company, you work to encourage a would-be customer to try your shop, and to come in today. Many of the same efforts translate to Twitter directly, such as offering sales promotions.

Others are new, such as curating and sharing information that makes your business appealing. You have special knowledge and can offer Twitter users nearly instant gratification (because you're just down the street). Let your followers hear about it.

For example, restaurants soon learn that photo-sharing of their dishes and signature drinks are paramount in commanding response. "This response is an open door to initiate conversation. Walk through quickly!" says publicist Mary Winkenwerder.

Extend the personal connection you make in the store. Just as an in-store salesperson might make a recommendation, the same advice can be shared as a Tweet.

For example, Nordstrom, the national department store, encourages its employees to use Twitter to better connect with customers. **@NordstromDave**, who works at the flagship store in Seattle, casually asks the customers he interacts with if they're on Twitter. If they say yes, he hands them a business card with his Twitter ID. His account shows a steady stream of personal customer recommendations, along with style tips and advice.

> **@NordstromDave** Travel much? Just received the newest color of Tumi's vapor series. **@NordstromSEA** twitpic.com/6o1awb
>
> **@NordstromDave @james3332** we do have the solos in both black and white … I'll DM the price

In some cases, when **@NordstromDave** is familiar with a customer's personal style, he sends a direct message tipping them off to a new product arrival. The real-time tip often generates immediate sales from the customer.

Keeping the Conversation Going After the Sale

In traditional retailing, the customer buys something and walks out the door. Several marketing techniques have been introduced in the last several years to establish an ongoing relationship, such as asking customers to sign up for electronic newsletters and loyalty cards. One of the newest is to ask the customer to follow you on Twitter, and provide incentives to make it worthwhile.

If a customer follows your Twitter account, you get more than the opportunity to share news, tips, event announcements, or sales promotions (all of which work fine in email newsletters). You can keep in touch with potential and existing customers. You can create a relationship that keeps your business top-of-mind, and—based on the customer responding to your Tweets or Retweeting the information you impart—encourage those customers to tell friends about your services.

Using Sales, Coupons, and Promotions

Retail stores are probably most familiar with sales and promotions. Consumers are motivated sharply by the opportunity to save money, and a Twitter-specific promotion can both give a customer a reason to visit the retail store today and provide you with tracking information.

Creating Trackable Promotions

The most obvious promotion is to create a Twitter-specific coupon. It's often hard to measure the direct value of Twitter, but this is one of the cases where it's easy to see an immediate return.

By Tweeting coded links to purchase pages, Best Buy (**@BestBuy**), the national electronics retailer, can monitor referral traffic to its website and, using promo codes, drive in-store purchases.

> **@BestBuy** Debut CD from country singer Hunter Hayes out tomorrow, $5.99 with this coupon! Valid 10/11-10/15. tinyurl.com/5umtec7 via **@BestBuyMusic**

You have a few options when it comes to setting up a Twitter coupon. You can do it yourself, or you can outsource the promotion to another agency.

Tweeting a promo code is straightforward. Include a discount code in your Tweet, or provide a link to a coupon that can be printed and redeemed in person. Make the code specific to Twitter so that you can understand which customers came from this channel.

> **@CarlsbadTavern** It's #NewMexicoMonday and the word of the day is "sopapilla." Say it to your server to receive a free appetizer today only! Enjoy!

> **@MuseumWayPearls** Take 10% off your entire purchase of #pearls with #coupon code "september" http://www.museumwaypearls.com/ #wedding

Also consider Twitter sweepstakes promotions. If users Tweet a certain message or use a certain hashtag, they can be automatically entered to win a prize.

If that's too much work—and for many retailers, tracking promotions is yet another task they don't have time for—there may be benefits in using a service to manage online promotions. Among the possibilities are these:

Klout, a service that measures social media influence, and ties free offers to qualified social media pundits. With Klout's perks program, your business distributes "perks" or coupons to the Klout users you deem to be both relevant and influential in your space.

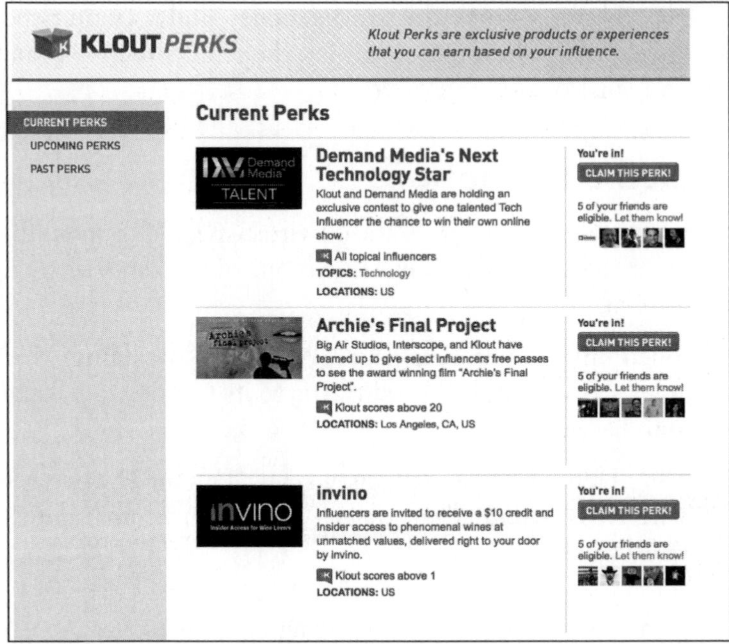

Klout lets businesses choose those who are eligible for perks based on topic influence, score, or other criteria.

Cloud:Flood is worth checking out if you're willing to gain people's interest by giving something away (cloudflood.com). You create a free product to give away to your website visitors, such as an eBook. You make a button on the Cloud:Flood site, linking to the file and a promotional page. You put the button that you just made on Cloud:Flood next to the freebie offering on your website. Site visitors see the freebie, and—here's where Twitter comes in—they must Tweet your link (or share it on Facebook) in order to get the free item.

OfferedLocal is a location-based marketing tool that makes it simple to create promotions, which can be distributed to your customers via Facebook and Twitter as well as location-based check-in services like Foursquare, driving more business to your place of business.

A Pearl of a Prize

Don't underestimate the value of a good online promotion.

Museum Way Pearls (**@MuseumWayPearls**), a luxury pearl jewelry company based in Boston, held a "Twitter Trivia Treasure Hunt." The company dropped several clues on Twitter, says Jacqui Trotta. Trotta did a random drawing from followers' responses and gave away gift certificates and a (very pretty) black saltwater pearl necklace. The winner of the necklace happened to be a blogger and did a write-up about the pearls on her blog—generating even more visibility for the small business.

The company also leveraged the contest for additional coverage. "We planned all of the questions in advance and put rules and regulations around the event," says Trotta. "We wrote up a press release and sent it to the masses. We were picked up in Luxist, National Jeweler, and more."

The winning name picked had to have all of the correct answers, but the barrier to entry was kept low. "They were all pretty basic questions about pearls and pearl jewelry," Trotta explains.

Sometimes people respond to a "special offer," take the freebie, and are never seen again. Museum Way Pearls had much better results. "Many of these people are still followers," says Trotta. "They shop throughout the year and during the holidays when we offer promotions on our Twitter page."

Create Incentives to Share

The "win" for many retailers is to motivate people to communicate about your business. An influential Twitter user sharing with her followers that she bought a product from your store can be worth far more than the cost of a promotion.

Incentivize customers to Tweet a message about your business, which "unlocks" or reveals a discount or coupon.

For example, Tasti D-Lite, the frozen dessert company, created a rewards program on its website. In addition to a regular in-store point system, the company added an extra social layer to motivate customers to share.

The business encourages Tasti D-Lite patrons to link their rewards card with social networks. By connecting to Facebook, Twitter, and Foursquare, consumers receive one point for every purchase they share at a Tasti D-Lite location. The company also regularly encourages people to respond in a public manner—which further widens their visibility.

> **@tastidlite** The first person to Tweet @ us once we hit 2,000 followers will receive a prize. Must be picked up at location 15888 Broadway, NYC

Building on Location-Based Services

You don't always have to reach out to your geographical community. A new set of services called *location-based services* (*LBS*) offers retailers the opportunity to increase in-store visits and foot traffic. Using LBS (sometimes called geo-location applications), the customers can find you.

DEFINITION

Location-based services (LBS) are a broad range of services that are based on or enhanced by information about the physical location of a user or device.

A whole array of mobile applications encourage users to self-report their whereabouts and to make recommendations to friends. These LBS applications, such as Foursquare, Loopt, and Gowalla, rely on mobile devices such as smartphones and iPads; they don't require the user to have a social media account.

However, all of them can announce the user's location on Twitter and Facebook, so it's worth the effort to sync your Twitter accounts with these services—and to explore the benefits you should offer their subscribers.

According to the Pew Internet Project, more than a quarter of American adults use a mobile or social LBS of some kind. Twenty-eight percent use phones to get directions or recommendations based on their current location. A much smaller number (5 percent of cell owners) use their phones to check in to locations using geosocial services such as Foursquare or Gowalla, or set up social media services such as Facebook, Twitter, or LinkedIn so that their location is automatically included in their posts on those services.

Those numbers are small, but the LBS marketplace is still young.

The Gamification of Marketing

One reason that LBS has taken off is that it turns a user's whereabouts into both a game and a recommendation service. As a user, you "check in" to venues as you move about a city, airport, or wherever else you might be.

Once you check in, your Foursquare friends know where you are. You can leave tips and unlock badges along the way. In many ways, Foursquare surfaces serendipitous encounters.

And—this is where retailing comes in—once a user checks in, Foursquare presents her with automated recommendations from previous Foursquare visitors for nearby restaurants, cafés, and other locations.

People can be motivated by "special offers," but they are even more captivated by games. In Foursquare, users earn points every time they check in, which can lead to virtual badges. By checking in, they earn freebies and coupon offers.

To get these offers, a user must become the mayor of a particular location, which means she checked in at a location more often than any other Foursquare user. The vendor determines the reward; for example, the mayor of a bar might get her first drink of the night free.

Foursquare for Retailers

The hook for Twitter marketing is that users can publish their check-ins on social media, which includes a link to the business location.

> **@Brett** Battlefield! (@ New York Penn Station w/ 72 others) goo.gl/13y8i
>
> **@misterclem** I just ousted Marine C. as the mayor of Pharmacie de l'Horloge on **@foursquare**! 4sq.com/bgOoeV
>
> **@newmediajim** I'm at Roti Mediterranean Grill (1747 Pennsylvania Ave Nw, at 18th St. NW, Washington) 4sq.com/pJXnSP

For merchants, the process is to claim your venue, create specials, and, optionally, use Foursquare's merchant platform. Among the possible specials, Foursquare suggests the following:

- A discount with purchase, such as "spend $50 and get $10 off"
- Something for free, such as a free dessert with the purchase of two entrées

- Special treatment, such as a seat upgrade
- Rewards for repeat customers, such as "free coffee on your fifth visit"

Business owners can get visitor statistics and other information to understand what's working.

This presents a huge opportunity for local businesses to increase their reputation and generate foot traffic. The clear benefit is more visibility for your business and explicit recommendations by users to their own followers. Foursquare users may not know your business is on Twitter, but you can benefit from their check-ins nonetheless.

MARKETING WIN

Butterlane, a cupcake shop in New York, Velcro'ed an iPad to the wall of its East Village shop, encouraging customers to use Twitter, Facebook, and Foursquare while waiting in line. What can you do in your shop to encourage participation?

Foursquare isn't the only location-based application. It is, however, the dominant player. Do investigate its competitors; the field is evolving quickly. However, this overview should give you a sense of what's possible with location-based marketing.

The Least You Need to Know

- When interacting with customers in person, follow up online and ask them if they're on Twitter.
- Use personal recommendations and one-to-one dialogue to your advantage. The more you can make customers feel special, the likelier they are to purchase from your brand.
- Take advantage of location-based services to attract more business.
- Use promotions to entice customers into the store.

Using Twitter as a Customer Service Tool

Chapter 17

In This Chapter

- Encouraging happy customers to become evangelists
- Turning "bug fixes" into opportunities to demonstrate your commitment to quality
- Incorporating customer feedback into product development
- Setting up your Twitter customer service workflow

Few businesses consider their customer support efforts to be a marketing role. Usually, companies think of technical support and customer service as a back-office necessity that ought to be hidden away. After all, if people need support, the implication is that the company's products are imperfect.

Yet by publicly providing help to customers and employees, you can build confidence in your brand and earn new customers. In this chapter, we show you how.

The Marketing Benefits of Good Customer Service

In previous chapters we have highlighted the benefits of engaging with customers and creating meaningful connections with them. Using Twitter for customer service is simply an extension of this effort.

As a marketer representing a brand, you are making a promise to customers and prospects, and setting their expectations for the quality of your goods and services.

Failing to deliver on that promise ultimately results in complaints and low customer retention. However, great customer service can turn critics into evangelists and transform one-time customers into repeat fans.

Online customer support is no longer an option: it's expected. According to a Burson-Marsteller survey, 19 percent of Twitter users seek customer support each month. If you aren't there to service them … your competition is.

The Payoffs of Public Support

People want to do business with companies that work to make us happy. We acknowledge that things aren't always ideal the first time; the restaurant order is late, or the flight is delayed. We're all human. But a company that goes out of its way to resolve a problem is valued far more than one that never lifts a finger to help.

For example, this customer submitted an online order of chicken wings. It didn't arrive on time. But the business ended up with at least one success story:

> **@glfceo** They lost my order, they apologized, refunded & served extra—gr8 #custserv **@wingstop**

This isn't just a case study; it's dinnertime. After seeing **@glfceo**'s Tweet, I (Esther) looked at the account and the website. Even if **@wingstop** doesn't have the best Twitter timeline in the world (obviously they haven't read all our advice), the company's timeline makes it clear what they sell and that they pay attention to customers. If they had a store near me, I would have ordered their wings! All in the name of book research, you understand.

Dealing with Failure in Public

Not every Twitter conversation about your company will be a positive one. Customer service tales, whether on Twitter or elsewhere, range from the mundane data dump to complex problem-solving. They come in several flavors: the good, the bad, and the ugly.

You have both an opportunity and a risk when you use Twitter as a customer support channel. The reward is that you help customers who might not have picked up the phone to call; you give them an opportunity to learn how dedicated your company is to customer happiness. It's a great way to get positive feedback, but it can just as easily turn into a fire hose of angry sentiments and skepticism.

However, unlike offline interactions, all Twitter conversations between brands and consumers are public and documented. Both your voice and the customer's voice are heard.

And that's its strength. You will find that people are delighted by contact with the company. No matter how rocky the relationship starts out, usually the customers become fans and evangelists. Simply by monitoring what people say about you and responding to their frustrations, you're using Twitter better than 95 percent of the companies out there.

In many cases, customers with complaints simply want to be heard and acknowledged. They want to feel that the company cares. It's not accidental that several well-known customer support IDs include "cares" in the name and are willing to help customers fix problems.

Good customer service, whether it's offline or on Twitter, should be personal, solution-oriented, and repeatable. The customer may not be a complete fan—you can't make everyone happy—but your actions usually dispel hostile or negative sentiments.

Turning Frowns Upside Down

One incident shows how a company can deal with an angry customer spewing vitriol across Twitter: the Kevin Smith and Southwest Air case study.

In February 2010, actor and director Kevin Smith boarded a Southwest Airlines flight. As an overweight passenger, he was asked to leave the plane as part of the airline's "size policy." Smith immediately took to this Twitter timeline and ranted:

> Dear **@SouthwestAir**—I know I'm fat, but was Captain Leysath really justified in throwing me off a flight for which I was already seated?

He then began a series of additional Tweets complaining about his experience.

Within six hours (on a Sunday), a customer service representative attempted to call Smith. The Southwest representative publicly Tweeted the following:

> **@ThatKevinSmith** Ok, I'll be sure to check it out. Hopefully you received our voicemail earlier this evening.
>
> **@ThatKevinSmith** Again, I'm very sorry for the experience you had tonight. Please let me know if there is anything else I can do.

Kevin Smith then Tweeted the following response:

> Via **@SouthwestAir** "Hopefully you received our voicemail earlier this evening." All lines checked, no voicemail message on any 323. Try again.

A few Tweets were exchanged, and it was clear that Southwest would not get Smith to retract his negative sentiments.

What Southwest Air did to follow up on the incident is a testament to its internal process and communication. Here's how they made the best out of a sticky situation, and what they did right:

- Someone was working on Sunday. They had designated decision-makers on call to handle tough scenarios, and guidelines to help staff know when to call in for reinforcements.
- They responded immediately. Rather than let the customer stew, the customer support staff engaged in a public conversation that signaled to lurkers that the company was listening and was working on a resolution.
- A vice president called Smith on the phone. 140 characters is too limited for emotional situations. When possible, take conversations offline.
- **@SouthwestAir** responded to everyone who Tweeted about the situation and explained the company policy. A blog post was published explaining the company rules and its remorse for what happened to Mr. Smith.

Silence is not an option in social media, especially when it comes to customer support. Although the dialogue might not always be favorable, a visible display that you're doing your best to make happy customers earns respect—and customer loyalty.

MARKETING WIN

When a company cares about making its customers happy—and lets that dedication show in public—people respond. You don't have to evangelize. Your customers will do that for you.

Market Research Opportunity

Social media isn't a new intersection for Marketing and Customer Support. In the 1980s, Borland International set up a customer support forum on CompuServe, which mainly focused on answering customers' technical questions about Turbo Pascal and other software.

What was exceptional about Borland's activity was that the customer service issues were fed into the software design process. That is, areas of frequent problems indicated to Borland's software developers that the company's products needed improvement in those areas. Moreover, the company CEO, Philippe Kahn, often engaged with users and helped to solve programming problems.

Borland enjoyed enviable loyalty for years, because the business turned a "support" activity into market research.

Customer support data gives you an insight into problems that you'd never think to ask in a traditional market research survey. That's an opportunity for innovation.

Look for the issues that come up regularly: How can the business improve its products and services so that these issues never arise? And what do users praise most often? Perhaps you should highlight those advantages in marketing materials.

Customer Service Workflow

Because your business aims to use Twitter primarily for marketing, you need to ensure that there's good communication between the customer service department and the marketing staff.

Customer service likely already has its contacts among the technical staff and other departments, but the speed of response on Twitter requires much better workflow.

Creating Cheat Sheets

Your customer support staff probably already has a checklist of questions to ask people who need support. That "messaging document" explains what to do or how to handle certain situations, including answers to a frequently asked questions (FAQ) guide to reference.

You can use the existing documentation, but consider the following additions:

- Create a list of answers your staff can Tweet in 140 characters or fewer.
- Add a brief "Twitter 101" one-pager that highlights definitions (DMs, @'s, RT's, etc.) and basics, so that new customer support staff aren't lost.
- Incorporate contact information for personnel who can make key decisions during off-hours.

Your website probably already has FAQs and other in-depth information meant to help customers. It's fine to suggest specific links to customers who don't know how to find it. That saves your time-starved customers from endless clicking on websites or navigating through lengthy telephone menus ("For a list of ways that technology has not improved the quality of life, press 3").

TWITTER TIP

Customers' need for FAQs and other information that's already on your site can be an early indicator that sites or menus need a redesign. If you get lots of Twitter inquiries about return policies, for example, you probably should make that information easier to find.

Interacting with the Social Media Team

The relationship between marketing and customer service is no longer what it used to be. Rather than exist as completely independent functions, the two must work closer together to create strong relationships between the brand and the customer.

Whether a Twitter account is owned by customer support or marketing, both teams need to be on the same page as far as goals, process, and procedures. At the end of the day, your objective is the same: to deliver an exceptional brand experience and improve the overall success of the company. Have regular meetings and briefings to discuss progress on the account. Share best practices when applicable, and leverage each other's work.

Make a point of setting user expectations. If you don't want users to associate your Twitter account with customer support, disclose that in your bio or background. Make it clear what your Twitter account is for and the best point of contact for customer support issues.

Tell Twitter users when your customer service staff are available; many companies include this information in the bio paragraph or as part of the Twitter background. Include the hours service is available if it's not offered 24/7, other customer service contact details, and any related Twitter hashtags used by your company.

Customer support can source testimonials and insights on behalf of the marketing team. The marketing team should brief customer support on major initiatives, campaigns, or promos in the event that they have to reference or support a particular program. ("I thought I'd get two bobbleheads with that special offer, and I got only one!")

As much as Twitter is about being transparent and open publicly, any organization using Twitter should also embrace this philosophy internally.

The Essential Customer Service Process

As reported by Tiffany Maleshefski in an Information Management newsletter, Frank Eliason (**@frankeliason**), who reinvented the customer service wheel at Comcast with **@ComcastCares** (and is now at Citigroup), summarized the customer service role in three steps:

- Apologize and acknowledge that there is a problem.
- Speed is imperative. "Respond within a few minutes if you can, especially for complaints," Eliason said.
- Be open and transparent, explain what happened as best you can, and resolve the matter quickly.

When you find someone complaining, @reply him to ask if you can help. Don't take an arrogant tone and don't tell the customer he screwed up.

> **@ATT @inthesegenes** Sorry to hear that, if you provide your zip code we'd be happy to look into this for you!

Ask if he'd like you to intervene and provide him the information they need. This may require an open conversation on Twitter, as the following example shows. Overall, that's a good thing because it demonstrates your company is ready for a dialogue that results in a happy user.

> **@louisgray** To enable Disqus, I need to enable Blogger Layouts. To do that, I need to be off FTP, and use Google custom domains. Too much work involved.
>
> **@danielha @louisgray** doh. how can we make it easier for you?

For the initial contact, sending an @reply works best. First, there are no restrictions on who you can reply to; plus, it provides a public and transparent face to your customer service. Others can see what you're doing, which helps reassure customers. It may even solve problems they were going to ask you about, saving you additional time.

But build an efficient and elegant way to take a conversation off Twitter and transfer it to email or phone.

If a problem is sensitive, the customer is extraordinarily upset, or you want to get in contact with a customer fast, either send her a direct message or give her a fast way to contact you, such as an always-staffed email address or even a personal phone number. Let the customer know you're there to help and go with her step by step.

> **@DellCares @CarynColgan** Caryn, If we can help w/ an issue, pls follow & DM your order nbr or service tag & email. We're glad to help. ^SV

MARKETING WIN

Don't underestimate the importance of responding in a timely manner. According to Twitter CEO Dick Costolo (**@dickc**), 40 percent of all Tweets come from mobile devices. Thus people are likely to Tweet you a question while they are in a store or out and about. A reply two hours later might mean you missed an opportunity.

Helping Users Know You're Available

Some users are savvy enough to search for the vendor whose help they want. Most won't even think of it. Your best opportunity for customer service is an outreach campaign to search for those who have problems—likely an outgrowth of your initial listening campaign.

If customers don't know that you're standing by to do them a service, it's a shame for you both. Blogger Jon Stokes wrote about a commuter rail problem he encountered when his journey home was disrupted by cows! (Really, we don't make this stuff up.) "Even though it was a very unusual situation, I wasn't too surprised, as I'd already seen a Tweet from the Chiltern Railway account before I had even left the FreshNetworks office," he wrote.

"It took me a while to learn that Chiltern Railway (**@chilternrailway**) even had a Twitter account, which is a shame," he said. "Their execution of Twitter for customer service is excellent and it has changed my perception of them for the better. Chiltern Railway are the only train company I have available to me, and before following them on Twitter my perception of them was neutral at best—viewing them as a means to an end. Now though, I feel much more involved and informed about the company and their service, and feel more forgiving when unexpected incidents like this one take place."

See? Success!

But few people in his area of the UK know that the railway is ready to support users with train status updates or to respond to problems. As Stoke suggested, Chiltern Railway could improve its promotion. "A quick-fix suggestion to this could be that the in-carriage scrolling LED signs on trains (giving a Welcome message, next stop, and other stop information) could have a simple 'Follow **@chilternrailway** on Twitter for travel news and updates,' which would surely reach the eyes of thousands of smartphone-equipped commuters."

MARKETING WIN

Remember in Chapter 2 how the Arizona Diamondbacks plastered its Twitter IDs everywhere, even on the scoreboard? Advertise your Twitter presence to users on packaging, signage, wherever it's bound to be noticed. Users may not remember your Twitter ID, but when they need support, they will remember that you have one.

A public dialogue does present challenges for the marketing department, which usually prefers to pretend that everything the company sells works perfectly and that no one will encounter difficulties. But when well integrated into your organization, Twitter can streamline the whole customer service experience, bolster your team's effectiveness, and improve your bottom line.

The Least You Need to Know

- Twitter usually works best for providing quick answers to relatively simple questions, such as directing customers to the specific online location where they can find more detailed information.
- Let followers know publicly that you're handling a sticky customer issue, but handle it offline with direct messages or other media.
- Make sure that customers who need your help are aware that your staff are on Twitter and ready to assist them.

Using Twitter for Business Communications

Chapter 18

In This Chapter

- Recognizing how Twitter shakes up traditional communications departments
- Connecting with journalists
- Handling a PR flap that explodes on Twitter
- Integrating your paid media spend using Twitter's Sponsored Tweets programs

Most Twitter marketing is run by the marketing or public relations departments, at least in larger organizations. These professionals are aware of many of the tenets upon which Twitter is based, such as connecting to influential people and thinking about how the business presents itself.

That gives Public Relations (PR) and Marketing Communications (MarCom) departments a leg up on many other businesses. It also means a new set of challenges—because Twitter is "just like" what they have done before—and yet so very, very different.

In this chapter, we speak of MarCom and PR as if they're interchangeable roles. They are not always, but in regard to Twitter, the sensibilities that apply to one apply equally to the other.

What's Different About Twitter for MarCom

While small businesses can just barrel in and try whatever seems right, most PR and MarCom departments have to weigh everything against company reputation, the existing way the organization does business, and … well, politics.

MarCom is often at the center of the maelstrom of business decisions, in touch with most departments, from technical delivery to the supply chain. They listen to everyone and usually have a pulse on what is happening across the organization. Their productive internal conversations with stakeholders can create effective organizational models that drive collaboration and communication. They can tear down the "organizational silos" that prevent crucial collaboration.

Yet PR professionals often play the go-between role; they can speak for the company but they are not the company. They interpret the executives but they cannot make all the business's decisions.

A Cultural Transition

Often, for PR and MarCom professionals, the hardest transition to make in Twitter adoption is a matter of culture. Some PR people need to make a major adjustment; others take to it naturally. Their executive staff has to make that transition, too—and that can cause friction, even (or especially) when PR naturally "gets it."

We speak here in the context of a worst-case scenario. Your MarCom staff might find this all blissfully easy. If your business is "naturally" transparent and open and based on easy communication with its customers, you're apt to think that we're making a big, hairy deal over a simple set of issues. If you do, consider yourself lucky. Not all your colleagues are in as enviable a position.

Compare this to press relations. Some companies (and some individual PR professionals) easily establish relationships with the reporters whose attention they want to attract. Others maintain an adversarial stance with the media, or fumble when they try to contact a journalist, and never quite manage to do it right.

In the 20 years that Esther has been a tech industry journalist, she's encountered PR people who understand the value of building relationships, who have no qualms about letting a company exec speak directly to a reporter without a PR person on the phone, and who see themselves as communication enablers rather than gatekeepers preventing access. As wonderful as those PR people are, they are not always representative of their profession. In our experience, effective PR people don't grasp just *how* bad the bad ones are.

MARKETING WIN

Esther wrote a highly regarded essay, "Care and Feeding of the Press," used regularly in college classes for PR professionals. It's somewhat dated now, but still valued. Find it at netpress.org.

So it is with Twitter. Some PR professionals take to it as a duck to water, accurately seeing this as a new way to connect with the people who matter. Others confuse Twitter with an RSS feed, trying to control a message as if the only megaphone in the room is their own.

The Challenge of Conversation

Traditional "old school" PR aims to create, maintain, and protect an organization's reputation. They want to present a favorable image, and narrow the gap between what the business intends to project and the public's perception.

The traditional way that businesses go about this process—at least bigger companies—is to attempt to control the message. The PR staff works earnestly to ensure that anyone who speaks for the company stays on point, reflects only the vision that the business has decreed, and never suggests that the organization is imperfect.

In the worst cases, corporate communication efforts present the company as a faceless entity with no soul, no towering identity. Rather, it's seen as a series of products and processes with employees behind the curtains. The intent is usually well meaning; these firms aim to show a consistent image.

MARKETING WIN

Twitter is disruptive to MarCom because it forces brands to have a personality. In today's consumer-centric world, having a real personality means engaging with the individuals you want to attract.

Engagement increases the likelihood of criticism, but it's a risk worth taking. The payoff comes in the form of loyal customers who are evangelists and brand ambassadors. It happens when your brand becomes more than just a business, but something that is both memorable and meaningful. Whether it's an advertisement, a press release, or an event, marketers can and should treat every touch-point as an opportunity to spark a conversation.

Perhaps the most important concept for MarCom to grasp about using Twitter for business (which applies to social media in general) is that it's conversational marketing, an expression coined by author and entrepreneur John Battelle. He found that advertisers who used their ads "as invitations to conversation"—or turned online conversations into ad messages—outperformed those who viewed ads as unchanging packages to be posted next to content.

If you are used to "old style" marketing (what Battelle calls "package-goods media"), you may be very uncomfortable with the new era, and thus may put too much energy into trying to shoe-horn Twitter into the way you've always done things. That's a recipe for failure. As Battelle wrote, "Big-brand marketers are, as a group, not particularly thrilled with the idea that they might find themselves in an environment where folks might poke fun at them, or criticize them, or call them out. In short, they were not used to *being part of the conversation*. But brands are conversations, are they not? Interesting."

FAIL WHALE

Even Southwest Airlines, today considered a poster child for social media marketing, started out on Twitter by doing what many companies do: automating its account to sync with its RSS feed. "We were failing to respond to anyone who was trying to start a conversation with us … we quickly learned that every social media channel has a different audience and a different purpose," Christi Day, the airline's Media Specialist, told Business Insider.

"Everything is now done manually. It takes more time, but it's called 'social' media for a reason," she added.

Getting Buy-In from Company Executives

It's entirely likely that your MarCom department understands Twitter and what it can bring to the company. But as you are well aware, if you don't get full support from the top of the organization, it's difficult to deliver results. In fact, consider the case studies throughout the book. *All* of them had executive buy-in, no matter the company size.

Obviously, it's best if you have the power or the influence to get buy-in from the company executives. If you don't, you need to earn it.

You can run into all sorts of objections from the executive suite, such as "We are a conservative business that keeps itself to itself." Or the CEO may believe Twitter is good for selling to consumers, but not good for business-to-business, or vice versa.

In that case, you need to convince the executives of Twitter's value to your type of business and energize them with the possibilities.

Show value to the boss, with particular attention to the following:

- Setting expectations on what you need
- Displaying a road map of how you'll build the Twitter program, starting small and building on success
- Identifying a reasonable time frame
- Showing data that demonstrates how your type of business is gaining business
- Getting it approved

Make the benefits, costs, and plan clear and understandable. If you can't explain it, the executives will think it's free and easy and will expect results immediately.

Also be sure to give careful attention to the initial Twitter marketing plan. You probably intended to pick a channel that gets results anyway, but in these circumstances you may need to fine-tune it to the exec's personal metrics.

One useful technique is to get the company executive involved and Tweeting personally. Even if he logs in only occasionally, he will get a sense of what Twitter can do. If the executives don't use the tool, they won't understand its usefulness, and a MarCom staffer will continually be swimming an upstream battle to prove why Twitter marketing works.

A Longer-Term Plan

MarCom departments in larger organizations also need to think carefully about the rollout. In one multinational business-to-business organization, the process from "Let's do Twitter" to a program that was well underway took a full year. For instance, explaining why the business should get involved and how it would be measured was a full month. Getting the legal department on board took six months. Don't expect a fast-track launch.

In these instances, add an additional education step to the Twitter plan. It should be run by MarCom, tuned to the executives and other key players who are deemed to represent the company on Twitter. Identify a relatively small set of people to be "social media ambassadors" during the initial phase, and give them permission to get excited.

Here's some of the items on the rollout to-do list to ensure the staff who will be Tweeting are prepared to do so:

- Build a deck with do's and don'ts to set guidelines for professional behavior online.
- Show best practices with examples of companies doing Twitter right.
- Offer an education series (such as "lunch and learn") on how to engage with people, how to get followers, and how to share information with value. (We like to think this book will help.)

The PR Role

MarCom has a special role in the company, from responsibility for communicating with the media to publishing press releases. The next sections detail a few unique Twitter twists.

Twitter for Announcements

Here's the easiest thing for you to do on Twitter: announce stuff. Make your big announcements on Twitter—and the small ones, too.

Your big news and press release won't change because of Twitter. Neither should Twitter change your effort to push that release over the wire or your pitch to journalists covering your industry. Plan to share the news on Twitter in conjunction with your traditional efforts.

MARKETING WIN

For news media, timing is everything. Don't wait for a journalist to see the press release on your Twitter feed. If the journalist is an important contact, send her the full press release via email before you release it in the wild.

When the timing is right, Twitter both complements your traditional press release and creates a viral effect. If you Tweet an announcement following the guidelines in Chapter 6—making it interesting, useful, and valuable—you can gain exposure with far less effort than by other means.

Sometimes all it takes is one influential Twitter user to share your content. Before you know it, your big news is shared by thousands.

Make a concerted effort to write a Tweet-able press release with these considerations:

- Create short headlines that fit comfortably in 140 characters.
- Don't try to say everything in the Tweet. Use anchor text and link to the full release.
- Give yourself multiple entry points. Consider breaking up an announcement into smaller components that can be shared individually, such as quotes, statistics, and video. Each should "work" standalone without reference to the other Tweets.

Announce minor new features, upgrades, service downtime, hardware upgrades, and other helpful company news. Twitter is great for announcing the "small wins" that aren't worthy of press releases but are interesting and cool.

Protecting the Company Name

Communicating in real time can be scary for companies. The good news is that the more strategic and thoughtful you are in your Twitter activities, the more you can anticipate worst-case scenarios and respond accordingly.

The real-time nature of Twitter is both a blessing and curse. Most of the time it's a huge opportunity, but as a few brands have learned the hard way, this leaves little room for error. One misstep and the entire Twittersphere can erupt. All you need for evidence are the examples in Chapter 3.

But it doesn't need to be that way.

Crisis Management

Not every company needs to go into serious "damage control" mode. We hope it never happens to you. But every PR department needs to be ready to respond to a meltdown if an employee leaks information, an executive says something inappropriate, or a business announcement generates hate mail as the result of, say, dropping a favorite product.

You know how we've applauded the speed of communication on Twitter? That fast turnaround can bite you, too.

For instance, just a couple of years ago, *Entrepreneur* magazine suggested, in an article about how to deal with PR disasters, "Don't just react in a knee-jerk way." In 2009, Samantha DiGennaro, founder of DiGennaro Communications, a PR and strategic communications agency advised, "Take a deep breath, take it all in, then come up with an informed plan of action." And tellingly: "Take a few days to formulate a response."

You don't have a few days. If the Twitterverse is hollering about your behavior, you need to respond *now*.

An effective crisis communication response requires three things:

- Report the facts to show you're on top of the crisis.
- Communicate what you are doing to fix the problem.
- Show empathy.

FAIL WHALE

If the company has a problem, communicate on Twitter. Tell your followers everything you can as soon as possible. Frequent status updates—even if just to say "We are investigating"—make people feel you care and are taking action. Err on the side of too much communication. Well, actually, in an emergency there's no such thing as too much communication.

Failure to do this results in bad things.

For example, in late 2011 Research in Motion's (RIM) BlackBerry BIS service went down across Europe, the Middle East, and Africa. Users served from the UK datacenter were unable to access email.

In coping with the problem, RIM demonstrated what one journalist called "an abject failure to communicate with its customers." It took six hours into the outage before Pavel from RIM's Twitter account gave "this content-free pronouncement," as Richi Jennings described it:

> **@BlackBerryHelp** Some users in EMEA are experiencing issues. We're investigating, and we apologize for any inconvenience.

"That's nice, but it's too little, too late," wrote an angry Jennings. "Where were you six hours ago, Pavel? And where are the frequent updates on the 'issues,' which paying customers have a right to expect? Oh, and what's all this about 'Some users?' It seems to me that it's all users served from the UK."

It got uglier before it was over. RIM's "just the facts" response failed on the last two bullet points; the company showed little concern about how the outage affected customers (until two days later, when the CEO posted a video apology), and it gave too few status updates.

The Red Cross and a Healthy Response

On the other hand, crisis management can be handled with class—and even humor.

Even though this PR flap was far less vital, we all can be certain that the initial message generated a moment of panic among the Red Cross's PR department. The Red Cross (**@RedCross**) undoubtedly depends on its reputation as a sober organization—in more ways than one.

First, a Red Cross employee accidently sent out a Tweet on the wrong account:

> **@RedCross** Ryan found two more 4-bottle packs of Dogfish Head's Midas Touch beer .... When we drink we do it right #gettngslizzerd

The employee explained: Oops!

> **@riaglo** Rogue Tweet frm **@RedCross** due to my inability to use hootsuite ... I wasn't actually #gettngslizzerd but just excited! #nowembarrassing

The Red Cross deleted the Tweet, and assured everyone all is well:

> **@RedCross** We've deleted the rogue Tweet but rest assured the Red Cross is sober and we've confiscated the keys.

So far, that might have been a "heh" (albeit an embarrassing one for the people involved). Here's where the story gets, well, cool.

Notice that the beer mentioned was from Dogfish Head Brewery (**@dogfishbeer**). Dogfish responded, and, rather than seeing this only as an opportunity to get mentioned, encouraged Red Cross donations using the hashtag.

> RT **@Michael_Hayek** #craftbeer **@dogfishbeer** fans, donate 2 **@RedCross** 2day. Tweet with #gettngslizzerd. Donate here http://tinyurl.com/5s72obb

People responded, and donations to Red Cross poured in like, well, free beer.

> RT **@hootsuite** We're donating $100 to **@RedCross** + beverage cozies to **@riaglo** & **@dogfishhead** http://on.mash.to/eQt9zB #gettngslizzerd

The reaction was humorous and provided the perfect level of humility to win people over. While it easily could have been treated as embarrassing and something to sweep under the rug, it turned out to be something really positive.

Interacting with the Press

You'll find several guidelines online on how to use Twitter with journalists—and these days, most journalists do use the service. It's too bad that most of those advice columns, written by PR people, are flat wrong.

Several PR professionals suggest that businesses should pitch articles to the press via Twitter as if it's yet another way to capture their attention. One "public relations princess" suggested this:

> "Ideally, it would be great to send these messages to a reporter as a direct message, but if all else fails, go ahead and say **'@JeffZeleny**, did you know that the most outstanding pork tenderloin sandwich in Des Moines is at Smittys?' (Of course, you'll want to come up with your own Tweet material) If the reporter does not respond, follow up with an email pitch."

As a longtime journalist, my—Esther's—response is *Ewwwwww cooties!*

Everything in media relations is about relationships. If the journalist covers your company regularly, then you may contact her. Certainly you should follow her, because she is an influencer whose opinions and actions are relevant to your company.

But contact by email, with a truly *personal* message. All journalists have a pool of PR people whose emails they readily open. However, some names in the From field are met with immediate deletion (usually accompanied by a stabbing gesture on the Delete key and a cussword). If you have an existing relationship, then you probably have more than 140 characters to say to each other, and a Tweet isn't long enough. It'll go to email soon, so just start that way.

If your target journalist previously has written about your company, it probably is okay to send a direct message that says, "Just sent you the press release about version 2.3; let me know if you have questions. Hope the cats are purring." That tells me to look for something in my inbox (with no *or else* implied). Because it's written to me personally (mentioning the always-Tweetable cats), it indicates that you read my Twitter feed.

Now if a journalist follows you on Twitter—so that you *can* send a DM—he must have at least some interest in your company. But a public @Mention calling his attention to your announcement, as suggested by the "public relations princess" blogger previously? Most journalists would probably unfollow you.

FAIL WHALE

Your first contact with a journalist should never be a pitch via Twitter.

So what *should* you do? Cindy Kim is among those PR professionals whose email messages get Esther's immediate attention. Kim suggests you create a private Twitter list: a directory of the media (and, depending on your industry, bloggers) your company cares about.

Create an online relationship with these people. Follow their conversations, she urges. Show interest in what they write and Tweet about. Read what they post and respond to it—not with a brand message, but as your professional self.

If you demonstrate that you are knowledgeable about the topics that matter to the journalist, you become a resource—not a pest. A Tweet much like this one led the journalist to follow Kim, followed by a conversation with the writer, which led to an interview for her CEO:

> **@KeyJournalistName** Great piece in Famous Newspaper Name. I love what you wrote about CEOs.

Kim advises: Think, "How can I be a resource to you?" rather than "What can you do for me?"

TWITTER TIP

Follow the media representatives who are relevant to your industry. Don't know where to find them? Visit muckrack.com, which lists all (well, most) journalists on Twitter and their media outlets. You can sort it by beat and follow each reporter directly through the site.

Treating Bloggers as Press

Much has been written about the distinction between the "real" press and bloggers. Even those of us who have been earning our livings for 20 years by writing down our observations can dispute the "What is a real journalist?" issues.

For the most part, it isn't your problem. Just as your customer service department shouldn't treat a Twitter user with 100 followers differently from one with 100,000 followers, MarCom should treat everyone from "Mommy bloggers" to *The New York Times* with the same respect. That's especially true for business niches where the bloggers have a large audience, and the traditional press is unlikely to respond to your earnest efforts for their attention.

Paying for Attention

Don't pin your business on getting into trending topics; it happens rarely, and usually as the result of a news event. But if your budget is big enough, you can take advantage of Twitter's forms of advertising. In 2011, the company released promoted Tweets, promoted accounts, and promoted trends. (Visit https://business.twitter.com/advertise/start/ to make contact with the appropriate department.)

Twitter currently offers advertisers three promoted products:

- Promoted accounts
- Promoted trends
- Promoted Tweets

Follow Me! Follow Me!

When you opt into the Promoted Account (or Sponsored User) program, your Twitter account appears as a suggested user to Twitter users who follow your existing followers.

Promoted accounts are basically a way to buy targeted followers for your Twitter account. You set the price you're willing to pay, provide keywords to target the right people (often a hashtag), and, they assert, your Twitter follower count should start increasing steadily.

With this paid-for promotion, you pay on a cost-per-follow (CPF) basis. You bid, say, 50¢ to $5 to have your account promoted at the top of an interest-targeted Twitter user's "Who to Follow" section. An advertiser promotes its account to build up a critical mass of loyal followers.

Your follower growth rate can increase exponentially from a campaign like this. Just keep in mind that it targets existing followers on your account, so the larger your account is to begin with, the more success you can expect.

Buying Your Way onto Trending Topics

Promoted trends are offered for a flat fee in the high tens of thousands of dollars per day. They're an exclusive buy that puts your chosen trend at the top of every logged-in Twitter.com user's trending topics list. You can use them as advertising to amplify the conversation about your brand or a related topic.

For example, a coffeehouse chain might target Twitter users who Tweet using keywords including coffee, latte, or café.

A promoted Tweet is a Tweet that you already published organically. Twitter has a proprietary algorithm that measures what it calls a "resonance" score: a combination of reach, rate at which a Tweet is shared, and how many interactions it has had (such as @Mentions and Retweets).

Brands can opt to take their organic Tweets and sponsor them by bidding on keywords. For example, if the hashtag #cybermonday was trending, a brand could promote a Tweet that said something like, "Can you believe it's #cybermonday? Check out this 2-for-1 deal at [link]."

When Twitter users click on #cybermonday, the promoted Tweet would appear at the top of search results. A tiny orange box saying "Promoted by [company name]" appears with each Tweet for disclosure.

Sponsoring Tweets

Advertisers use promoted Tweets to Tweet to the most relevant users beyond their core followers.

Promoted Tweets are offered on a CPE (cost-per-engagement) basis. You pay your bid price when a user clicks on, Retweets, replies to, or favorites your promoted Tweet (likely between 20¢ and $5). Promoted Tweets are currently available in

Twitter search, where they're keyword-targeted, and are being tested in user timelines, where they're interest-targeted. (The rules may be different by the time you read this.)

You may want to target a Tweet at people who have already opted into your brand, such as a thank-you promo for fans, or to remind Twitter users about something you know brand fans care about.

Brands with budgets have seen tremendous success with these types of campaigns. The *Wall Street Journal* reported that brands have seen 8 percent engagement rates on these types of sponsored Tweets. In our experience working with clients, follower growth has increased by 2,000 percent in a matter of weeks.

Tweets Talk

With these programs, you buy attention. Not adulation or control.

Unlike traditional advertising, you are placing sponsored Tweets in an ecosystem where their success is contingent upon conversation. If you promote something that isn't well received, you may be subject to an onslaught of response that isn't always a positive reflection of the brand.

For example, McDonald's spent $80,000 to promote the return of its McRib sandwich—a significant marketing investment. But the Twitter conversation included a lot of negative comments, such as, "McRib is back and it's as bad as I remember."

If you're going to engage in a paid Twitter program, have a monitoring system in place, and ensure that it parses for sentiment. If it becomes overwhelmingly negative, you may want to pull the plug on the campaign. Despite the negative exposure, McDonald's still found that the majority of Tweets produced a positive sentiment and that the investment was worth it. Your situation may be different.

Companies that truly want to embrace Twitter and brand themselves as a company worth following need to learn how to be relevant, social, and transparent. These use all the skills you've developed—and teach you new ones.

The Least You Need to Know

- Twitter can be integrated into all MarCom efforts. It's an opportunity to give your brand a personality.
- Assume that every Tweet is being recorded and can be shared out of context.
- If you have budget to spend and take Twitter seriously, consider opting into its Promoted Tweets campaign.

Integrating Twitter into Your Marketing Mix

Part

5

Just having a presence on Twitter is not enough. Your online and offline marketing efforts should be an integral part of a single story: helping people find out what you offer, and making it easy for them to acquire it.

Twitter is just a single part of that. It's one component of a larger social media strategy, and has to dovetail appropriately with Facebook, Google+, and other online communities. You also need to use your other online and offline properties to let people know that your company is on Twitter and ready to engage with them. Here's how to unify Twitter with the rest of your outreach efforts.

Aligning Your Twitter Strategy with Other Online Marketing

Chapter 19

In This Chapter

- Tying your Twitter identity into your company's website
- Finding work and soliciting job candidates
- Encouraging site visitors to interact with your company

Our attention has, naturally, been on helping you learn to use Twitter and to understand the Twitter community. But Twitter is not a universe unto itself (however often it may seem that way). Ultimately it's just one more site on the Internet—no matter how important it may be to your business.

People who are on Twitter already have many ways to discover your company's presence and to engage with you. However, a world of customers, business partners, and suppliers may be ignorant that you're using the service. Here's how to change that with your online properties.

Incorporating Twitter on Your Company Website

You may be new to Twitter, but you aren't new to the web. Most businesses create a website before the ink on the incorporation papers is dry.

We assume that your existing website is at least adequate for current needs. You may not be an expert at web design, you may fumble at search engine marketing, and you may still run a website that's an electronic brochure. Yet after all these years in business, you probably have amassed a fair amount of content on the site, whether it's white papers, an online catalog, or a company blog.

The problem is, for a surprising number of businesses, there's no connection between the corporate website and its Twitter presence. That's just silly. The business website should help customers find your social media presence, engage with you, and proclaim their affection for your brand.

Help People Find Your Social Media Presence

The simplest ingredient to add to a business website is an "ad" that tells site visitors to follow you on Twitter. The Twitter "bird" and the "t" are now recognizable-enough icons that in many cases you can minimize the screen real estate requirements and get the message across.

Independent bookstore Powell's highlights its Twitter accounts prominently on its homepage with an icon. No explanatory text is necessary.

It's far from standard practice because this is still too new for anyone to have established expectations, but most often the Twitter icon appears on the top right of the home page or in the site's footer.

Feel free to debate with your web designers how prominently the ad should be placed. That's a matter we leave between you and them. The important thing is that it's evident to casual observers that your business is looking forward to conversing with them on Twitter.

TWITTER TIP

Find the Twitter-approved logos and images at http://twitter.com/about/resources/logos.

One Twitter logo is effective if your company has only a single Twitter account. If your business maintains several accounts for each brand or role, it's a wise idea to feature an easy-to-locate web page that helps site visitors connect to the right people or department. (Often, this is under Contact Us or About Us.)

For example, Vanderbilt University encompasses many organizations: everything from a medical center to a fine arts gallery, each of which has its own Twitter feed. (Imagine how confusing it would be if they didn't!) The university website pulls them all together at http://social.vanderbilt.edu/twitter/ to make it easier to locate the right account.

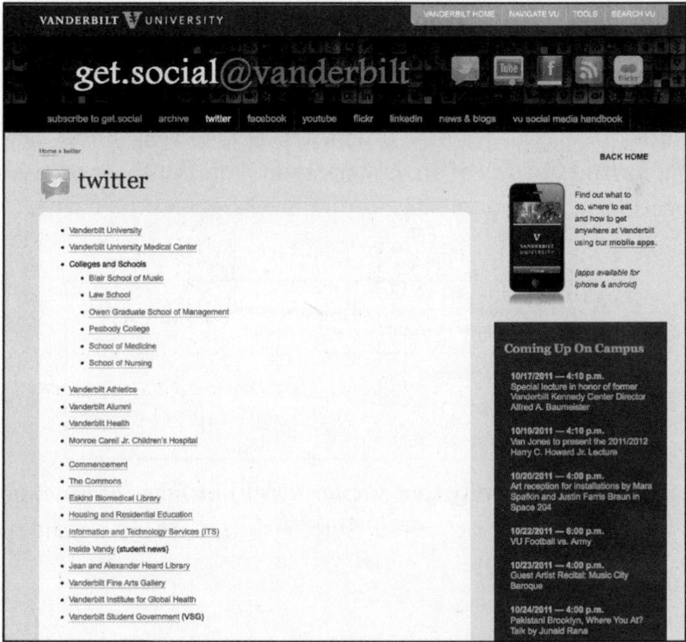

Vanderbilt University's social media page

It is essential that someone keep this information up to date. Having Twitter accounts that are out of date is just as bad as your website displaying a street address for the offices you outgrew two years ago.

Encourage Site Visitors to Share Your Content

Most organizations publish websites with some sort of dynamic content. Perhaps your company has a blog. Maybe the website has individual pages that list products. Or you publish technical information that helps customers make use of a technology or get the most out of the products you sell.

If it's good information, people value it. And if they like it, why not make it easier for them to share it?

Most websites can easily add a "Tweet this" button to any page. That's good for you, because it means that people are amplifying your message with no effort on your part. If someone Tweets your blog post, she writes her own text in the Tweet (or, optionally, uses the page title as default text).

Heck, you don't even have to have a Twitter account of your own for this, because the Tweet appears on the reader's account.

Even better, adding social bookmark buttons is incredibly easy. Most blog software and content management systems have a Twitter plug-in ready to go. Or you can use any of a number of freely available buttons, such as "AddThis," which are recognizable by many Internet users. In the worst case—which isn't bad at all—you can add a two-line bit of JavaScript to the bottom of a blog post (search on "TweetThis" for the code). It's easy to find dozens of such tools that even the most tech-shy can use for website integration.

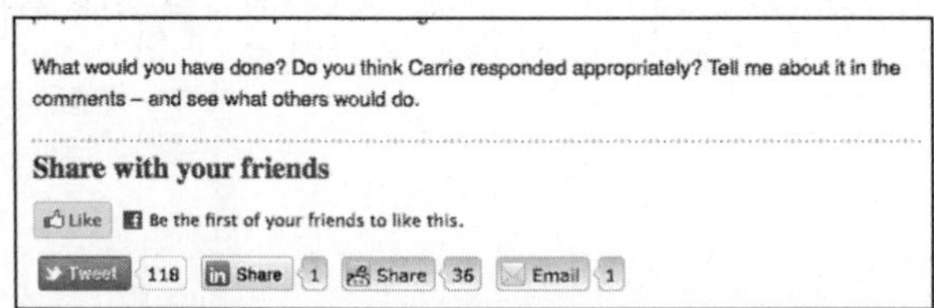

Most content management systems can integrate a social sharing bar that users easily recognize.

Don't limit this functionality to blog posts, however. Almost any type of content can be shared: catalog items, FAQs and help documents, how-to videos, and conference announcements.

Removing Site Barriers to Entry

Well before social media came on the scene, many businesses yearned for contact with their customers and sales prospects. It was fairly common for a business website to exhort people to sign up for membership in some way before the user could post a blog comment, get an email newsletter, or download a white paper.

Because the sales department was in charge of such ventures—it's lead generation, after all—the signup forms were laden with required fields that helped the Sales team, but regularly irked site visitors.

Online registration is still a viable option for any business (they do show engagement!), but the requirement for a casual visitor to register is often a barrier. Thoughts from the visitor's standpoint emerge as, "I don't know who you are, and you're asking for personal information? You want me to spend 10 minutes telling you, a stranger, about my company size and my intent to purchase something I haven't even learned about yet? Just to *look*? I'm outta here." Unless the user is already committed to the cause or has a burning desire to respond—which usually means a readiness to criticize using potty-mouth language—few bother.

MARKETING WIN

Want to attract people to your web-based services without requiring an arduous signup? Ask them to "pay with a Tweet." This is an excellent way to give information away, as long as the site visitor is willing to Tweet a link to your webpage.

The tool vendor Simply Measured, for instance, gives a "freebie" analysis for a single Twitter account, in return for a Tweet telling the world about the company.

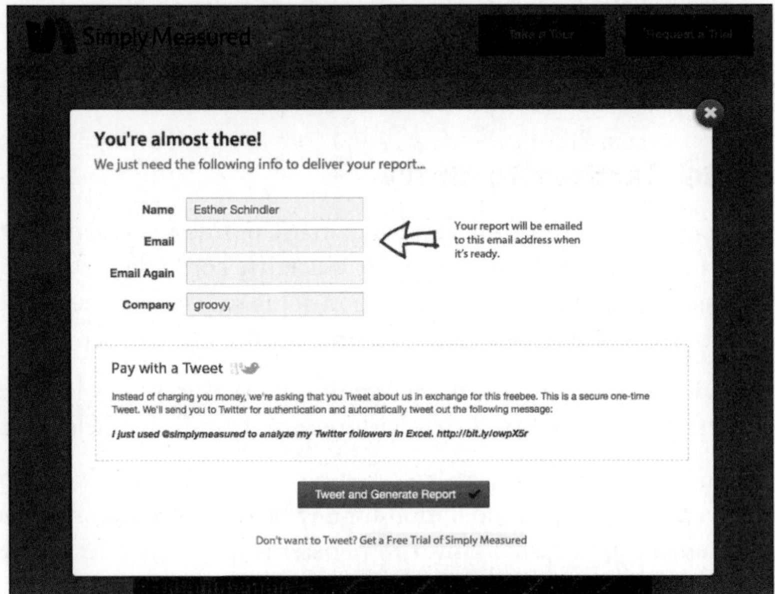

Simply Measured requires users to "pay with a Tweet."

If you want to create a true online community—on your site or on Twitter—then it's best to keep the barriers to entry low. You want people to wander in and look around without making them feel as though a security guard will frisk them at any time.

As longtime community managers know, initial registration should ask for little more than an account name and email ID. Yet policing memberships and participation, especially in volatile or sensitive communities, is a major pain.

Using Twitter IDs as Site Logins

One solution is to give site visitors the option to log in to your site using their Twitter ID. Twitter takes care of authentication (using a technology call OAuth) and offers a modicum of control. (At least you don't have to worry overly much about a troll logging in under five different identities to Astroturf a discussion.) Users already know their Twitter IDs and don't have to remember yet another password. And it's far easier for your staff to manage.

For example, the "Simple Twitter Connect" plug-in for WordPress uses Twitter's latest authentication mechanisms. If the site visitor is already logged in to Twitter, he doesn't need to add his account name or password. Clicking the **Connect with Twitter** button redirects the site visitor to Twitter for approval, and then returns him to where he came from, only now with Twitter credentials available for use.

Twitter logons are also built into many web tools with which your developers are probably familiar. For example, IntenseDebate is a highly regarded third-party commenting system. The service is famous primarily for its core features such as threaded comments and user ratings. Of particular note is IntenseDebate's ability to notify Twitter when someone makes a comment. This feature helps the commenter showcase what she's yakking about online, and also gives the originating site (yours) more attention on Twitter.

The advantage to users relying on social log-in (which may also include MySpace ID, OpenID, Facebook Connect, and other options) is that it may increase signups and thus widen the marketing funnel. The disadvantage is that your Sales department doesn't collect an email address or other information, and you don't know who the participants are.

TWITTER TIP

Want even more online community? Tweetboard (currently in testing) is a fun and engaging micro-forum type application for your website. It pulls in your Twitter stream in near real-time (with a delay under one minute), reformatting Tweets into threaded conversations with unlimited nesting.

Instead of expending the energy to get customers' email addresses, encourage them to become followers on Twitter. They will tell their friends, bringing more people to your site. Best of all, you do very little; they do the work.

Displaying a Twitter Feed on the Site

With yet more tools from Twitter and external vendors, you can (relatively easily) display a Twitter stream on your home page or on any web page where it seems appropriate. This isn't always a no-brainer, but we do encourage you to seriously consider the options.

The most common way to display a Twitter stream is one's own account, usually showing the last three to five posts.

For example, ComputerWorld prominently highlights its most recent articles in the feed, which also serves as a quiet reminder to a casual site visitor that the magazine has a Twitter feed; the visitor can click on **Follow** without leaving the ComputerWorld site.

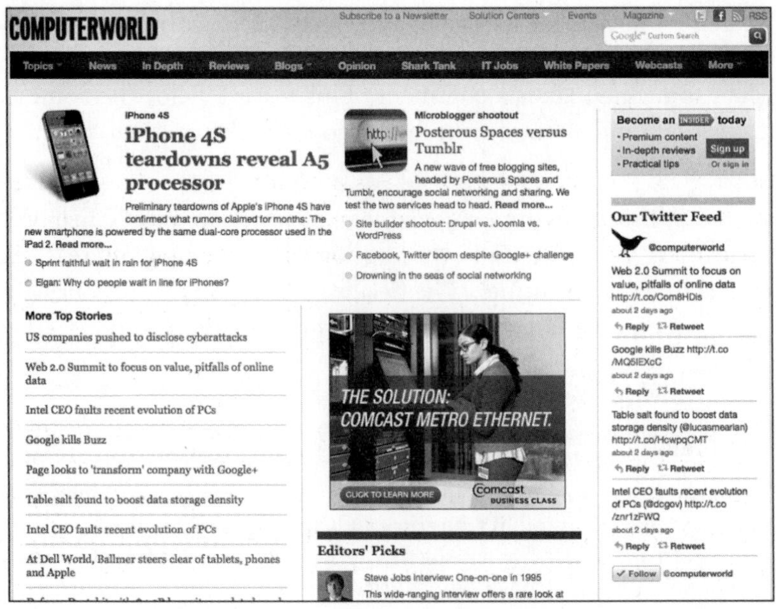

*ComputerWorld (**@computerworld**) displays its own account on its home page.*

The difficulty with this type of integration is that it can be repetitive (and repeat itself, too). If your Twitter feed primarily announces new blog posts, and the feed appears on your blogs, the site visitor sees another reminder of the same blog posts she is looking at online. The extra information is irritating.

If your Twitter account is more conversational and demonstrates engagement with followers—which this ComputerWorld example does not—it's a far more viable possibility.

On the plus side, many business websites are largely static. A Twitter stream showing that you're actively communicating can be a very good thing.

Assuming you *are* communicating. A company Twitter stream with the most recent Tweet displayed from three months ago is unlikely to impress anyone.

MARKETING WIN

Think beyond the home page! One of the best ways to integrate your company's Twitter stream onto the website is on blog posts. Frequently, another site links to an older blog post, or a web search lands the visitor on an oldie-but-goodie post. A Twitter stream displayed alongside that post demonstrates what you are doing and talking about *today*.

It's a good bet that if someone enjoys your blog, notices your Twitter stream, and likes your last five Tweets, she will follow you. Then you have *another* way to engage with her.

While "Look at us!" is the most common way to integrate a Twitter stream with a website, it's far from the only alternative. The Twitter feed can be set up to display anything: a Twitter account, a Twitter list, Mentions, or hashtags.

For example, Software Quality Connection, sponsored by SmartBear Software, publishes articles of interest to software developers. Each blog post has an assigned term to use in the Twitter stream that appears on the right side of the page.

In the example, an article about the lessons from Monty Python for the computer industry is accompanied by the results of a Twitter search for Monty Python. While that isn't inherently related to software development, it helps site visitors find more information that appeals to them—and the sponsor's intent is to demonstrate that it understands software developers' concerns.

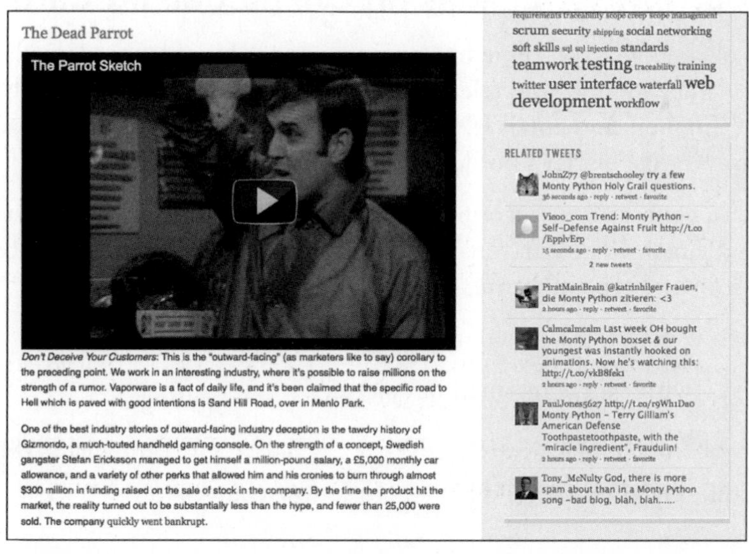

A Twitter stream integrated on a website can include anything you like. Even dead parrots.

Including Twitter Links on Company Pages

The previous suggestions are simply the beginning. Twitter has a rich set of application developer interfaces, so if you can imagine a way to "mash up" your site with Twitter, it's probably possible.

Need more ideas? Here are a few.

Optimize website landing pages for Twitter promotions. When you promote a special offer on Twitter, consider creating landing pages especially optimized for each offer code. This can help you track the promotions that are most effective, learn which codes are Retweeted and shared, and improve your effectiveness.

Use @Mentions as a source of testimonials. Don't be shy about using testimonials and love-notes for your brand. Incorporate them into your web copy or use them as callouts throughout the site.

Tweet the company newsletter. You've already gotten used to the idea of sharing company blog posts on Twitter. Consider other company-generated material as well.

For example, in addition to its core email marketing features, Aweber can Tweet the newsletter. The newsletter delivery service created a way to convert RSS to email to Tweet. This becomes yet another entry point for a direct marketing campaign, especially if the newsletter makes it easy to subscribe.

Treating Your Twitter Link as an Online Calling Card

If you are old enough, you remember a time when a business card displayed only a few items: name, address, and telephone number. Gradually, other fields were added, such as fax numbers and email IDs. Then business cards became outmoded and we all switched to vCards, but let's not let facts get in the way of a good analogy.

The point is, your Twitter account is now as much a calling-card item as your phone number and email. Whether you Tweet personally or on behalf of the brand, consider including it in any type of online communication:

- Sign your email with your Twitter ID.
- Use Twitter links in email newsletters.
- Include your Twitter account on forums and other correspondence.
- Explicitly ask your blog readers to follow you.

Finding Work and Workers

Because Twitter is a conversation, it's a remarkably good way to find the people to work for you or to find your next job. Twitter is all about connecting people who share interests, after all—and there is nothing quite as connective as "Come to work with us."

Finding Staff Through Twitter

HR professionals are using Twitter to find great talent. You often see people share job listings on Twitter or announce that they're seeking their next big opportunity.

> **@nickdenardis** We're Hiring: Full Time LAMP Web Developer at **@waynestate**! http://j.mp/pgoFJY #job #detroit #lamp #highered
>
> **@Insight_PR** We're hiring! Please RT: Digital Communications Executive—Consumer bit.ly/mXxzn2 #jobfairy
>
> **@flyingdog** Want to join the Flying Dog Pack? We're hiring an Experiential Specialist: http://ow.ly/64quE

The people you most want to attract are those who already care about your brand. Anyone who already follows you ought to get a point for passion, if nothing else.

Larger companies should consider creating a separate Twitter account purely for job listings. This has been successful for AT&T (**@attJOBS**) and MTV (**@mtvnetworksjobs**).

TWITTER TIP

Don't count on your job applicants to know about your company. Use hashtags to attract people with specialized expertise. These examples use #lamp and #highered to improve the chances that someone in higher education or with LAMP (technical) skills will find out about the job opening.

Finding Gigs

Even if you aren't in the job market, Twitter is useful for helping people find consulting assignments, employment, and contracting work. Many individuals today use Twitter to find job opportunities.

In many ways, your Twitter account says more about you than your resumé does, such as how networked you are or your social media know-how.

Back in 2007, Alexa Scordato (**@Alexa**) was a recent college graduate and looking for job opportunities in Boston. She found Aaron Strout (**@AaronStrout**) on Twitter who at the time was the VP of Social Media at Burlington-based Mzinga. She Tweeted, "**@AaronStrout** Looking for a full-time job in Boston. Is Mzinga hiring?" Within minutes he sent her a message requesting a link to her LinkedIn profile and a few short weeks later, she had the job.

Alexa isn't the only one. Five years ago, a freelance writer responded to one of Esther's Tweets about editorial opportunities. The writer included a link to her website and a friendly comment about her availability. Pam has been writing for Esther ever since. At least $50,000 of income has resulted from that first perky Tweet.

Alexa and Pam aren't alone. There are thousands of case-studies where employees and employers connected online versus the traditional job application or career site.

The Least You Need to Know

- Integrate Twitter into your existing website to encourage people to follow you and to amplify your content.
- Website integration should be deeper than the home page. Build it into blog posts, help desk information, and landing pages.
- Treat Twitter as another vital contact point, giving it equal weight to your company's telephone number or physical address.

Aligning Twitter with Offline Marketing

Chapter 20

In This Chapter

- Taking your Twitter marketing into your external media
- Leveraging your commitment to customer dialogue
- Brainstorming new ways to highlight social media engagement

There is a world outside our computers.

This may be shocking news. Some of us check our email before we brush our teeth. Our best friends (and co-authors) live thousands of miles away, and often we have never met in person. The notion of getting in a car and driving to a store, rather than using an e-commerce site, is an astonishing revelation. And we have several true friends whom we call by their Twitter names, like "**@hotclaws**" or "**@socosoco**."

Yeah, maybe we don't get out much.

But your customers probably *do* interact with that real world. (Do you know it *rains* there? Amazing.)

While your target customers can find out about your Twitter presence with Twitter searches, websites, and blog posts, the people you want to reach aren't always online. You can, and should, attract their attention when they are out and about, too. In this chapter, we show examples of how to do so.

Being Found

Consider the following scene: a landscaping business van driving down Scottsdale Road with a large sign advertising the business. The sign offers loads of information, one nugget being a Twitter ID.

Unless you were actively looking for a landscaping service, you probably wouldn't remember the company name. You certainly wouldn't recall the phone number. But a Twitter ID is at least as memorable as a URL—and likely shorter.

At the Corner of Main Street and Twitter

As we emphasized in the last chapter, think of your Twitter identity as a standard part of your contact information. Just as a delivery truck advertises the company name, phone number, and web address in its role as traveling ambassador for the business, you should include your social media participation, too.

MasterCard's subway billboard includes social media icons.

Should you emphasize it? Maybe, maybe not. You have finite space to work with on a billboard, print magazine advertisement, or other offline media.

But do include the information, because—with ever more people mobile—the Twitter account tells people both how to find you and who you really are.

The mobile component is becoming an integral part of shopping, especially for retailers. According to eBay CEO John Donohoe, research shows that half of all retail customers access the web at some point in the buying process, whether to research or to comparison shop. Increasingly, they do that online research on their smartphones while in the store, Donohoe told the audience at the Fall 2011 Web 2.0 Summit.

Television advertising, such as this spot from Education Connection, can showcase social properties.

Emphasizing the Local

People—especially young people—are coming to expect your business's participation at both a local and personal level. Whole Foods has both a corporate ID (**@wholefoods**) and accounts for most of its individual stores (such as **@wholefoodsSF**). If you don't let local customers know that you also respond locally, how else will they know?

For example, the Best Buy in New York City (**@bestbuyunionsq**) asks its customers to follow them. An individual customer might not remember the specific Twitter ID, but he is sure to remember that his nearby store has one.

Best Buy customers are assured that the store's staff is accessible.

Being Engaged

The reason that you use Twitter for marketing is to create a connection with your customers. For many consumers and even business users, that's a new perception. The fact that your company is looking for a dialogue, and not promising only a sales call and a see-ya-later, sets you apart from the competition.

Why not exploit that? It's one of the things that makes you better than the other guys.

Demonstrating Commitment

Let's say your business is committed to customer service. You set up a customer service Twitter account to ensure the business delivers on its promises of quality. You applied an entire chapter's worth of our advice, teaching your staff how to reach out on Twitter to find those in need, streamlining the customer service workflow for customer follow-ups, and feeding the lessons learned back to the development and product marketing departments.

Don't forget to tell the customers about it, too.

For example, Best Buy's sales claim is that its staff is more knowledgeable about electronics than that of other chains. It has backed up that assertion with a **@Twelpforce** Twitter account, staffed by a large crew of customer service agents who respond to user questions.

To ensure that customers (and people just browsing in the store) know that customer service "comes in the box," each store prominently displays the Best Buy marketing message.

Best Buy advertises is Twelpforce service inside the store.

Emphasizing Service

KLM Royal Dutch Airlines took its commitment to customer service to new heights with its Live Tweet campaign. The airline used Twitter to make the business more personal, and to get across the message that live staff are always standing by, ready to respond to any customer within an hour.

During the campaign—which KLM turned into a television advertisement—140 employees were used as a live Tweeting medium for one day. Each person held up a single keyboard character, and, as a group, the employees spelled out Tweets as replies to the Tweets that KLM received.

The purpose was to highlight KLM's social media services, to let people know that there are people on Twitter 24/7 waiting to help out. The message was not really, "KLM is on Twitter," but rather that the airline is invested in being as accessible and helpful as possible.

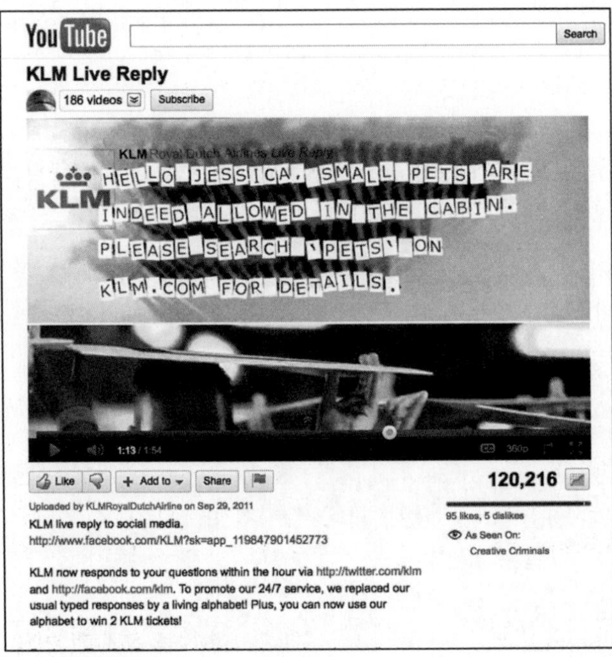

KLM replaced its usual typed responses by a living alphabet for 24 hours—and used it in a TV ad.

Beyond "Sign Up for Our Newsletter"

Another reason behind your decision to create a Twitter identity is your desire to build a connection that lasts beyond the moment.

Your customer is in your restaurant *now.* If she follows you on Twitter, she will—at a minimum—think of you every time she sees your Tweet in her timeline. If she doesn't, you have no clue when she will think of you again.

Think of all the ways you can get the "Follow us!" message across in your marketing materials. Maybe a "Follow us on Twitter" card in the restaurant check. Perhaps a brochure in a monthly bill, or at least social media channels stamped on the back of the envelope.

Our favorite independent bookstore includes a logo'ed bookmark with each book sale. Although the business has a Twitter account, its name isn't included on the bookmark. Tsk.

Reflecting Your Community Knowledge

Examine every customer touch-point. Encourage your staff to talk about social media where relevant and where possible, such as the Nordstrom salesman we mentioned in Chapter 16.

Consider, too, the behavior of your customers—and their willingness to Tweet about your business while they are actively engaged in it. Remember the Arizona Diamondbacks, which put fans' Tweets on the scoreboard before the baseball game began? Fans get the ego boost of appearing in front of thousands of other people—and the fans' followers are reminded that their friends were having a good time at Chase Field.

Cupcake store Butter Lane (**@butterlane**) in New York is aware that customers regularly wait in line. The company—which was featured on a Food Network TV show, "Best Thing I Ever Ate"—mounted an iPad on the wall, and encourages its customers to participate in social media while they are in the queue. The proprietors are also aware of the attention it's earned from bloggers, and it rewards them publicly.

You might not mind being in line at Butter Lane if you can get on Twitter.

The Testing Ground

Let online marketing inform your offline marketing. It's common for businesses to push whatever was successful offline into the online arena. However, few use the opportunity of switching this around.

With Twitter analytics, you have a platform to test marketing campaigns quickly and cheaply. You can discover which topics are Retweeted most often, and make note of the phrases customers use to describe their pain points and the solutions they find (whether yours or someone else's). While online behavior is not always a map to offline purchasing habits, it's more informative and far cheaper to do it online than with expensive market research and focus groups.

Being Inspired

Part one in your offline Twitter marketing efforts is to get noticed. Part two is to engage with customers.

But the entire process becomes special—and rather exciting—when you think in terms of connecting other people with one another.

Encouraging Community Building with Tweetups

You don't have to look for offline opportunities. You can create them.

One way to do so is to organize Tweetups, gatherings of people who have connected via Twitter or other social media, who have an interest in your industry or product category.

You can get in touch with vendors, suppliers, and other people with whom you can form partnerships. You can organize lunch with other people who share your same business role; for instance, many towns have monthly Tweetups for social media directors or web developers.

But think beyond your own needs. Give your loyal customers a reason to meet one another and to tell you how wonderful you are.

For example, the Arizona Diamondbacks' Tweetup included a special price in a reserved section, $10 off food at the ballpark, a t-shirt to commemorate the occasion, and a "town hall" meeting with team executives and baseball players. This was a reward to followers, and it helped active fans meet each other.

TWITTER TIP

One useful tool for creating Tweetups is Twtvite.com, which is a little like evite.com for social media. Twtvite invitations are easily shared on Twitter, Facebook, and other social networking sites.

The website manages RSVPs, automates calendar entries, prints name tags, and displays a map for the venue. People can leave comments for anybody interested in the Tweetup, and the software captures related hashtags. You can embed Twtvite onto your website, too, making it easy to get the word out to those who aren't on the invitation list.

Going Big

Sometimes, even for the best-known brands, it seems like there just isn't that much to say. Some brands can have a conversation about their customers' day-to-day needs, the way that Pampers (**@pampers**) discusses parenting issues. But others … well, how much is there to say about pudding?

So Jell-O (**@JelloMoodMeter**) created a Twitter-powered billboard at the corner of West Broadway and Grand in New York City. The billboard is essentially an outdoor version of the Jell-O Pudding Face website, which monitors the world's mood based on the number of smiley-face and sad-face emoticons posted to Twitter.

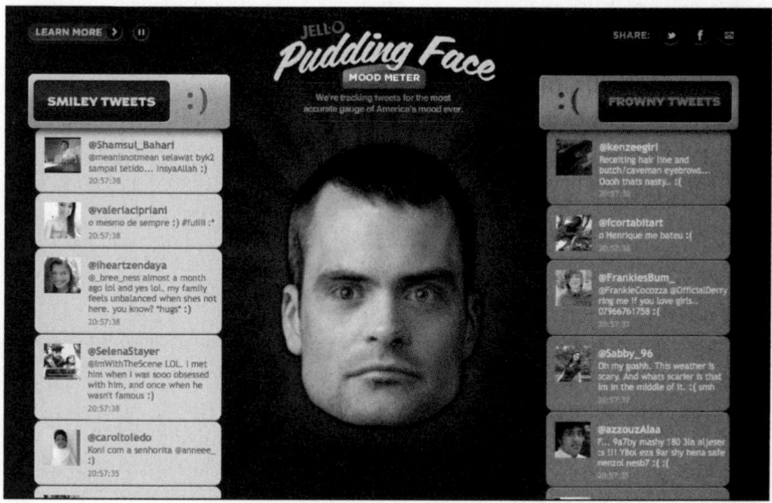

The billboard is modeled on the jellopuddingface.com, which shows a visual update of the world's mood based entirely on emoticons.

Jell-O's advertising agency monitored Twitter for two months, and found a consistent global average of 1,200 smiles :) and 800 frowns :(per minute. The billboard pings Twitter every seven seconds, searching for the emoticons and adjusting the percentage—and the face—as necessary.

When the mood starts to dip, the brand uses Twitter to give out coupons to the randomly downcast.

> **@JelloMoodMeter @Jumpeii** Oh man. The only thing that helps a frown like that is a little pudding. Dig in. pdnf.ac/bqj #PuddingFace

And that puts a smile on *our* faces.

The Least You Need to Know

- Use your offline media to create a connection with users and encourage them to continue the conversation.
- Your message should not be merely, "We are on Twitter" but rather, "We use Twitter to provide you with better service."
- Don't be shy. Explore new ways to connect with your customers.

Appendix

Glossary

DM (direct message) A private message sent only to the individual account.

Fail Whale The image users see when Twitter experiences an outage. Specifically it means that Twitter is unavailable, such as due to system overload. Often generalized to mean any kind of failure.

follow To subscribe to Tweets from a single user or Twitter ID. Following someone means you see his or her messages in your own timeline. Twitter lets you see all the people you follow and also who follows you.

hashtag (#) The # symbol identifies keywords or topics in a Tweet. Hashtags become instant search terms and help users categorize their messages.

HT (hat-tip) The process in which you rephrase another user's Tweet with your own words, and then credit the person for sharing on Twitter.

Mentions (@Mentions) Highlighted messages of a specific Twitter ID, created by including an @ before the account name (e.g., **@Brett**). Twitter highlights @Mentions in that user's Twitter stream.

@reply A Tweet directed to another user in response to his or her update. The difference between an @reply and an @Mention is that the reply has the username at the beginning of the Tweet (e.g., "**@estherschindler** You're right: That's wonderful chocolate.").

Retweet (RT) Resend the contents of someone else's Tweet to your own followers.

Timeline or **Twitter stream** The list of Tweets from those you follow that appears on your Twitter home page.

trends/trending topics When a topic becomes popular on Twitter, it's listed as a "trending topic." These topics, displayed on the home page, may take the form of short phrases ("Michael Jackson") or hashtags (e.g., #RoyalWedding).

Tweet A message posted to Twitter, containing 140 characters or fewer.

Twitter handle The same thing as a Twitter name or Twitter ID. Your Twitter handle is how you are represented on Twitter and to all users.

Index

A

B

C

D

E

F

G

H

I

J

N

O

P

Q-R

S

T

U-V

W-X-Y-Z

CHECK OUT THESE BEST-SELLERS

More than 450 titles available at booksellers and online retailers everywhere!

978-1-59257-115-4

978-1-59257-900-6

978-1-59257-855-9

978-1-61564-069-0

978-1-59257-957-0

978-1-59257-869-6

978-1-59257-471-1

978-1-61564-066-9

978-1-59257-883-2

978-1-59257-966-2

CD INCLUDED!

978-1-59257-908-2

978-1-59257-786-6

978-1-61564-118-5

CD INCLUDED!

978-1-59257-437-7

978-1-61564-112-3

ALPHA

idiotsguides.com